SCHOOL CULTURES:
UNIVERSES OF MEANING IN
PRIVATE SCHOOLS

INTERPRETIVE PERSPECTIVES ON EDUCATION AND POLICY

George W. Noblit and William T. Pink, **Series Editors**

SCHOOL CULTURES:
UNIVERSES OF MEANING IN PRIVATE SCHOOLS

Mary E. Henry
Washington State University

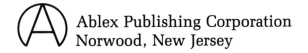 Ablex Publishing Corporation
Norwood, New Jersey

Library of Congress Cataloging-in-Publication Data

Henry, Mary E.
    School cultures : universes of meaning in private schools / Mary
E. Henry.
        p. cm. — (Interpretive perspectives on education and policy)
    Includes bibliographical references (p.   ) and index.
    ISBN 1-56750-022-6. — ISBN 1-56750-023-4 (pbk.)
    1. Private schools—United States—Sociologial aspects—Case
studies. 2. Educational anthropology—United States—Case studies.
I. Title. II Series.
LC49.H46   1993
371'.02'0973—dc20   92-42686
                                                                  CIP

Ablex Publishing Corporation
355 Chestnut Street
Norwood, New Jersey 07648

For my nieces and nephews,
Kurt, Mark, Tara,
Thomas, Jonathon,
Erin, Miriam,
and Jacob

CONTENTS

CONTENTS

CREDITS

"Blurred Genres: The Refiguration of Social Thought," by Clifford Geertz. Reprinted from *The American Scholar*, 49(2), Spring 1980, 165–179. Copyright © 1980 by the author.

"The Constitution and Private Schools," by Erwin Chemerinsky in *Public Values, Private Schools* by Neal E. Devins (ed.). Philadelphia: The Falmer Press, 1989. Reprinted with permission.

"Ethnography: An Anthropological View," by George Spindler and Louise Spindler in *Education and Cultural Process: Anthropological Approaches* (2nd ed.) by George Spindler (ed.). Prospect Heights, IL: Waveland Press, 1987. Reprinted with permission.

Managers of Virtue: Public School Leadership in America 1820–1980, by David Tyack and Elisabeth Hansot. New York: Basic Books, 1982. Reprinted with permission.

Japan's High Schools, by Thomas Rohlen. Copyright © 1983 The Regents of the University of California. Reprinted with permission.

"The School Class as a Social System: Some of Its Functions in American Society," *Harvard Educational Review*, 29(4), 298–381. Copyright © 1959 by the President and Fellows of Harvard College. All rights reserved.

Preschool in Three Cultures, by Joseph J. Tobin, David Y. H. Wu, Dana H. Davidson. Copyright © 1989 by Yale University. Reprinted by permission of Yale University Press.

FOREWORD

In a time of multiplicity and preoccupation with choice, a study of alternative educational realities holds particular interest. Taking an ethnographic and qualitative approach, Mary Henry turns her lenses on two distinctive "school cultures": that of Waldorf School, oriented to the "natural" and to a philosophy called "anthroposophy," and that of St. Catherine's, a fairly traditional Episcopal school devoted to academic growth and accomodation to contemporary technological society. Not only is the account of each one's mythology, symbolism, and rituals fascinating in itself. So is the description of the various ways there are of structuring meanings in a consumerist, individualist society. To a degree, as Dr. Henry shows, fundamental values and beliefs are filtered from the larger culture through the moral and social fabrics of significance woven by each school. At once, schools like Waldorf School and St. Catherine's offer to their students existential alternatives of considerable moment. In each case, young people learn that there are modes of living and feeling (and, perhaps, worshipping) very different from those dominating the culture at large.

Both schools under study here exist in the same rural community of Southville. This suggests that they tap generally similar populations, and that there are overlaps with public school clienteles. Not only is the reader challenged to confront the very idea of alternatives in an unusual framework, but he or she becomes involved in the ongoing cultural conversation with regard to private schools and their place in a democratic society.

Parochial, "Free Christian," experimental, technical, or socially exclusive, private schools have often been called "protest schools," meaning that they are at odds with mainstream education in some particular or general sense. This book makes clear the range of dissonance or "protests" that become audible to anyone who chooses to hear. As the author says, an acquaintance with the variety of what is possible cannot but make discussions of the pros and cons of "choice" more intelligent and informed. Freedom itself takes on far more meaning when people become acquainted with a full extent of options or alternative possibilities. And this book gives fascinating content to the alternatives its author has observed.

Because she has viewed each school as a live culture, a process of making meanings, the worlds she reveals disclose unexpected depths as well as surfaces. The reader is given an experience analogous to one that might be had in visiting an unfamiliar civilization under the guidance of an especially sensitive anthropologist. Myths, symbolisms, rituals, art forms: the usually submerged components of school life are made present. This is because the schools are deliberately rendered as "cultures," in light of distinctive traditions and history. Not only do matters of curriculum and value become clearer when viewed in such a context, but potent questions about the social and spiritual live of children are framed, as new insights into the ecology of schooling in this country begin to emerge.

Much will be learned about the nature of culture and contemporary studies of culture in the pages ahead. In addition, there will be the great pleasure of witnessing with a sense of immediacy the day-to-day action in Waldorf School and St. Catherine's. The view is that of the participant observer who makes no claim to total objectivity, but who presents a multifaceted minidrama whenever she communicates what it is like to be there at a celebration or a ritual, to attend to diverse ways of learning and being, and to recognize the play of symbols that gives rise to diverse, forever-changing realities. This wise and well-written text opens doors to new conceptions of meaning, selfhood, and educational policy. There is much to discover ahead.

Maxine Greene
Teachers College
Columbia University

ACKNOWLEDGMENTS

I want to thank many people for their help. The book began as a Ph.D. dissertation at the University of Virginia and was re-written while an Assistant Professor in the Department of Education Administration and Supervision at Washington State University. Heartfelt thanks to the administrators, teachers, parents and students in the schools studied. Your contributions are evident on every page of this book. A number of people have also been inspirational mentors to me and directly contributed through ideas and discussion. Without them this book would not have been written. I want to especially thank Eric Bredo for all the help and advice with this project. Words cannot convey my debt of gratitutde. Peter Hackett, Jennings Wagoner, and Ellen Contini-Morava at the University of Virginia, were also extremely helpful. The Commonwealth Center for the Education of Teachers, University of Virginia, provided financial support for the study during the dissertation stage. Thanks also to Ian Henry for his part in helping to make this work possible. The following people kindly critiqued chapters at various stages: Eric Bredo, Peter Hackett, Jennings Wagoner, and Ellen Contini-Morava, University of Virginia; Donald LaMagdaleine at the University of St. Thomas; Cynthia Dillard, Gisela Ernst, Terry Ford, Mona Roach, Ed Rousculp, Steve Rowley and Sherry Vaughan at Washington State University; and Kathleen Warren,

University of Idaho. Jim Carroll drew the form drawing on the computer. The expert guidance of editors William Pink and George Noblit and the folks at Ablex, Carol Davidson, Sharon Jehlen, and the rest of the staff, also meant a great deal to me. Friends, students, and colleagues too many to mention by name helped turn research and writing into a joyful endeavor. Particular thanks go to Pat Krysinski for her many kindnesses, Donald Reed and Gail Furman for thoughtful discussions, Walt Gmelch and Don Orlich for practical advice and encouragement and Bernie Oliver for administrative support. I also want to thank people who have inspired me over the years: Bronwyn Davies and Fred D'Agostino, University of New England, Australia; Jim Kaminsky, Auburn University; Dell Hymes and Valerie Sutter, University of Virginia; Ray McDermott, Stanford University and the shining example of Maxine Greene, Teachers College Columbia. Finally, and most importantly, thank you to my family in Australia: Walter, Kath, David, Robyn Jeanette, Kurt, Mark, Tara, Ben, Robyn Jane, Erin, Miriam, Jacob, Tim, Ann, Thomas and Jonathon Gardiner.

1

REVISITING SCHOOLS AS CULTURES

WALDORF SCHOOL

Southville,[1] *December, 8:20 a.m.* A huddle of teachers, students, and parents stand in a field of snow. They talk and laugh, some exchanging home produce, eggs, and goat's milk; the children play. Soon, the parents drive off on a narrow country road. The children hike with their teachers up the trail to school. Snow crunches underfoot. The lake is frozen. Someone throws a stick on it as he walks past, to see if the surface will crack. Horses stand quietly by, their bodies responding to the winter's chill. The trail leads to rustic cabins at the top of the hill. At school the children play again for a short while, swinging on a rope suspended from a tree or running in the snow. One of the bigger boys rings the school bell. Ding, dong, ding, dong. It is an old bell made of steel and set on a wooden post. The children then move to their classroom-cabins, set on the hill in a circular fashion, like tribal huts. They file quietly into class. As they

---

[1]Pseudonyms have been used for the names of all people, schools, programs, and the community in this study. All figures (school enrollments, fees, etc.) referring to Waldorf School, St. Catherine's, and the other schools in the Southville community refer to the 1989–1990 school year, when fieldwork was undertaken.

enter they shake their teacher's hand. It is a warm, yet formal greeting. "Good morning. How are you today, Sunshine?" "Very well, thank you, Mrs. Jones." Inside there are things to do: coats to hang up, shoes to take off, friends to talk to, and school bags to be put away in the hat room, which is also a bathroom. When they have done these things the children stand behind their wooden desks. Teacher faces her 13 fourth and fifth graders. "Good morning, children." "Good morning, Mrs. Jones," the children reply. Without any signal to begin, the children and the teacher recite a verse:

> The sun with loving light
> Makes bright for me the day.
> The soul, with spirit power,
> Gives strength unto my limbs.
> In sunlight shining clear
> I reverence, O God,
> The strength of human kind
> Which Thou as gift of love
> Hast planted in my soul
> That I may love to work
> And ever seek to learn
> From Thee stream strength and light;
> To Thee rise love and thanks.

The children sit. Mrs. Jones notices that no one is absent or late today.

ST. CATHERINE'S SCHOOL

Southville, same day, 8:05 a.m. A retinue of cars stream past the white painted fences and rolling fields leading up to the school. Parents follow the set procedure for dropping off children as laid down in the school handbook. Arrows and signs assist the uninitiated. Mrs. Wright stands on the pavement as the cars circle past. She greets students as they get out of the cars; sometimes she talks briefly to parents. Mr. Moore, the director of the Lower School, is also there for a short time. The children then enter the building with its wide corridors and bright windows. In the classrooms the children play video games on the computer, talk to their friends, put their books away in their lockers, and get ready for the first lesson. At 8.15 a.m. an electric bell sounds in all rooms in the building. The bell signals the commencement of official school time. Students and teachers have 5 minutes to be ready. At 8.20 a.m. another bell sounds. The homeroom teacher stands at the front of the room. Twenty children face her. They stop talking. "Good morning, fourth grade." "Good morning, Mrs. Wright." "O.K. Let's stand for opening exercises." Everyone stands and faces the flag. With right hands over their hearts, the teacher and the class say clearly:

> I pledge allegiance to the flag of the United States of America,
> And to the Republic for which it stands,
> One nation under God
> Indivisible, with Liberty and Justice for all.

The Lord's Prayer follows, said with heads bowed and eyes closed. ". . . For ever and ever, Amen." Then there is one beat and the class begins begin singing loudly and quickly:

> My country 'tis of thee,
> Sweet land of Liberty,
> Of thee I sing [thump, thump—as students hit their desks]
> Land where my father died,
> Land of the Pilgrim's pride,
> From every mountainside,
> Let Freedom reign [thump, thump].

"Have a seat. Quickly. We're late. We'll be late for Reading today. Is anybody absent?" Attendance is checked by the teacher. She asks for lunch orders from children who are buying their lunch. Students who are excused from Athletics or are going home early produce notes from their parents. Children who came late are sent to the office to register their lateness. Any changes in routine for the day are announced. Students are told to listen carefully and be prepared. "O.K. Go to Reading."

SCHOOLING AS CULTURAL PROCESS

Two schools, two rituals to begin school each day. Are they the same ritual or are they different? In both schools there are familiar themes—parents dropping off youngsters, the greeting upon arrival at school, play time, getting ready for class, the bell ringing, teacher taking charge, lunch preparations, attendance, and opening verse. These are the rules and routines that are part of our knowledge of schools. Memories of our own school days are clouded with these rituals; as teachers we have played a role in them. But what they mean may be obscured. If the American flag has always been in the fabric of school life, participants may not even notice it, let alone consider its meaning. And even somewhat similar routines may have completely different messages embedded in them.

Rituals such as those just described help define a school culture of beliefs, attitudes and actions into which students are socialized. School culture is not, however, a static phenomenon; it is a process. Rituals are part of the process, facilitating change as well as orienting people to a school's prevailing order. The school, in turn, is located in wider society, so a school may be promoting a broader set of concerns in addition to those relevant to everyday life in any one school.

This is an ethnography of two private elementary schools, a Waldorf school (referred to as "Waldorf School") and St. Catherine's, a college preparatory school, in Southville, a Southeastern U.S. community. It is an interpretive inquiry into school cultures, seeking answers to the question: What cultural meanings do the schools create? The approach has been to analyze day-to-day life in schools in terms of what the schools do, not to study the effects on those in the schools.

Private schools were selected as part of a sector of schooling that is rapidly expanding. 5.3 million students are now attending at least 22 different types of private schools (Toch, 1991, p. 67). Private schools have the potential to offer alternative ways of approaching schooling. Here are school settings that are structured quite differently to public schools. Private schools may be completely autonomous or have only partial ties to the state. They are rarely answerable to school districts or to any of the state and federal bureaucracies that govern public schooling. If we want to know about different ways of doing school and social dynamics in diverse schools, then private schools provide a functional setting for this purpose.

The level studied is the elementary school (students aged 5–12 years). At St. Catherine's this was referred to as the "Lower School" (Grades 1–5), a division of the larger school (Preschool–Grade 12). At Waldorf School elementary school was called Grade School (Grades 1–7). (Waldorf Kindergarten, comprised of a nursery class and two kindergartens, is on a separate location.) Though the focus was on the elementary schools, attention was also given to whole school programs to understand linkages and contexts.

The lower level of schooling is critical to a child's social and moral development. Durkheim emphasized the significance of the child's initiation into school. He differentiated between two stages of childhood. The first stage is within the folds of family life, and nursery school is essentially a substitute family. Then, in elementary school, the child beginning to leave the family circle is initiated into a larger environment (Durkheim, 1961, p. 17). Whether schools do initiate students into the values and attitudes required of a nation's citizenry, as Durkheim and other functionalists maintain, or whether schooling is determined by class interests, as radical theorists claim, has been debated for some time. It is also the case that schools evolve within their own particular environments and are concerned with creating distinctive meanings. The part thus played by schools in developing a school culture into which children are socialized deserves our attention and is the focus of this study.

The book has been written for experienced educators, scholars, and practitioners who "know" schools yet are wanting access to new ways of looking at schooling. The study shows different meanings of school life, uncovering defining metaphors and elaborating on school processes and their cultural content. The metaphors provided here are those of a "holistic model" at Waldorf School, and an "academic elite model" at St. Catherine's, the college-preparatory school. Both metaphors differ from the so-called "industrial model," which has come to dominate our view of public schools. The study provides an opportunity for scholar-practitioners to reflect on their own philosophies and practices. Teachers can gain insight into, and recognize the potential impact of what they are doing. They can enrich their own teaching experiences through exposure to the variety of ideas contained in these schools. Researchers, too, can enhance theory building. Familiar notions about culture are given new wrinkles and made unfamiliar. Also, for those interested in interpretive inquiry, the study is a useful example of qualitative research conducted from an anthropological standpoint.

By focusing on school culture, some of the particulars of schools, their own distinctive features, are able to be examined. Schools too often are treated in the literature as if they are all the same. Context is deemphasized in much research, since it is concerned with controlling variables. The richness of school content and processes is often flattened, because the impetus for research has become in many cases to produce a measurable result that can be applied to other situations. If any differentiation in schools is recognized in research it is often along a two-dimensional scale: "good" versus "bad" schools, "middle class" versus "working class," "traditional" versus "progressive," "public" versus "private" schools. These overly simplistic characterizations can be as harmful as they are helpful. The ethnographer or researcher who studies school culture has the potential to reveal, not only how schools are the same, but also how they are different. School processes and meaning systems, their cultures, have tended either to be ignored or treated as if they are, in Page's (1990, p. 50) words, "manipulable levers for change."

The organization of the book is as follows. The first two chapters introduce the reader to the study and its theoretical framework of culture theory from a symbolist and postmodern perspective. Chapter 2 explores the notion of culture in depth, laying the groundwork for successive chapters focusing on school cultural themes. Chapter 3 begins with an introduction to the schools' historical legacies, which is further drawn on, as appropriate, in later chapters. A school's history affects its culture, for many of the structures and guiding principles of schools have their origins in past traditions. In addition, societal "rules" concerning private schools, as laid out in landmark court decisions, are also traced, for they figure into the cultural possibilities of schools. A typology of schools is then outlined. The schools are placed within a general framework of schools and in relation to other schools within the community. The myths, stories, and "philosophies" created by and about schools can also help define them as demonstrated in Chapter 4. Chapter

5, in turn, analyzes the curriculum proper and its evaluation system as a value-laden entity that figures largely in generating particular beliefs and actions. What is taught, and how it is taught, contain implicit and explicit cultural messages. The analysis of culture is further extended in Chapter 6 by looking at rituals as significant practices which undercut or support other dimensions of school life. Festivals, celebrations, and special events, as well as everyday rituals, are documented and analyzed for their symbolic messages. Finally, in Chapter 7 the uses of time, space, and social relations, including pedagogy, are compared across the two schools. The concluding chapter ties the analysis together and draws conclusions about the "universes of meaning" created by each school and considers their differences in educational and social terms. For those readers interested in methodological concerns, an Appendix outlines the fieldwork process and covers the procedures employed.

FIELDWORK

In looking at schooling as a cultural process, an assumption is made that ideas and understandings can be found in collective life through anthropological fieldwork. Such work is interpretive, and therefore evocative, raising as many questions as it answers. The rewards, however, are those of looking inside real schools and seeing what people do, what they think, and what they desire.

Clifford Geertz (1980), the well known American anthropologist, draws attention to the explanatory power of an anthropological approach:

> interpretive explanation—and it is a form of explanation, not just exalted glossography—trains its attention on what institutions, actions, images, utterances, events, customs, all the usual objects of social-scientific interest, mean to those whose institutions, actions, customs, and so on they are. As a result, it issues not in laws like Boyle's, or forces like Volta's or mechanisms like Darwin's but in constructions like Burckhardt's, Weber's or Freud's: systematic unpackings of the conceptual world in which condottiere, Calvinists, or paranoids live. (p. 167)

The researcher lives in a particular social world for an extended period of time in order to see through participants' eyes and analyze their cultural world. The aim is not to provide final answers or a perfect consensus, but to refine debates and stimulate thought.

To study in cultures requires an appreciation for observation, symbolism, and nuance. Some aspects of culture are hidden, such as values, norms, and meanings. Other aspects of culture are clearly overt, such as rituals, celebrations, and leaders. However, even overt acts and phenomenon have a meaning that may be held up for interpretation and analysis. Whether a school event has a covert function of indoctrination, control, growth, or even obedience, for instance, can only be understood in the context of other events. Thus, a teacher who engages in a daily ritual to nature in his or her classroom may be engaging in any number of activities. For instance, he or she could be supporting the Green Peace movement, or showing human control and domination of nature, or, as in the Waldorf School in this study, using nature to teach in a holistic and aesthetically enriching way. In another school the activity may simply be a time-filler without any conscious motive or purpose.

The Spindlers (1987a), among other anthropologists, empha- size the importance of penetrating manifest, overt cultural content for the hidden dimensions:

> we find that the implicit, tacit, and hidden levels of culture are most important. They are what explain puzzling persistencies that are there over time under a surface level of change, some- times even dramatic change . . . . Many models for research and analysis used by both social scientists and educators do not permit the study of the very processes we have discovered are the most important—those aspects of the continuing dialogue be- tween students and teachers that are hidden beneath the surface of behavior. (p. 154)

Prolonged engagement and persistent observation are necessary to discover meanings. Surface representations are sometimes misleading, requiring the anthropologist to remain both open to suggestion and sceptical at the same time. The study of school cultures was therefore carried out through close observation of, and involvement with, administrators, teachers, students, and parents in schools.

The study took place throughout the 1989–1990 school year, with the previous year spent becoming acquainted with the schools. The preliminary year of involvement prepared the way for the study. Data were generated and analyzed concurrently. Three main methods of data collection were employed: (a) observation, (b) interviews, and (c) the study of documents. I spent on average a full day observing in each school every week, being involved in and recording virtually every aspect of school life. Classroom lessons, playground behavior, assemblies, chapel (at St. Catherine's), sports days, festivals, ceremonies, parent and faculty meetings, and the anthroposophical study group (at Waldorf School) were studied. Extensive notes were taken, which included such details as time records, spatial and social relational maps. Observational data were aided by the video-recording of lessons and events. Video technology, combined with detailed notes, and view of a larger context than a video frame permits, allowed for a close analysis of the social settings. Interviews were also conducted with administrators, teachers, parents and students. The interviews varied in length from 40 minutes to 2 1/2 hours. They were conducted throughout the year's period of fieldwork, frequently after school or in the evenings following a day of observation. Questions asked of interviewees varied due to the interactive nature of the interview. Interviews were audiotaped and later transcribed for analysis. In addition, documents, written materials, and curricula were studied to assist in the search to uncover school cultural meanings. These included faculty and student guides, parent handbooks, student publications, calendars, parent notices, faculty meeting minutes, and school demographic and other data.

The last phase of the study (1990–1991) was spent reworking material and reviewing videotapes, audiotapes, and documents, with an aim to refine the interpretation. It should also be noted that cultures of schools do change over time; therefore, we cannot assume that the schools described and analyzed here are identical to those same schools today. The cultural themes that were found and the intimate portrayal of life in schools is not intended to be a blueprint for other schools, but a characterization of schooling developed *in situ* that may sensitize educators to some of the broader implications of taken-for-granted cultural phenomena in schools.

AN ANTHROPOLOGY OF PRIVATE SCHOOLS

This book differs from the bulk of research on private schooling, which has been directed at a quantitative comparison of test scores with those of public schools. The aim has frequently been either to laud the public school system, or to evaluate critically public schools by drawing attention to their more successful private school counterparts. The classic study in this vein was Coleman, Hoffer, and Kilgore's (1982) comparison of public and private high schools. They argued that private schools produced higher levels of student achievement than public schools with comparable students. Chubb and Moe (1990) then updated the study, arguing that the private school model of a competitive market system would serve public schools well. State control of education was seen as the problem, and in Chubb and Moe's view all one needed to do to revitalize schooling was to create a market system. Any group could thus start a school, meeting only minimal government criteria to be a public school. Good schools would flourish; the bad ones would die. However, Chubb and Moe seem to have little recognition of the inequalities that such an approach would create, nor do they acknowledge the potential for divisiveness. Moreover, the Coleman results on which Chubb and Moe place so much faith have been challenged. Other researchers using the same data have found insignificant or no differences in student achievement between private and public schools (James & Levin, 1988, p. 3). School culture and other qualitative and intangible school differences may be more important than achievement scores in shaping students' motivations, attitudes, and skills that lead to future success (Haertel, James, & Levin, 1987, p. 3).

A cultural perspective allows for a more complete view of a school than other analyses allow. Instead of isolating administration or classroom management in order to study them, for instance, the school is properly conceptualized as an *ecology of people and events*. Rather than separating dimensions of schooling, they are considered as interacting elements in an ecology we call school. It follows, then, that, if policies are to be effective, they need to be informed by such an analysis.

The study also contributes to school restructuring literature by providing school comparisons. Reform proposals have begun to encourage the growth of diversity in public schools, for example, Grant (1988). Schools known as magnet or alternative public schools have been promoted in recent years. There are now thousands of these public school alternatives in the U.S. (Barth, 1980, p. 18). Such schools differentiate themselves according to public demand in a free enterprise manner: an artistically oriented school in one community, a technical school in another, an academic school, and so on. Public alternative education is touted as a means toward achieving "educational excellence and equity in our schools and correcting social injustice in our society" (Young, 1990, p. 126). The present study of private schools adds to our view of what schools can be. The study illustrates schooling based on philosophical foundations that are distinctly different to regular public schools and may provide stimulating ideas and possibilities, as well as insights into potential problems for yet to be proposed alternative public schools.

At St. Catherine's a strong academic orientation is combined with an emphasis on character development. Waldorf School, on the other hand, offers an alternative to the "age of the machine" so readily embraced in U.S. culture. Schools are shown responding to a rapidly changing modern world in different ways. Waldorf School advocates less materialism and a return to nature, an alternative to the prevailing U.S. culture. St. Catherine's contrasts sharply in its promotion of more science and technology, although tempered by a social concern. The study also draws attention to the costs and benefits of distinctive school types. Indeed, many of the arguments surrounding the controversy over tracking students (e.g., Oakes, 1985) apply to schools. We need to think again about the question of whether schools ought to be pluralistic from within, and essentially the same across the country, or differentiated according to demand and local conditions.

The simple dichotomy between traditional and progressive education is also shown to be far too simplistic. St. Catherine's, a traditional and conservative school, also has some liberal or progressive overtones. And Waldorf School, an essentially progressive school, contains much that is representative of the traditional school of thought. For instance, the authority of the teacher is central at Waldorf School, which contrasts with the school's insistence on a democratic organization of "working within a circle." Two varieties of schooling, and the complexity of their educational and social foundations, are made apparent.

The study also highlights the importance of symbols in schools. Students' lives are keenly affected by the values, ideas, beliefs, and attitudes of those around them. Private schools experience less internal disagreement over what symbols are appropriate, for parents and teachers self-select their school and create a school that complements their own value system. Private schools are also not compelled to admit or retain any student. Countercultural elements are thus reduced. However, this raises another issue, that of private schools exerting a strong control over students' lives through the manipulation of symbols and perhaps coming close to Goffman's (1961) "total institution" concept. Ironically, Waldorf School argues that it prepares students to "respond in powerful and positive ways to whatever challenges to freedom and demands to conformity are placed on them," and yet conformity to Waldorf School culture is strong. Ought private schools be free to set their own agenda in this regard? And what of private schools' relationship to the state? Would it be acceptable to found a school on radically antistate principles, for instance? The study draws attention to these and other social foundational concerns. Probing, enlightening, seeking to find what "is" and then to explore what this "means" for schools, characterizes this book.

UNIVERSES OF MEANING CONCERNING THE WORLD, OTHERS, SELF

School cultures are shown to have tremendous educational and social implications. First, we need to consider the way schools make sense of the larger world, their view of nature and the "cosmos." Second, the form of relations to others that is encouraged in schools is important, not only in the immediate context, but as a foundation for social life. And third, the perceptions of the individual or "self" developed in schools is surely critical to a student's growth and development. Schools implicitly adopt a particular lens or set of assumptions about social reality, nature, and human nature. While my emphasis is on the meanings or philosophic foundations embedded in schools through symbols, we are not simply talking about symbols and school philosophy. Symbols manifest themselves in concrete and tangible forms, in curriculum, school organization, rituals, the use of time, space, social relations, and so on. Tangible and intangible aspects of life in schools are described and analyzed in successive chapters. While the book also focuses on *particular school cultures*, the findings have relevance to a much wider audience. Educators from a variety of backgrounds might want to further consider the meanings of school cultures and where they stand in relation to perceptions of the world, others and the "self."

Perception of the World, Nature, the Cosmos

Waldorf School promotes the idea of humankind as part of the cosmos. Interconnectedness with nature and the world, and the development of spiritual understandings, are considered at least as important as academic concerns. The school promotes the idea of the world as an organic whole and seeks to educate the child to feel at home in that world, rather than experiencing the anomie and aimlessness that is seen as a problem in modern postindustrial societies. Spirituality is a core value in the school, although no one religion is taught. Spirituality is seen to arise through the development of reflectiveness and intuition through aesthetic experiences, particularly those involving nature and the natural world. The arts, music, painting, modeling, movement, eurythmy, and so on, are some of the processes that are seen as helpful in integrating cognitive, emotional, kinaesthetic, and spiritual learning. Students are also educated in a way that minimizes national boundaries and instead looks to a connected view of a world global village.

St. Catherine's, on the other hand, promotes the idea of humans "above" nature. St. Catherine's adopts a traditional academic view of the world, one that privileges logico scientific knowledge and divides the world into somewhat separate spheres, such as social, economic, political, and religious lives. Thus, the school encourages both religion and science as somewhat separate entities. In this view God is "above" nature, and humans are to use their knowledge of science and scientific processes, tempered by spiritual and social concerns, to make decisions about nature and the social and physical worlds. In the Waldorf school's organic or *holistic* conception of the world, knowledge is taught in wholes rather than in parts, and through storytelling rather than through abstractions. The rhythms of the school day are thus cyclical at Waldorf School, compared to a more linear and divided mode at St. Catherine's, where an *academic elite* model of schooling prevails. The differences in school cultures can be seen across school goals, practices, and outcomes. For example, Waldorf School has a largely oral curriculum built around the notion of interdisciplinary studies and "weak" boundaries (Bernstein, 1971). Arithmetic is thus taught, using music, rhythm, dance, poetry and writing, by the same teacher, who stays with the child for an extended period of time, ideally 8 years. The curriculum at St. Catherine's is, instead, a written document with "strong" boundaries and subject specialists who teach discrete areas. Many other examples and detailed analyses of the schools' views of the world and nature will be found in successive chapters.

Relations to Others

The form of relations to others in Waldorf School is personalized, stressing community and equality. The individual child is recognized and encouraged to develop in unique ways, but as a part of a small society that is the school. Strong community affiliations between teachers, child, and the home are apparent. The practice of teachers staying with the child for a long period of time is illustrative of the personal approach that is taken. In many ways the school has a feminine or nurturing culture. Teachers visit each child's home at least twice a year and constantly work towards strengthening school–community bonds. St. Catherine's social relations also emphasize personal connectedness, but from a more professional standpoint and with a view towards developing the child's intellect. The school's intention is to foster rationality and cognitive growth along with other aspects of development. Both schools intend to prepare students to be able to live in the outside society in the future, as well as to be strong, community supporters in the present. However, St. Catherine's places more emphasis on academics and preparation for the future in the wider external society; Waldorf School tends to focus more on all-round development through the senses, and for the here and now in the local school-community.

Perceptions of the Individual or "Self"

In Waldorf School the individual is recognized as an important being; indeed, children are viewed as special "gifts" from God. Reverence for the child goes back to Rudolf Steiner, the founder of the Waldorf School movement, who is regarded as an inspired teacher or leader of the school. In Steiner's public lectures he continually thanked the higher powers who had sent children down to earth. As an example of this reverence for the child, each morning and afternoon teachers shake each child's hand as they enter and leave the classroom, extending warm messages of encouragement. Contact between the child and the teacher is personalized. Each child is recognized as a unique individual. The emphasis on the uniqueness of the individual can also be seen in the school's "evaluation" system, whereby teachers represent each child in poetry or narrative form. No grades are given. Thus, each child inspires the teacher to convey the essence of that child's development to his or her parents. The use of an artistic form of expression is consistent with the school's holistic approach to teaching and learning.

At the same time as emphasizing the whole child, Waldorf School also follows Rudolf Steiner's theory of stage development, where the individual is seen to progress through fixed stages of development of three 7-year periods: 0–7 years is the "willing" stage; 7–14 years is the "feeling" stage; and 14–21 years is the "thinking" stage. Thus, kindergartners are not encouraged to read, since the stage of readiness is not thought to occur until after the child has lost his or her "baby teeth" around the age of 8. In its adherence to stage theory, the school thus also upholds a belief that children possess some universal qualities that are not just unique to the individual. In contrast, at St. Catherine's the approach is that the individual's development is able to be accelerated and perfected through a variety of experiences, tests, and challenges. Children in kindergarten and even preschool are exposed to print and encouraged to explore with prereading and writing activities. Waldorf School places more faith in natural development and the child's inner unfolding. School culture in one context is organic and aesthetic in form; in the other context it is academic, instrumental, and rational.

CONCLUSIONS

Understanding and critiquing schools in terms of their conceptual model of teaching and learning, in this case holistic or academic elite, and their moral vision, is necessary if we are to know what schooling is really about. As Dewey (1938, p. 48) points out, the moral life of schooling cannot be split off from its intellectual function: Collateral learning, the formation of attitudes, likes, and dislikes, is at least as important to students' own futures and society's well-being as any other knowledge or skills they might gain.

One of the outcomes of this book is therefore the sense of potential it offers us as educators to envisage the creation of alternative school cultures, and to be informed consumers of schools. We are led to ask, for example: What is a school promoting with regard to relations to the world, others, and the individual? What is it that a school stands for? What is valued or worth fighting for in a particular school? Studies of different forms of schooling serve to stimulate thought about the mission of public schools. Criticism of schools frequently focuses on alleged fragmentation, alienation, and isolation. The study provides tangible examples of schools that have a coherent culture, a strong web of meaning by all involved. Both schools seek to provide an answer to social and educational ills. Both schools have a clear idea of education and the educated child, although they pursue quite different goals in different ways.

The idea of looking at these schools as religious environments is also introduced. Waldorf School has the appearance of a secular school with no specific religious instruction, but this belies the school's emphasis on spiritual and religious values. The verse in the opening ritual described earlier, which reveres God and nature, was written by Rudolf Steiner. Steiner was a "prophet" who proclaimed a particular doctrine that has now been adopted by people all over the world. Those parents who call themselves anthroposophists and follow Steiner's "spiritual science," or anthroposophy belief system, and Waldorf educators and parents in general, tend to hold certain moral values. A central belief is that of a nonmaterialistic worldview. Interestingly, people with Catholic, Jewish, Protestant, and other religious faiths find anthroposophy and the Waldorf view compatible. Neither is St. Catherine's a secular school, like public schools, although it is nondenominational. The school does not teach a particular religion or doctrine. Nevertheless, even though students from a variety of religious groups attend the school, they are required to attend chapel, where a distinctively Christian and Episcopal inspired message is given, despite efforts to diversify by including hymns and prayers from all churches. Religion in its various forms is shown to underpin teaching and learning. Waldorf School might be criticized for emphasizing spiritual concerns more than political ones (Uhrmacher, 1991, p. 264, also makes this point). For instance, the school does not seem overly concerned about the underrepresentation of minority students in the school. For those of us who are concerned with social justice and equity, Waldorf School's focus on spirituality while downplaying social action and social problems merits further consideration.

The study also breaks new ground in its attention to holistic education, an underresearched area. Waldorf schools are perhaps one of the best examples of holistic education yet developed, although they have remained relatively closed off from educational discourse and research. To my mind, educators and social scientists have much to learn from Waldorf schools, just as those in Waldorf Schools would benefit from dialogue and interchange with others. Public school educators are able to see in Waldorf School a form of education that demonstrates an interconnection of culture and environment. Waldorf School advocates for its students an aesthetically enriching life in harmony with nature. Its emphasis on all natural materials and a curriculum focused on music and the arts is fascinating and

unique. This contrasts with the academic, rationalist, individualistic, and competitive ethos of St. Catherine's. Waldorf School
asserts a romantic, progressive, and somewhat escapist view of
education that has charm and appeal as our world becomes
increasingly more depersonalized and dehumanized. St. Catherine's, on the other hand, is traditional and academic. At first
glance one might reach the conclusion that Waldorf School is a
more humane and democratically consistent form of education.
However, this position might be questioned on the grounds of
exclusiveness: Is it democratic in character, or a special interest
group with little relevance to the larger society in which it is
located? St. Catherine's faces the problems of our modern
society in a different way, by teaching students to compete
successfully, to excel in a competitive world, but also to hold
onto traditional values and retain a humane attitude toward the
world. Finally, when the wider U.S. society values instrumental
values, individualism, and competitiveness, the implications for
Waldorf School, which is trying to establish different norms, are
profound. Will the oppositional school culture of Waldorf
School also prepare students well for U.S. society, or will they
be illprepared and at odds with mainstream society? The study
raises these and other important questions about schooling,
while celebrating two fine and unique examples of schools.

2

A SYMBOLIST AND POSTMODERN THEORY OF CULTURE

CULTURE AS SYMBOLISM

Looking at schools as cultures allows us to perceive the dynamic quality of schools. Schools are no longer simply institutions, but viable living organisms, human creations with unlimited possibilities. A group of people making up a school is seen to be actively devising solutions to commonly held problems. Their solutions and collective understandings are then passed on to new members, subtly changing in the process. A symbolist theory of culture recognizes these various problems and solutions and emphasizes the symbols that people use to convey their meanings. It attends to the points of view of the people in the situation. The meaning of culture to participants is held to be all important for its role in uncovering new dimensions of schooling. Describing and interpreting school cultures becomes a way to "see" and "show" what schools are really about beneath their presented "face." In this study a symbolist view of culture grounded in and developed through fieldwork is then refined by drawing on a postmodern critique to explain some of the ambiguities and discontinuities in school cultures.

We shall first consider the culture concept. Culture is a historically developed system of symbols, both verbal and nonverbal, which contains a group's pattern of meanings about the world, others and themselves. In other words, culture is "a system of inherited conceptions expressed in symbolic form" by means of which humans "communicate, perpetuate and develop their knowledge about and attitudes towards life" (Geertz, 1968, p. 641). Viewing culture as a pattern or web or meanings means that while we can study parts of the system, this is not the same as understanding the culture as a whole. Culture is considered as an ecology of interconnecting parts. Changes in any one part of a culture may affect other parts of it, although this is not always the case; cultures have some partial independencies. The metaphor Geertz uses to illustrate culture as a whole, and yet that also contains partially independent elements, is that of an octopus. The octopus' tentacles are separate from one another and from the octopus' brain, and they are also connected, making a "viable if somewhat ungainly entity" (Geertz, 1973, p. 408). Geertz argues that the analysis of culture comes down not to an overarching master plan or heroic "assault" from the top-down, but to a painstaking bottom-up searching out of "significant symbols." A workable theory of culture is to be achieved by "building up from directly observable modes of thought to determinate families of thought, those that are more clearly defined and then to more variable, less tightly coherent but still ordered 'octopoid' systems of thought" (Geertz, 1973, p. 408).

The meanings encoded in symbols are many and varied. For instance, cognitive elements of culture are those ideas about the world that people use to interpret their own behavior and the behavior of others. Evaluative components of culture are those areas where people place a value on things, for example, moral codes and ethics. "Conceptions of the desirable" or shared values that serve as guidelines for behavior would fall under this rubric (Yinger, 1982, p. 23). Expressions of feeling, including sentiments, moods, motivations, and ambitions are also culturally embedded (Rice, 1980, p. 213). This is not to say elements of culture can be separated; ideas, values, and feelings are interconnected. However, it is helpful to remember that culture is made up of a variety of human responses expressed in symbolic form.

Symbols encode meanings. They make them accessible. Symbols can be any number of "signs" that "signify" (Geertz, 1973). Words, stories, myths, music, paintings, objects, and technology can all be symbols. So can events and activities, such as rituals and ceremonies. Even institutions, behavior, processes and social relations can serve as symbols (Rice, 1980, p. 214). Receiving a high grade at St. Catherine's, for instance, is not valued in itself, but for what it stands for, as a sign that the student has "done well" academically and is expected to garner future rewards. When Waldorf School refuses to give grades and instead has teachers write prose and poetry and paint pictures to convey messages to children and their parents, this is symbolic of the school's commitment to a holistic model of education and to the aesthetic realm.

In the symbolist view of culture there is much that the researcher intuits or pieces together from tacit knowledge by immersion in a culture, rather than logically deducting the argument in the abstract. Because culture is about social rela- tionships and human thought and behavior, which has its own informal logic, it can only be studied within the ongoing pattern of life. One cannot study pieces of a culture analytically, out of context and in terms of their logical interrelationships alone. Cultural meanings can only be found through prolonged engage- ment in the field, a process of "inspecting events" for their symbol systems (Geertz, 1973, p. 17).

It is the relations among symbols that help us to understand culture. The meaning is not discernable from any one particular symbol, but rather from its association with, and relation to, other symbols. Context is all important. The researcher then has to interpret the symbols, for meanings are problematic and sometimes ambiguous. We cannot simply match a meaning code to a symbol. Instead, the process resembles a kind of trial and error, learning by discovery approach whereby the researcher tries to discern the uses and meanings of symbols in a particular context, much as natives learn their cultures in the first place.

The researcher then uses imagination, seeing into the meaning of things, rather than just seeing things. To analyze social life we are interested in the drama of human existence, the "games" of life, the complexity of life's "drama" and the "texts" we write and enact (see Bredo, 1990; Geertz, 1980). What becomes impor- tant for analysis is the search for rules, representations, atti- tudes, and intentions.

When viewing social life as a game, best represented by Erving

Goffman's (1959) work, people are seen to make moves and play a game with socially constructed rules. The social group is seen to create its own "little universes of meaning in which some things can be done and some cannot (you can't castle in dominoes)" (Geertz, 1980, p. 171). People are viewed as strategists, playing the game according to their self-defined motives: "I wonder," Prince Metternich is supposed to have said when an aide whispered into his ear at a royal ball that the Czar of all the Russians was dead, "I wonder what his motive could have been." When playing the "game" of life, people are seen to make an effort to keep up appearances and present a public "face" in "front regions," much as a poker player keeps up pretences in order to be successful. "Back regions" provide a much needed place for people to then let go of pretences and relax away from the public eye (Bredo, 1990).

Likewise, a drama metaphor is a useful way to analyze social life. The drama metaphor has been around at least since Shakespeare: all the world's a stage, men and women are merely players, they have their entrances and exits, and so forth. And, as Geertz points out, the concept of role, which is central to sociological analysis, has dramaturgical origins (Geertz, 1980). Ritual theory, too, is rooted in a view of life as drama. Theater and religion in particular use ritual to bind their social meanings. In the anthropologist Victor Turner's (1988) interpretation, the drama of social life leads to differences and conflict which are then resolved through ritual, such as feud, litigation, sacrifice or prayer.

> If they succeed, the breach is healed and the status quo, or something resembling it, is restored; if they do not, it is accepted as incapable of remedy and things fall apart into various sorts of unhappy endings: migrations, divorces or murders in the cathedral. (Geertz, 1980, p. 173)

In turn, looking at social life as a text involves constructing a text to represent a social entity and then interpreting that text:

> To see social institutions, social customs, social changes as in some sense "readable" is to alter our whole sense of what such interpretation is and shift it toward modes of thought rather more

familiar to the translator, the exegete or the iconographer than to the test giver, the factor analyst, or the pollster. (Geertz, 1980, p. 176)

Researchers working in this vein, for example, Becker (1986), study the social text in terms of the "relation of its parts to one another; the relation of it to others culturally or historically associated with it; the relation of it to those who in some sense construct it; and the relation of it to realities conceived as lying outside of it" (Geertz, 1980, p. 177). A consideration of boundaries, "who's in and who's out in the social group," and of the rules for inclusion and exclusion, becomes important (Bredo, 1990).

A holistic and symbolist view of culture thus focuses on face-fo-face interaction (culture as "game"), collective intensities (culture as "drama") and the imaginative forms of life as they are socially constructed (culture as "text"). To focus solely on one or the other would be to consider only a part of the buzz and confusion and noise that is culture. Culture is not only about situated motives, but about authority and persuasion and exchange and hierarchy. Culture is not just a text that is read or translated; people also create their own meanings in the situation. Culture is like jazz. There may be a musical score, but the genius of jazz is in its impromptu and creative side, with an exploration into what could be. Culture is very much a process.

A POSTMODERN PERSPECTIVE

A classic account of cultures as closed systems does not accommodate the multifaceted nature of modern 20th-century society with its fragmented cultural systems. A postmodern perspective adds some conceptual detail that is missing in an overly bounded and integrated view of culture. For instance, however much a particular school may wish for schooling with a certain view of the world, it is virtually impossible to prevent the cross-fertilization of other ideas and ways of doing things. People in modern society are not isolated and are therefore subject to many, and often conflicting, loyalties and points of view. Even for the somewhat self-contained schools in this study, the fact remains that they are characterized by multiple perspectives. As an example, Waldorf School seeks to promote a nonmaterialistic world view, but the influence of Big Business through such activities as grocery shopping at large supermarkets (rather than a community/village store), and exposure to videos and television, are in many ways inevitable. The school may attempt to create normative control through such means as advising parents to limit their children's exposure to television, and the practice of teachers visiting children in their homes, but this control has limitations. From the time they begin school students also face the likely prospect of entry into a career in the "outside world." Moreover, people uninitiated into Waldorf School philosophy (e.g., new students and sometimes faculty) are constantly coming into the school. Proper Waldorf School ways of doing things are often quite different things for different people in the school. Depending on the background and experiences of those in the school, for example, Jewish, Sufi, Buddhist, or Christian, Waldorf School may be perceived in a conflicting manner. Moreover, at St. Catherine's, a traditional college-preparatory school, there is also no possibility of the school defining its ideas and values and automatically going about the business of transmitting them. It can try to do this, but the diverse, fragmented, and ever-changing dimensions of school culture prevents its careful regulation within a single, unified system. This is not to deny the strength of school cultures, but simply to point out that they are systems of meanings derived from many sources of input and comprised of multiple and often contradictory meanings.

Peshkin's (1986) study of a Baptist academy, and Cookson and Persell's (1985) studies of private schools, did not find such diversity of experience. They argued that the schools they studied were "total institutions," thus likening schools to jails, convents, and cloisters where there is virtually a monopoly by a particular socialization agency. There were many ways in which the schools I studied could have been cast in terms of a theory of total institutionalization, for there was much that fit this framework. However, this would be to overlook anomalies such as Waldorf School parents shopping at one of the large modern supermarkets to get credit for receipts to buy a computer for the school office—this in a school where there are no computers and many parents want it to remain that way for moral or philosophical reasons. A postmodern perspective adds the conceptual detail that is missing in overly neatly integrated theoretical constructs. Cast in postmodern terms, a symbolist theory of culture was able to provide a credible framework for piecing together the puzzle of school cultures.

But what does it mean to be *postmodern*?[1] To the sceptic, postmodernism seems to be yet another "ism" characterized by unintelligible rhetoric. In demystifying the term it is useful to consider postmodern thought in the context of premodern and modern thought. Premodern is that period of thinking marked by many worldviews prior to the rise of Western consciousness about five centuries ago. Western consciousness then came into its own as the key to modern thinking with its notion of *perspective*. Perspective spatialized or rationalized sight, as can be seen in mathematical geometry, modern engineering and machinery. Measurement became all important:

> The combination of the abstractedness of numbers as symbols that measure, with perspective, a way of relating those numbers as symbols to the visual world, leads to a sense of space as measured, as extending outward from a given point; ultimately the world is measurable—epitomized in Galileo's maxim, 'to measure everything measurable and to make what is not measurable capable of being measured'. (Turner, 1988, p. 73)

Modern thinking also meant clearly defined academic boundaries. In anthropology social reality was represented as "stable and immutable, a harmonious configuration governed by mutually compatible and logically interrelated principles" (Turner 1988, p. 73). History in a linear sense, technical rationality, the supremacy of the "individualistic, competitive person (implicitly male) who exercises restraint and represses desires in the interest of more 'rational' goals: power and control," these are characteristic of modern consciousness (Spindler, 1978, pp. 22–25).

The postmodern turn rejected the one point perspective and

---

[1]Alan Toynbee is said to have coined the term *postmodern*, with Ihab Hassan giving it prominence and Benamou (Benamout & Caramello, 1977) in *Performance in Postmodern Culture* lending the term even greater specificity (see Turner, 1988, pp. 72–76).

began entertaining instead ideas of multiperspectival consciousness. Ideal models of social structure, as touted by functionalism
and various types of structuralism, gave way to multiperspectival time and the study of processes as performances. A prede-
cessor of this position was Erving Goffman's (1959) *The Presentation of Self in Everyday Life*. For Goffman "all the world's a
stage" in terms of social interaction. It is social processes with
all their ebb and flow, flux and performance, that are central:

> Goffman, Schechner [1977] and I constantly stress process and
> processual qualities: performance, move, staging, plot, redressive
> action, crisis, schism, reintegration, and the like. To my mind,
> this stress is the 'postmodern turn' in anthropology . . . Post-
> modern theory would see in the very flaws, hesitations, personal
> factors, incomplete, elliptical, context-dependent, situational
> components of performance, clues to the very nature of human
> process itself, and would perceive genuine novelty, creativeness,
> as able to emerge from the freedom of the performance situation,
> from what Durkheim (in his best moment) called social 'efferves-
> cence,' exemplified for him in the generation of new symbols and
> meanings by the public actions, the 'performances' of the French
> Revolution. What was once considered 'contaminated,' 'promis-
> cuous,' 'impure' is becoming the focus of postmodern analytic
> attention. (Turner, 1988, pp. 76–77)

Social performance as a process became a legitimate object of
study. Social life became conceived of as made up of performances.

To translate these ideals into a coherent cultural framework,
we will draw on Gerholm's (1988), work which identifies a
number of postmodern features of culture in a theory of ritual.
First, the plurality of perspectives is salient. For example, even
within any one ritual there are any number of different vantage
points from which it may be approached. A ritual seen from a
teacher's point of view is quite different from that of a student
also taking part in the ritual. A second feature is that none of the
participants, neither teachers nor students, "moves within an
unquestioned cultural whole." They all live in a somewhat
fragmented cultural universe combining elements from various
cultural systems (Gerholm, 1988, p. 194). Third, for each individual participating in a ritual it will have a unique meaning.

There is not just one correct and official version of what a ritual "does" or "means." There may be a correct view of how to perform a ritual and a culturally developed interpretation, but this does not guarantee an individual's experience of it. Moreover, the ritual is embedded in a social context, the general situation, that also informs the ritual. It is not just the ideas and ways of doing and meaning in the ritual that are important, but also the "general occasion of the ritual as much as the ritual itself" (p. 195) that affects an individual's private experience of it. Finally, tradition is reinvented through ritual. Whatever the official institutional purpose, ritual serves to orient people towards a particular tradition. A tradition has roots in the past, but is updated to serve current needs. Thus, in Gerholm's example, when a Hindu woman living in Trinidad dies, her husband and son, who are not religious, nevertheless insist on a proper Hindu funeral for her. The meanings they derive from it are not seen as inauthentic, but rather as fitted to their circumstances and needs.

Thus, the postmodernist turn, which views culture as paradoxically fragmented and characterized by a plurality of perspectives, adds a significant and new dimension to Geertz's definition of *culture*. Since my concern here is with messages sent by schools, a symbolist and Geertzian view of culture is implicit in my work. However, I needed to be mindful of accepting Geertz's definition uncritically. His view has been criticized for creating "beautiful structures" and assuming a "homogeneous culture so that individual versions are more or less identical" (Gerholm, 1988, p. 199). A symbolist and postmodern view of culture gives credence, not only to totality, unity, or structures, but also to culture as process and as performance.

MICRO- AND MACROANALYSES

Much of the literature on schooling is driven by macro- or grand theorizing. Culture writ large, the idea of a larger system organizing peoples in many different contexts, is the concern of macrotheorists. Bernstein (1977), for instance, argues that schools are the primary agent of ideological control by the state, that schools socialize students into the dominant society, and that society, in turn, is reproduced through schooling. Similarly, Apple and Weis (1983), Aronowitz (1973), Bourdieu and Passerrou (1977), and Giroux (1983) are all concerned with situating schools in a sociopolitical context. Apple's "hidden curriculum," Bourdieu's idea of "cultural capital" and "habitus," and Giroux's "hidden curriculum" all explain what goes on in schools in terms of their connections with the larger society; the middle class culture of the school teaches students to adopt middle class values. Schools are seen to do much more than simply teach subject matter and skills; they socialize students into a prevailing ethos: "Values, virtues, desirable ways of behaving—these are, intentionally or not, conveyed through social structures, settings and the ways in which knowledge is distributed" (Greene, 1983, p. 3). Students are taught to internalize values that would be useful for "good" workers in society, for example, respect for authority, punctuality, cleanliness, docility, and unquestioning acceptance of and conformity to the social order. In Bowles and Gintis's (1976) *Schooling in Captialist America*, the social class background of students is held to interact with their schooling experience and result in the production of a family's position in the hierarchy of labor. Those students from more advantaged backgrounds gain positions of power and authority, while "working class kids get working class jobs" Willis (1977). Anyon (1989) further differentiates between classes of schools, showing how the more prestigious schools are preparing upper middle-class kids for positions of power and authority, in contrast to working class schools, whose mission is to prepare workers.

But American public schools have traditionally been in the business of socializing the working class and bringing a middle-class value position to the masses: "With a shock of recognition we note today that the schools are educating for docility, or that they operate to reinforce a rigid class structure, or that teaching methods and curriculum content are saturated with a middle-class value bias. These are precisely the grounds on which American schooling was initially justified" (Vallance, 1983, p. 20). The aim of public schools was historically, after all, to provide for equality of opportunity, to assimilate immigrants, and to civilize and moralize the populace for the good of the nation. To prevent religious groups from using schools for their own purposes, it was constitutionally decided that church and state should separate. Henceforth, public education and other matters of civil policy were conducted without religious elements.

Schools are nevertheless not simply puppets of the dominant mainstream society. They have their own unique concerns and their own "poetry" of people and events. Whether public or private, all schools are not the same. What often occurs is that macrotheorists apply a macrotheoretical grid to particular case studies which are assumed to inform us about general sociocultural phenomena. Overinflation of the results of the case study can occur. As Bredo (1990, pp. 8-9) points out, macrotheorizing can also reduce what one is able to find in a particular setting. The fixed framework or theory forces interesting anomalies into a conforming pattern. Much of the complexity that is able to be included in a microstudy is thrown out. Microstudies, on the other hand, focus on the local level. Culture writ small deals with particulars. One culture in a specific time and place is studied. Those who study both culture writ large and small focus on similar aspects of culture—social relations, education maturation, religion, and so on. They differ in whether these are considered in essence locally specific or universally shared.

It is also possible to bring both perspectives into the analysis. McDermott and Roth (1978) urge abandoning the micro-versus-macro distinction on the grounds that macrostudies "need to be verified by an interactional record" and because micro studies "have been showing how ordinary behavior can reveal much of the machinery for the workings of social structure" (pp. 322-323). The benefit of a dualistic approach is that the anthropologist is able to focus on local culture which is anthropology's sine qua non, yet in doing so the study is able to illuminate influences from the broader cultural level that are salient at the local level.

In my view we have not paid enough attention to the local level, and in particular to qualitative differences in schools. While there have been many top-down social reproduction studies concerned with showing how the dominant social order is reproduced, it is also important to learn about processes and social dynamics within and across schools. In this study I am mainly concerned with accounting for the distinctive cultures of just two schools in a way that provides insight into their cultural processes. At the same time illuminating these tiny threads out of the patchwork quilt of all possible schools is worthwhile, both for the insights into the particular settings and for the questions this might raise about a theory of culture, and the role of schools in inculcating cultural mores. In Geertz's (1973, p. 313) words, analyses should be both particularistic and descriptive on the one hand, and general and theoretical, on the other.

THE STUDY OF SCHOOL CULTURES

The research tradition of viewing schools as cultures goes back at least to Waller's (1932) *Sociology of Teaching* and owes a debt to the many studies done by George Spindler (1982), George and Louise Spindler (1987a, b), and their students. Wolcott (1973, 1976, 1977), too, has long been a champion of cultural studies of schooling. *The Man in the Principal's Office* has remained a classic in the field, and Wolcott's (1987, 1988, 1990) many other works have showed us a great deal about the cultural basis of human ideas and actions. McDermott (1976), Noblit and Pink (1987), Peshkin (1986), Sarason (1971), Spradley and McCurdy (1988), Stephens (1967), and Van Maanen (1988) are just a few of the key people who have made significant contributions to the field of cultural studies. In this section I will not attempt to survey the field, but to draw attention to some of the different interpretations of school culture.

The Culture of the School

One way of looking at school culture is as institutions with their own set of practices. *School culture* is defined as composed of phenomena, such as academics, crowded public settings, and recitation (Page, 1990, p. 54; Sarason, 1971). Schools are seen as distinct from other institutions, hospitals, jails, convents, and so on. The roles of teacher and student, and the public's perceptions of what schools are for constrain schools in certain ways. Typically, researchers adopting this perspective study similarity in schools, see Mehan (1978), Sarason (1971), Stephens (1967), Waller (1932). Everhart (1988), for instance, finds a "culture of the school" within progressive schools. He studied three junior high "schools of choice." They were newly founded progressive schools, one public and two private, located in a city he calls Seaside on the west coast of the United States. The schools were staffed and attended by the largely middle-class liberal constituency that characterized the town. While the schools were "progressive," Everhart claimed they were less progressive than a "Summerhill or Waldorf school." His intent was to look closely at the symbolism used in the schools. He found consistencies across the schools and emphasized the similarities in their cultures. Everhart concludes that the symbolism in all three schools centered around "openness," meaning individualism, independence, and self-reliance. He criticizes the schools for their inability to conceptualize social relationships based on collective thought and action (p. 175). In his view, self-reliance and independence is only a part of human development; social and collective organization and interdependence is also important. The dominant pattern for schools to be top-down and to educate for independence was shown to occur even in schools with alternative ideologies. A gap also existed between informal student culture and a more formal school agenda, "despite progressive intentions" (p. 200). In other words, *doing school* has come to mean a set of fairly rigidly defined practices. Nevertheless, in Everhart's study, the alternative schools were at least partly successful in an endeavor to form a different model of *doing school*. The schools' application of academic knowledge to everyday life, the relatively "open" atmosphere with a high degree of student choice and parental involvement, the emphasis on "how to think" rather than memorization, and the fact that students enjoyed going to school meant these schools were somewhat different to regular public schools. Thus, those who study and write about the culture of the school remind us that as a society we have created a set of assumptions about and practices that we call "schooling" and that it is salient to take a step back and deconstruct the familiar and to think about alternative cultural possibilities.

School Culture from Teacher and Student Perspectives

Another way of looking at school culture is to take the perspectives of teachers or students. Metz (1978), for instance, focused on teacher cultures in schools. She identified two teacher cultures. One group was composed of teachers with the student centered or "developmental" teaching philosophy, the other group was made up of those teachers with the "incorporative," or academic, teaching philosophy. Metz raised the issue of there being more than one culture in a school: "There need not be just one culture in the school. And at Hamilton there was not" (p. 175). Her concern was with authority and control in schools from the points of view of people in the relationships. Here *culture* was defined primarily as social relationships between teachers and students, which is just one of the elements in the broader, holistic view of culture developed in the present study.

Cusick (1973) focused instead on school culture through the eyes of students. He conducted a case study of a public high school, or more specifically the experiences of three boys in an attempt to understand "the perspective used by those students to deal with their school" (p. 3). Cusick observed and examined the phenomenon of "student groupness and some of its effects." He concluded that the prevalence of tight inschool student groups was a natural but unrecognized consequence of the school's organizational structure (p. 216). The school, like other "large, impersonal, bureaucratic future-reward-oriented organizations that make up the bulk of America's economic and social life" was seen as demanding "only a part of the whole person" (1973, p. 220). Provided the students accepted school rules and limitations and adjusted to organizational life they were free to seek other rewards, primarily through peer group friendship. Cusick viewed schools as a "factory-like" "transmitter of our society's culture," a maintenance subsystem of the larger society (pp. 219–220). Cusick's analysis of the sociocultural characteristics of the school, with its "batch processing," routinization of activity, specialization, fragmentation, vertical organization, and compartmentalization of knowledge, is illustrative of an *industrial model* of public schools (pp. 208–209). While Cusick does not claim that the school studied is representative, he does believe it is "not unlike most secondary schools" (p. 219). Cusick (p. 222) would like to see schools more responsive to the whole student in a Deweyan sense, where the learner is involved in setting goals and the means to attain those goals.

Eisenhart (1990, p. 53) is also concerned with students' mean ings. She begins by noting that "not all schools send the same message to students," and that even schools in the same district may promote different cultural patterns. Eisenhart points out that theories that explain poor performance in school based on discontinuity between home and school fail to recognize that, in some cases, it is precisely the differences between home and school that facilitate some students' progress. She cites Jacob's (1984) study in Puerto Rico, which showed that caregivers of less proficient students routinely copied the literacy activities of school, whereas families with more proficient students invented their own out-of-school activities, thus making school more "discontinuous" for proficient students (Eisenhart, 1990, p. 53). Eisenhart then explores the notion of *created meanings* by different groups. She stresses the dual process of deriving meanings from previously created culture, and also the recreation and negotiation of new emergent meanings: "when groups or individuals with different inherited or (previously) created cultures interact, meanings have to be negotiated, and from this process comes a new created culture of the interacting group" (p. 56). In particular she focuses on cultural differences in the less successful groups, less proficient students, low ability readers, and gender differences, in order to discern culturally created meanings. Eisenhart claims that we have traditionally invested too much attention looking at simplistic cultural groups based on ethnic minority versus mainstream, when student performance in school is more likely to be influenced by cultural groups that the students *themselves* create, such as ability grouping, gender, athletic prowess and popularity (1990, p. 59).

School and Community Studies

Cultural differences between school and community are also studied. A good example of work in this vein is Heath's (1983) *Ways With Words*. Through an intensive 10-year-long ethnographic investigation of two communities in the Piedmont region in the Carolinas, Heath discovers cultural patterns in the communities of Roadville and Trackton that differ from that of the mainstream culture of the Towns People. The middle-class school is seen as oriented toward the values of the Towns People and essentially views Roadville and Trackton in "deficit" terms.

Heath's definition of *culture* centers around language, the children's "ways with words" and "how their teachers learned to understand their ways and to bring these ways into the classrooms" (p. 11). Heath actively engages students and teacher in ethnography in an attempt to build bridges of understanding between home and school. Teachers were made aware of how language is valued and developed in the differing communities, which then helped them to adapt teaching methods in order to connect home skills with school skills. Children, for instance, were taught to begin to observe the communication styles of many different people within the communities. However, after Heath's departure teachers who had successfully used her ethnographic strategies abandoned them. High test scores and "excellence" were thought to be more easily attained through the formerly used conventional schooling practices of recitation and drill and disregarding language and cultural differences. Where the present study complements Heath's work and addresses a new area is in its attention to schools as cultures and communities in themselves, not as mere institutions patronized by communities. Particularly in the case of private schools—but this may also apply to public schools—the school stands for and upholds certain key values, beliefs, and practices consistent with a school-community. If the school-community is heavily invested in schooling then it is no longer a matter of imposition of the school on a reluctant community, but an authentic nurturing of the community's young people.

School Culture as an Instrument of Social Reproduction

School cultures are also be seen as sites for social and political meaning making. McLaren (1986) uses reproduction theory to show how rituals in a "tough" inner-city Catholic school in Toronto, Canada, reproduce existing class, ethnic, and generation divisiveness. He was concerned that the "figure of Christ" had been reduced to a "silent accomplice in the act of symbolic violence and an invisible partner in the process of cultural reproduction" (1986, p. 13). Like Giroux (1981, 1988), McLaren is concerned about the oppression of marginal groups in society and the role of schools in perpetuating dominance and subordination. He urges students and teachers to form "new alliances with popular constituencies such as women's movements, gay rights, the peace movement, and the workers' movements" (1986, p. 253). McLaren's view of culture emphasizes ritual: "culture is fundamentally formed by interrelated rituals and ritual systems" (p. 5). McLaren suggests that schools' impoverished environments could be improved by deliberate attention to the creation of rites: "Perhaps a school procession could be orchestrated in which students would proceed from a nearby parish to the school (perhaps carrying a statue of the Virgin); the statue could then be rotated among the neighboring schools and kept in each school for a month. Students could then make moral and/or academic pledges during the time the statue resided in the school" (pp. 237–238).

Some studies of schools thus emphasize what they can tell us about the wider culture in which they are located. Every school is not unique, argues Page, "but neither is it the case that schools are all the same." Rather, schools are seen to "filter the broad manuscript of the wider culture" (1990, p. 52). Page sees the various schools in the U.S. as translations of a master text that is U.S. culture: "Just as Madame Bovary survives in inspired and insipid translations, so do U.S. schools vary as they render America lively or otherwise in the texts they construct." Similarly, in their analysis of "culture" in a white middle class school, Goldman and McDermott (1987) found evidence of competitiveness that they believed was part of an American ethos of competitiveness: "In American society, we have little choice about how to use competition. It seems to have a life of its own. It is everywhere, and it operates without regard for the people it measures and records. We do not do competition. Competition does us" (p. 298). Teachers in the school they studied consistently used competition as the motivator for learning. When teachers downplayed competition, students actively resisted these efforts. Deering (1989), too, emphasizes competition in U.S. schools, giving it a rather unflattering gloss.

Mainstream (white, middle class, androcentric) American culture and our schools are steeped in imagery and myths of individualism and competition. . . . Even in team sports, we find ways of singling out especially noteworthy individuals for recognition. Eight years of rhetoric from the Reagan administration about up-by-the-bootstraps initiative, and competing with the Japanese and Russians have bolstered the sense that individual effort and competitiveness are the ways to get ahead in America and the world. (p. 30)

The portrayal of competition and individualism as endemic in schools, and emanating from wider social values, once again focuses on the way schools reproduce fundamental qualities of the larger culture in which they are located.

Schools as Corporate Cultures

Another approach to the study of school culture is to view it as an entity which can be altered to bring about "school effectiveness." Researchers typically use a clinical model, drawing on the work of consultants in business who study managerial career development and the process of socialization, for example, Schein (1985). The "pathway" to educational "excellence" is considered to be built into school culture. In this view, teachers, administrators, parents, and the community are all playing their part in establishing and maintaining certain traditions and symbols that set the school apart from other schools. Deal (1985) particularly emphasizes history, and urges schools to codify and pass on their historical traditions and legacies. Developing a shared identity and sense of purpose is held to arise out of a school's experiences and history. However, he recognizes that both innovation, new rites and practices, as well as tradition are important to prevent becoming obsolete or losing one's roots and identity (Deal, 1990, p. 423). Deal (1990) further contrasts what he calls "cultural bonds" or "shared purposes, values, traditions and history" that promote a sense of community in private schools, with "rational bonds" or top-down "rules, roles, functions, penalties and formal authority" that he believes exist in public schools (p. 417).

Sergiovanni (1990, pp. 88-90) builds on Deal's ideas and attempts to provide school leaders with a template for the fostering of a "culture of excellence." The first step he proposes is to consciously explore and document the school's history: "Great accomplishments meld with dramatic failures to form a potentially cherishable lore." A second step would be to "anoint and celebrate heroes and heroines.'' Those individuals who succeeded in showing the school's values, such as a student who once struggled with math and later became a well-recognized physicist, would be used as role models, and tributes paid to them. Sergiovanni then suggests the building of sacred rituals and ceremonies that testify to the importance and significance of shared values. Like McLaren (1986), Sergiovanni argues that school rituals can be used to enhance a school's potential as an educative and social environment. He outlines an example of a ritual, a matriculation or enrollment ceremony for elementary, middle, or high schools. He describes parents and children attending a dignified service in their "best clothes." Students would march into the auditorium and take up their seats at the front of the room. On the stage flowers and candelabra would signify the import of the occasion. "Pomp and Circumstance," or another suitable piece, would be played, while faculty in academic gowns make a colorful procession into the room. Speeches would be made, followed by each student making an oath, such as promising to study hard, to do their best, to uphold values and traditions, not to let down their parents, and to aim to help run the country one day. The ceremony would conclude with the school song, a ceremonial exit and a reception (1990, pp. 89-90). A fourth step in this view of building school culture would be to cultivate the art of telling good stories about the school and the people in it. Myth making built around events and accomplishments that embody the values of the school is considered essential to a strong culture. Finally, Sergiovanni, again drawing on Deal's work, recommends that informal power networks, such as those headed by secretaries, custodians, and old guard teachers, be identified and consciously "worked": "schools need to identify these people, to integrate them into the mainstream of activity, and to reward them for the important positive contributions they make" (p. 90).

Sergiovanni's analysis assumes that principals, his audience, are able to carry out these steps and create a school culture. However, administrators typically attribute much greater power to their own actions than their observers or subordinates attribute to them. His proposal to consciously create school culture, while useful in highlighting some cultural elements, is overly simplistic in its assumption that one person, the princi-

pal, can change the face of school culture. He or she may indeed
effect some changes, but what is missing in this analysis is a full
recognition of culture as a collaborative affair, and one that is not
easy to predict: by introducing A into the ecology this may not
lead to the B that you had hoped for, but rather to X or XYZ. I am
not denying that principals can effect positive changes in
schools. They can. I would simply caution people against
adopting a "cook book—one recipe fits all" approach to the
creation of school culture. A principal may be well served to
understand the culture of a school, to be sensitive to its ethos,
traditions and ideals, and to view *the school as an ecology*
characterized by interdependence, rather than setting out as an
all-powerful individual administrator who is going to singlehan-
dedly change school culture. In Deal and Peterson's (1990, pp.
36–79) case studies, for instance, there is no sense of the
principals being assisted, and interacting with others to create
meaning. It is as if the principals have an omnipotent vision that
they then imprint on the school in their own individual way.

School Cultures as Webs of Meaning

Anthropologists such as Spindler (1982) (and the author of the
present study) look at schooling as a cultural process with an
aim to uncover defining metaphors through prolonged engagement in the field. *Culture* is the relationships and webs of
meaning that people "spin" in a particular social setting. As an
example in this tradition, Lesko's (1988) study of a midwestern
coeducational Catholic high school focuses, not on how to create
culture to gain excellence, nor on social reproduction or ine-
quality produced by schools, but rather on institutional culture,
the inside social and cultural relationships. She examines rituals
as central to culture and finds tension between "caring" (or
community) and "contest" (or individualistic competitive striving) in the school (1988, p. 110).[2] Lesko claims that public

---

[2]Interestingly, Varenne (1977) argues that it is the tension between community and competition that characterizes U.S. culture at large, a point under-
scored by the Spindlers (1987a, p. 152) in their discussion of "pivotal
concerns" or debates in American culture between: "freedom and constraint,
equality and difference, cooperation and competition, independence and
conformity, sociability and individuality, Puritanism and free love, materialism and altruism, hard work and getting by, and achievement and failure."

schools place too much emphasis on competition, evidenced in abstract and fragmented teaching and learning practices, and that they could learn from the Catholic school example of a dual emphasis on both achievement *and* a "religious-based education emphasizing character and morals" (1988, p. 19). Lesko's study has some parallels with this study in its focus on school cultural dynamics in process. Also, St. Catherine's, in the present study, embodies some of the same concerns about social responsibility (like Lesko's "caring"), in addition to an emphasis on college preparation or "contest." Waldorf School is less concerned with "contest," but even here the school intends to prepare students well for whatever futures they might hope for themselves. The present study is broader, however, than Lesko's. Her view of culture is of "systems of thought" expressed through ritual and myth (1988, p. 22). Lesko adopts a mainline Levi-Straussian (1963, 1979) synchronic and structuralist approach, and I include both structural and historical dimensions. History does not figure into Lesko's account, yet to my mind cultures are both created through day-to-day interaction as well as shaped by concerns outside the immediate present.

Clearly, the approaches to school culture are by no means alike. Just as there are literally hundreds of definitions of *culture*, so have researchers attempted to study it from a range of perspectives. We will now turn to the holistic view of school culture implicit in the present study.

What is School Culture?

School culture is a set of relationships, beliefs, values, and feelings shared by those who make up a school. Administrators, faculty, staff, parents, friends, students, and others create school meanings. Schools promote a particular orientation toward the world, toward others, and toward the individual or "self." For instance, they may socialize students in an attitude toward success, even if it is not attended to in an overt way.

A central aspect of school culture is shared meanings, even if the meanings are built around tensions and contradictions. People acknowledge one another as "belonging." For example, a person's allegiance to a particular cultural group or school signifies a set of guidelines for thought and behavior. A culture also needs a contrasting group or culture with which to define itself. The opposing culture helps give people in a cultural group a sense of itself and some clear boundaries: "we stand for X and not Y like those others."

This study shows five interconnected domains of analysis in a theory of school culture that focuses on the messages that schools send. First, we need to consider the *historical* and *social context* in which a school is embedded. Every school has an historical heritage, albeit in some cases only a recent heritage. What is aspired to, valued, and upheld today bears witness to past people, events, and standards. Even if we are not interested in change, we cannot properly understand the present without seeing it as rooted in its own time and place. A second consideration is the stories, *myths, and "philosophies"* of schools, which help define a sense of collective purpose and intentionality. It is in the telling and retelling of a school's stories that its culture gains meaning. A school's written philosophy, likewise, is a human creation designed to encourage commitment and loyalty to the school, and though it may only bear a thin resemblance to the created culture, it is nevertheless part of the web of intentions and meanings. Moreover, since schools are in the business of deliberately, as well as covertly, engendering ideas, beliefs, and values, the content and process of schooling is scrutinized. A third domain of analysis, the *curriculum* and *evaluation*, therefore centers on what the school does to educate the child, and on the measures it uses to evaluate performance. What kinds of things are taught in school, and how they are taught, are important elements in the dialectic of school culture. Moreover, symbols are used in rituals and ceremonies to restore and create culture. They are not just a reflection of the cultural system. *Ritual* is thus a fourth domain in the theory of school culture. The social world consists of signs and meanings that are dramatized in the form of ritual. Rituals stand for and display certain ideas; they also help perform actual functions. For example, they transform students into seniors and initiate students into school. Rituals are clearly much more than prescribed acts. The fifth domain, which I have called *time, space, and social relations*, takes into account a school's ecological context. Schools occupy physical space in varying ways. Their "lives" span particular time periods. They use time and space differently in their day-to-day realities. And they grow and flourish because of social relationships. It is through social interaction, people working together, sharing problems and triumphs, and communicating with each other, that collective meanings are made.

School culture is shown to be at the interface of individual and collective responses to the problem of how best to educate the child. The two schools in this study approach the problem in their own distinctive ways that can be seen in their cultures or symbolic and interpretive systems of meanings. Because culture is historically and socially developed, we begin with a focus on the schools' roots. We will consider the court decisions that have impacted private schools, raising a number of controversial private school debates; and we will place the school within a context of other types of school.

3

HISTORICAL AND SOCIAL CONTEXT

For the ethnographer no less than the historian, the events and social constructions of time past need to be known. They affect the present. Geertz (1973) writes that much of what we need to comprehend a particular event, ritual, custom or idea is insinuated as background information before the thing itself is directly examined. In the case of school cultures the background that is salient includes both a local and broader context of people and events. In the local context the specifics of a school's founding, its history, mission, goals, and so on has a bearing on contemporary cultural mores. In addition, a school's relationship to other schools in the community may affect its character and identity. And in a broader context, the outcomes of state and federal legislature are also often significant in setting limits on what is possible for schools.

We will begin with an introduction to the schools, then give some background on private schools more generally as they have been affected by legislature, for the courts regulate private and public schools. Over the years they have set parameters that constrain what a school can be. This is of interest because of what it tells us about the changing U.S. social and political situation and how private schools fit in. Schools arise in a context, forging their identity and mission in response to local conditions as well as those emanating from the broader society in which they are located. Finally, I will review some of the variety of private schools that are flourishing today, placing Waldorf School and St. Catherine's within a general framework of types of school.

WALDORF SCHOOL, ST. CATHERINE'S, AND SOUTHVILLE COMMUNITY

St. Catherine's is a traditional college preparatory school, preschool through grade 12, divided into three schools: Upper, Middle, and Lower. The school has 365 students in the Kindergarten through Grade 5 division, and a student body largely made up of the children of professionals. One part of the school was originally founded in 1910, although the school known today as St. Catherine's resulted from a merger in 1970 of a school founded in 1955 and the 1910 school. The original school was an Episcopal girls' boarding school, and the newer school was also founded by an Episcopal priest and a group of parents and citizens.

> The school was owned by the Episcopal Church prior to 1970 when the school merged and bought itself from the Episcopal Church. They remained associated with the church to some degree but two years ago severed connections with the state Episcopal Church Schools organization. Now we only have weekly chapel and a required religion course in the Upper School which is a scholarly approach to religion. It is an Old and New Testament course where students are required to read The Last Temptation of Christ. Chapel involves ministers from many different faiths, mostly the various Protestant Christian sects, but we have had the Rabbi. We have had teachers do chapel, and we have had a Catholic priest come, and the Captain of the Salvation Army . . . . We have folk who think the school is too religious and people who think we are not religious enough, and everything in between. (Interview, administrator)

Over the years the school's Episcopal links have been deemphasized, though the school remains a member of the National Association for Episcopal Schools and a member of the Council for Religion in Independent Schools. The current headmaster is a Doctor of Ministry and Master of Divinity in the Presbyterian Church and a philosophy scholar. In practice this means that, while the focus is more on universal moral themes than sectarian in approach, the orientation remains Christian:

> I had some problems with the original chapel. It was too denominational, too baby Jesus for me. And over the years they've modified that, too. But sometimes the guest speaker will still get too baby Jesus. Most of them though are really talking about morals and ethics that are true in every religion. A true samaritan is from the New Testament, but it's not a new idea at all. (Interview, teacher)

Religion is an important part of the school's heritage. The school's approach to religion is a scholarly one, and one which underlines the school's college-preparatory charter.

St. Catherine's is oriented heavily toward scholarship. It seeks academic excellence and social exclusivity for its clientele and is modelled on the prep school tradition which goes back to the ideals of the Anglican (Episcopal) British boarding schools. Like the British public schools, St. Catherine's is wealthy and established. St. Catherine's boasts assets of $7,543,000, including 60 acres of prime real estate on which the school is located, and an endowment of $1,320,513. Fees vary with grade level: around $4,000 per year for the elementary grades, and up to $7,000 for the higher grades. A tree-lined avenue leads up to the school, which is located in an area also populated by exclusive country clubs and old Southern mansions. The school buildings are of brick construction, designed in a style that Robert Sommer (1974) describes as "hard" architecture, with a linear and angular style.

Waldorf School is a less well-known type of school. Waldorf schools draw on the philosophy and teachings of Rudolf Steiner (1861-1925), an Austrian philosopher, scientist, romantic, and follower of Goethe. It was Steiner's life task to "gain an understanding of materialism" and to "transform" it (McDermott, 1984, p. 10). Goethe, Steiner's mentor, also affirmed the positive role of subjectivity in gaining knowledge of the world beyond a materialistic conception. The first of these schools opened in

Stuttgart, Germany, in 1919. In the U.S. there are now some 69 schools belonging or affiliated with the Association of Waldorf Schools in North America (AWSNA), and three member teacher training centers, two in California and one in New York (AWSNA, 1988, p. 14). Sixteen of these are "sponsored" schools, 25 are "federated" schools, and 28 are "member" schools of AWSNA. "Member" status is coveted. Other "unofficial" schools also consider themselves Waldorf schools. It is estimated that there are over 50,000 Waldorf students in 500 schools worldwide: 100 in North America and 400 schools in 27 countries, including Brazil, South Africa, Holland, Switzerland, Australia, Finland, England, North and South America, France, and Germany (Armstrong, 1988, p. 44; Southworth, 1990, p. 60).

The Waldorf school studied here is a "federated" or associate Waldorf school that has not yet gained its officially sanctioned membership to AWSNA but considers itself Waldorfian in every way. The school is located in rented cabins in a campground just a few miles from a university town. The school was founded in 1982 by a small group of parents who had heard about Rudolf Steiner and anthroposophy (Steiner's "spiritual science" belief system) and wanted to try an alternative form of schooling. The school started with 12 students in a single kindergarten and it now has 120 students, nursery through Grade 7: 45 children in nursery school, and 75 in grade school. The founding parents were concerned that the school would be a "proper Waldorf school," following the tenets of Waldorf schools and with a Waldorf trained faculty. However, the school soon found it was necessary to be flexible and to consider applicants for teaching positions who were not Waldorf trained. The school now has a mix of Waldorf trained and ex-public school teachers. Many of the original families are still with the school. These parents argue that the school's mission has not changed:

> We wanted then and we want now to provide Waldorf education following Rudolf Steiner's principles. We wanted our children to have a structured form of education that was not like public school. Most families are seeking a more spiritual and holistic education. But it's not religious dogma that we are teaching. It's more of an attitude the adults have of the child as an evolving soul

and they are willing to stay with the children to guide those souls.
(Interview, parent)

Steiner's anthroposophy movement provides spiritual and emotional leadership for the school. Anthroposophy is a philosophical/
spiritual belief system seeking "new age" truth through medi-
tation, discipline and restraint. It aims for cultural renewal
through knowledge of the spiritual world. Connecting spiritual
and intellectual worlds is considered essential for the development of human wisdom.

Throughout its brief history, Waldorf School has struggled
financially. Fees are set at around $2,700 per year and adjusted
to suit family circumstances. Some parents provide service for
reduced tuition, and children of faculty are not charged fees.
However, the school's financial situation is expected to improve, for the school has gained an increasingly affluent clientele. Originally, the school was attended primarily by the
children of "crafters and carpenters," but its population now
includes a number of Southville's professional families. The
school has had to come to terms with the tradeoff between
having a viable and financially secure school and allowing some
of the tenets and principles of the school to be relaxed. The
school is adamant, however, that it does not want to become a
school with a reputation for elitism, like St. Catherine's, nor
does it want to have fees that are prohibitive. Most of the parents
are college educated, and many of them have European backgrounds.

The two schools are located in Southville, a middle-sized,
fairly wealthy Southern university town (population 100,000).
The community's economic base comes from education, tour-
ism, retail trade, agriculture and light manufacturing. In the last
few decades the city has shown an increased interest in private
schooling. Nine of the 10 elementary private schools in Southville were established in the 1970s and 1980s. St. Catherine's is
the exception (the original girls' boarding school founded in
1910, and the new school in 1955). Economically, the community is thriving, evidenced in the construction of new office
buildings, shopping centers, accommodation and convention
centers. Thus, one might expect the growth of specialized
schooling, given the existence of affluent neighborhoods and a

social and political climate that has entertained the idea of "choice" in schooling in recent years.

COURT DECISIONS ON PRIVATE AND PUBLIC SCHOOLS

While interest in private schooling has recently increased, it is not a new phenomenon. Private schools have always been part of the American educational scene. They have existed as an entity quite separate from public schools and separate from government regulation. However, the private sector has been largely invisible. Research efforts are hampered by the view of many of the "gatekeepers" in private schools resisting public intrusion or scrutiny in what they have staked out as a private concern. Since private schools are frequently not subject to state or federal educational mandates, they have little financial or administrative incentive to participate in research ventures. Also, private schools, operating on a market economy, can and do go in and out of business at a steady rate, making up-to-date documentation of their demographics a difficult task. Researchers and policy makers for the most part ignore private schools. They refer to "schools" when they usually mean a figurative institution modelled on public schools. Yet 12% of all elementary and secondary students in the U.S. attend private schools of various persuasions, and private schools comprise 25% of the total number of schools (U.S. Department of Education, 1991, p. 1). Private schooling is a vibrant and growing school sector, no longer just an Eastern urban tradition, nor one dominated by Catholic education. Private schools are now in all 50 states in both religious and secular forms.

One of the key issues concerning private schools is that of "choice." Americans hold firmly to the values of individual rights to private property and freedom of choice, which more and more parents feel applies to schooling. Tension has been created by the liberating aspect of individual choice and its potentially fragmenting aspects for the state. Private or independent schools are seen by critics as serving parents who object to the values being taught in public schools. Indeed, the "choice" principle was founded on the struggle between individual rights and the state. "Choice" goes back to 1925 when the Supreme Court, in *Pierce v. Society of Sisters,*[1] upheld the right of parents to enroll their children in private schools at their own expense (Kraushaar, 1972; Rebell, 1989, p. 37; Tyack, 1968). The Society of Sisters, a Catholic group that ran a number of schools, challenged the Oregon Compulsory Education Act which "held parents criminally liable for any failure to enroll children under the age of 16 in a public school" (Rebell, 1989, p. 39). The Oregon Compulsory Education Act was seen by opponents as having roots in anti-Catholicism as promoted by the Ku Klux Klan and Oregon Scottish Rite Masons. The problem for the Supreme Court was to decide between the state's interests in Americanizing its citizens, and upholding individuals' rights to their own religious and other belief systems as laid down in the First Amendment.

The question became: Would private schools undermine the role of schools to socialize children into American culture? What if schools began instructing in languages other than English, so that subcultural groups would no longer contribute meaningfully to the dominant culture? If the child is not to be a "mere creature of the state," might it not also be possible that the child might be "a mere creature of other systems of authority that create their own total world of socialization outside of the state" (James, 1988, p. 2)? The contradiction was resolved by way of a compromise; all children were required to attend school, and parents were also given the right to choose for their children private schools which may teach different values to the state. However, by opting to leave private school funding responsibilities to parents, the state intended that the vast majority of parents would continue to support the public school system. And private schools were protected by the stipulation that the state could impose basic demands in satisfaction of compulsory schooling laws on private schools, but those demands were not to be so stringent as to invalidate private school interests or incorporate private schools into the set of public schools (Yudof, 1982, p. 230).

In 1972 in *Wisconsin v. Yoder*[2] the Supreme Court further

---

[1]Pierce v. Society of Sisters, 268 U.S. 510 (1925).
[2]Wisconsin v. Yoder, 406 U.S. 205 (1972).

emphasized parents' rights in the religious upbringing of their children. Amish parents sought exemption from state compulsory attendance laws. It was decided that Amish parents who had educated their children to the eighth grade would not be forced to comply with the additional 2 years of education required by the state. The questions became: Who has the right to inculcate values, parents or the state, and which values are to be inculcated? This decision once again was a compromise. The state was assured its future citizens were being educated to a certain extent, and parents exercised their rights to freedom of religion.

Another area where the court has placed constitutional limits is the teaching of religious and political values in schools. In the 1960s the Court reinforced the idea that the state must be neutral in regard to religion.[3] Once again in 1980 the Court further argued in *Stone v. Graham*[4] that public schools should be neutral: Kentucky law requiring the posting of the Ten Commandments on the walls of public school classrooms was ruled unconstitutional. The only way religion could be studied in public schools was as history, ethics, or comparative religion (Levin, 1987, p. 104). This is noteworthy because the omission of religious teaching from public schools is undoubtedly one of the reasons for continued and considerable private school patronage.

The tension in many of the cases is an ongoing concern for private beliefs and the state's interests in promoting its "fundamental values." The "long arm of the state" can be seen to intrude into school affairs in a way that many private school advocates find objectionable. As an example, *Edwards v. Aquillard*[5] in 1987 was concerned with values in the public school curriculum. The dispute was over a Louisiana statute that required equal teaching time of "creation science" for every period of evolution taught. The statute was invalidated by the court. Private schools, in contrast, have the possibility of setting their own limits and creating their own norms and values, sometimes in opposition to the state's ruling.

---

[3]Abington School District v. Schempp, 374 U.S. 203 (1963).
[4]Stone v. Graham, 449 U.S. 39 (1981).
[5]Edwards v. Aquillard, 107 U.S. 2573 (1987).

Yet another important court case in terms of its affect on private schooling today was the well known *Brown v. Board of Education* in 1954.[6] The case concerned a national value issue: Ought Americans to have the right to desegregated schooling? The court ruled in the affirmative, and the nation reacted with affirmation in some quarters, anguish in others, and decided subterfuge elsewhere. Institutionalized segregation had a long history that would not be easily overturned by a legal ruling. In the South, in particular, reaction to desegregation was intense. The 1-year delay before enforcing the *Brown* ruling that was granted by the court to allow for smooth integration was used to devise alternative plans. Schools in parts of the state were closed. Approximately "13,000 pupils in the state were left with no public school to attend" (Ely, 1976, p. 74). Most Southville students, however, found some form of schooling. Private schools in Southville, and emergency classes in homes and churches, were full to capacity. New private schools were formed, including St. Catherine's, founded in 1955.

Desegregation was eventually achieved in the public schools, but not without a considerable loss of students to new private schools, a trend that increased as the years went by. This was not only a Southern phenomenon:

> White flight from public schools has been a national phenomenon. The more aggressive the desegregation efforts, the greater the flight to private schools. For example, the estimated enrolment in Southern private schools organized or expanded in response to desegregation increased from roughly 25,000 in 1966 to approximately 535,000 by 1972. (Chemerinsky, 1989, p. 280)

It remains speculative, however, to link the growth of private schools in Southville with the Brown decision, and information on the private school movement in the state is limited. Nevertheless, the linkage appears strong, given the predominance of white students in private schools and the timing and continued growth of private schooling. Some of the people interviewed argued that desegregation had been an important factor in the founding of their schools. No doubt there were many other

---

[6]Brown v. Board of Education, 347 U.S. 483 (1954).

considerations involved, such as those centering around family values.

Public funding for private schools is another key private school issue. In 1983 the Supreme Court decision, *Mueller v. Allen*[7] clarified those conditions under which public support for private education could be found constitutional (Olson, 1991, p. 10). The court ruled that Minnesota's state tuition tax deduction was legal, since both public and private school families could apply for tax relief from school costs (Cooper, 1988b, p. 174). Once again we see a compromise whereby private school interests are neither disregarded nor privileged. To this day the controversy continues over the issue of public funding for private schooling. Proponents argue that public monies should be used in ways that allow people to select a suitable education for their children. Opponents counter that public institutions are available for everyone, and that those who elect not to support it ought to pay for the school of their choice. Private schools are seen as elitist, undemocratic, and detrimental to the nation because of their exclusionary function, the stratification of society by class, and the demoralizing effect on those in the public schools.

President George Bush, however, does not think private schools are undemocratic. In the "state of the nation" address of 1991, President Bush, while dealing with the Gulf War, nevertheless addressed some domestic concerns. For education he selected the word *choice* to indicate his orientation. In April 1991 he also presented an education plan called *America 2000: An Education Strategy*, which advocated competition among schools and the creation of brand-new experimental schools that could be private or public (Ostling, 1991, pp. 52–53). Again, in the 1992 "state of the nation" address the president announced that "more choice" for parents was critical for the creation of "new American school." He also praised the 30 schools across the nation already involved in *American 2000*. Bush's politics serve as symbolic reminders of the federal government's ideology, which includes an emphasis on testing, preferably standardized and publicly reported, a commitment to greater teacher control, and significantly for private schools, allowing parents

[7]Mueller v. Allen, 463 U.S. 388 (1983).

choice of schools. Also, Bush's Education secretary, Lamar Alexander, who has two children in private schools, believes that "a child ought to have a choice with public dollars of any school that is willing to be publicly accountable," and that aid for religious schools is "as American as apple pie" (Ostling, 1991, p. 53). What all this means in practice has yet to be determined, for the federal government provides only 6.2% of elementary and secondary funding. However, the debates over government support for private schools continue, and the variety of schools in both public and private sectors is increasing. Moreover, the idea of choice is currently being instituted in new proposal plans at federal, state and local levels.

Several proposals are indicative of the "choice" initiative: (a) President Bush unveiled a $200 million plan in February 1991 to reward districts that develop choice policies enabling parents to select among a variety of public or private schools. (b) Also in February 1991 the Detroit Board of Education agreed to consider using public monies to allow some private schools in the city to become public, thus raising the issue once again of what constitutes public education. The plan seems to be saying that private schools that meet some public regulations, for example, to be nondiscriminatory, publicly accountable, and meet some common outcomes, would be "public" even though not "government" schools. (c) Town officials in Epsom, New Hampshire, in December 1990 authorized tax cuts for property owners who would sponsor high school students in their private education. (d) In September 1990 Milwaukee became the first city in the U.S. to experiment with a private-school voucher plan. The plan uses state funds to pay for some 260 low-income students to attend private nonsectarian schools. By limiting choice to private nonsectarian schools, they have strategically managed to sidestep arguments over any violation of the constitutional separation of church and state. In addition, by focusing on low-income students the program created a new following. Thus, private school choice was demonstrated to be not just a middle class or Catholic concern. The idea was popularized that choice could benefit minority and low income students. And, (e) Coalitions lobbying for choice plans for both private and parochial schools are multiplying around the country. Some groups are aiming to use legislation to gain vouchers for parents to send their children to public, private, or parochial schools of their choice. Others are concerned with gaining the right to use public money for private schools (Olson, 1991, pp. 1, 10, 11).

The difference between recent choice proposals and those of the 1980s is that formerly it was a federal government initiative calling for large national expenditures, and that this time the movements are primarily local in origin (Olson, 1991, p. 10). Nevertheless, powerful and influential people have been instrumental in promoting the choice cause. The Brookings Institute, a Washington political "think tank," published Chubb and Moe's (1990) *Politics, Markets and America's Schools*. It called for an educational system based on choice whereby private schools would compete for students. The authors claimed that private schools produced better achievement rates, and that private schools functioned more effectively because of their greater autonomy.

But this raises the issue of whether autonomy for private schools would still be possible if they were publicly financed. Government funding may mean government regulation. In the present study, Waldorf School, though financially insecure, did not want public monies, because of the strings attached. The school avoided government regulation. Similarly, Christian fundamentalists who once supported choice in the 1970s and 1980s no longer want choice and its attendant federal and state intervention. The Catholic lobby, on the other hand, has increased its efforts for government funding. They point to the alleged failure of public school reform movements, claiming that their schools are more effective and cost efficient. A recent Rand corporation study of effective Catholic high schools in New York City and Washington, DC, is cited as proof of its claim (Olson, 1991, p. 10).

Private schools are an underresearched sector, but they are now the focus of considerable political attention. One theory to explain the resurgence of interest in private schooling is that those belonging to the Baby-Boom generation, that is, born in the aftermath of World War II, are now at an age where they are selecting schooling for their children. Having grown up with affluence and a distrust of government, "boomers" now desire excellence and choice in schooling. They are thus part of a growing constituency in favor of privatization (Boas, 1986). As one of my colleagues belonging to this generation put it, "we have a system of mass, industrial-style schooling in an age of designer everything else." Tyack and Hansot (1982, pp. 249-250) also write:

> the resurgence of privatism, the newborn faith in the market system, the ambivalence of nervous liberals about their own prospects, and the desire to cut back on public services and redistributive social programs are ominous signs that even the modest commitment to equality of the last generation is waning. Many politicians now seem convinced that Americans need MX missiles more than school lunches and Title I. Advocates of vouchers and tuition tax credits for private schooling suggest that family choice should reign supreme and that education is more a consumer good than a public good. And if people who have choice believe that public education is a mess—as the media insistently say—why should sensible people send their children to public schools at all?

Whether the movement toward choice will slowly fade or mark a turning point in American education is unknown. [As this manuscript goes to press the new leadership of President Clinton offers hope for increased support for public schools.]

But with government and grassroots moves to increase options in kinds of school, we need to know much more about varieties of schooling. Unless we wish to support, with taxpayers' money, diverse options that we know little about, it behooves us to study schools in all their variety. Just as no scientist ignores a new species, neither should educators overlook their more rare and exotic species of schools.

THE ECOLOGY OF PRIVATE SCHOOLS IN SOUTHVILLE COMMUNITY

Though the courts pass legislation on "private schools" as if they belong to a single class of schools, they are by no means similar. Private schools come in a distinctive array of organizational structures and value orientations. This is true at the national level and at the local level. Not all the variety present at the national level can be found in Southville, but there is a fair representation. The following discussion is intended to give an overview and to provide points of comparison.

In 1989, at the Ethnography in Education Forum in Philadelphia, we began to address Dell Hymes's (1980) question "What kinds of school are there?" (see Bredo & Henry, 1989). Hymes suggested that we know much more about American Indian cultures than we do about school cultures. We are, he said, about 100 years behind in this regard. The study sought to portray schools ethnographically and to characterize the nine private schools that we had been studying for a year. Our comparisons were made on the basis of values, curriculum, and pedagogy.

The usual categorization of private schools is into "religious" (81% of all private schools), and "independent,"[8] or those schools that are not affiliated in any way with a church (19% of all private schools) (U.S. Department of Education, 1991, p. 68). However, such distinctions are not finely drawn, and it is more useful to look at schools' underlying social and value orientations. For instance, even schools that are not overtly religious schools may have an emphasis on the spiritual growth of students. This applies to both St. Catherine's and Waldorf School.

We characterized the schools instead along three dimensions: religious, technical and social. The religious schools were mainly Christian, although Waldorf School has a broader social and mystical view of spirituality, with an emphasis on nature. Technical schools emphasized efficiency using the natural and behavioral sciences. Socially oriented schools were liberal or progressive in their values and sought to establish a strong school-community. The schools were not always clearly of one orientation; there was some overlap. Thus, some schools adopted both technical and social values, religious and social, or religious and technical. Waldorf School holds both social and religious values. And St. Catherine's has elements of all three. At the time of the initial study, we categorized St. Catherine's as religious. However, extended fieldwork over the following year, and subsequent work, showed that it emphasized religious, social and technical values. The school has a strong scientific and technical approach, along with upholding religious and social ethics.

---

[8] See the special section on independent schools in the Spring 1991 *Teachers College Record, 92, 3*.

We also found that the schools differed in the way that they approached their academic missions. Some schools were "prep" schools, aiming to accelerate students through school at a high level of achievement. Other schools aimed at "normal" standards, which they based on public schools. Still other schools took on a "remedial" function, tutoring students who had been failing, in an attempt to get them up to "normal" levels. One of the socially oriented schools, Waldorf School, was less concerned about the academic hierarchy, although well aware of the standards that other schools were using (Bredo & Henry, 1989, p. 6). A typology of the schools along religious, social, and technical dimensions follows. I have drawn on the initial study (Bredo & Henry, 1989), and my own research (Henry, 1989, 1990, 1991, in press), while broadening the discussion to include some examples of schools not found in Southville.

Religious Values Schools

Religious schools of many kinds comprise 81% of the total number of private schools. Of the total number of private schools 39% are Catholic, 42% of varying religious persuasions, and 19% nonsectarian (U. S. Department of Education, 1991, p. 68). I am arguing, however, that some of the 19% of nonsectarian or independent schools with no official church affiliation may also be "religious" in orientation. Thus, we have two kinds of religious schools, those that are doctrinal religious, and those that seek spiritual growth in students in other ways.

Prevalent in the community of Southville are "Christian Schools," which comprise three of the ten private schools in Southville. Christian Academy (Kindergarten through Grade 12, with only 23 students in all) was founded in 1982 by a local Baptist church and continues to operate out of the church building. Most of the parents attend that same Baptist church, though the school is officially nondenominational Christian. Its mission is to create a Christian environment as an alternative to the "morally corrupt public schools." Students are seen as in need of moral guidance and salvation. In this school the day begins with hymns, prayers, and the Pledge of Allegiance, then students work on materials from Accelerated Christian Education (ACE), a mail-order curriculum publisher in Texas. For most of the day, students work quietly at individual study carrels. They request help from the teacher by holding up a small American flag. The director sees the orderliness and tightly structured nature of the school as "these kids' salvation."

Holy Trinity school (Kindergarten–Grade 12) was founded in 1984 as a nondenominational Christian school, although its student body is predominantly comprised of the congregation of a large Presbyterian church in town. Its enrollment level stands at 200. Teachers in the school claim that the school was founded in reaction to perceived weaknesses and lack of moral education in the public schools. The school offers a "Great Books" curriculum, with obligatory classes in Bible and biblical history. Parents also attend special religious seminars. The school claims, however, that it is not forcing Christianity on parents and that the school's academic orientation is more important. The school inherited the building, students, and debts of a previous Christian school, which had, in turn, taken over from another Christian school founded in reaction to desegregation. The present school has a small minority of African-American students.

The growth of Christian schools such as these is so nationally widespread that some claim that they open at the rate of one per day (Cooper, 1988a, p. 31). There are approximately 5,000 to 6,000 Christian day schools affiliated mainly with fundamentalist Baptist churches in the U.S., with an enrolment of approximately 1 million students (Reese, 1985, p. 175). Once loyal supporters of the public schools, these parents lamented the "moral decay" of public schools and reacted by establishing their own schools. Public schools were once considered "God centered" but are now seen as "humanistic, if not atheistic" (Interview, Baptist fundamentalist headmaster).

The Catholic school system, in contrast, was created in reaction to the "prejudice and open hatred in the Protestant-dominated public schools in the nineteenth and twentieth centuries" (Cooper, 1988a, p. 20). Roman Catholics objected to the reading of the protestant bible in public schools, and alleged discrimination against the Irish (Kaestle, 1983, p. 171). Since 1870 Catholic parochial schools have existed in substantial numbers. However, after the civil war, public schools became less overtly Protestant oriented and more acceptable to Catholics. Public schools shifted their focus from a doctrinal religious base to a more secular one, and assumed a central position as "publicly funded centrally regulated and professionally managed institutions" (Kaestle, 1983, p. 221). Thus, a gradual decline in support for separate Catholic schools has occurred. Eighty five percent of all private school children were Catholic in 1965, and by 1988 this had dropped to only 54% (Cooper, 1988a, p. 22). The reasons are not clear, but are likely to be associated with increased affluence and the lowered Catholic birthrate, as well as reduced numbers of priests and nuns in teaching orders. In Southville, with an absence of Catholic schools, local informants argue:

> We would like to have our own schools, but the priest said it just isn't worth it. Here in the South the distinction is not so much whether you are Catholic or Protestant, but rather to do with whether you are fundamentalist or not.

Religious boundaries of various kinds, whether Catholic versus Protestant, Christian versus Fundamentalist Christian, and so on, are clearly important and subject to revision based on changing social contexts.

Rapidly growing religious schools are those of the Lutheran Church (up 265%), Jewish (up 37%), Moslem, and Buddhist faiths (Cooper, 1988a, p. 24). Lutheran church schools totalled 4,067 in 1990 with an enrollment of 372,840 students (Lutheran Church, 1990, p. 4). While none of these schools are in Southville, it is significant that there are a fair number of Jewish children at both St. Catherine's and Waldorf School. Waldorf School also has some Moslem and Buddhist students. Another fast-growing religious sect is that of the Seventh Day Adventists, with 1,324 schools and an enrollment of 81,507 students (Cooper, 1988a, p. 24). Greek Orthodox Schools, Society of Friends (Quaker) Schools, Mennonite Schools, (Dutch) Calvinist Schools, and Assembly of God Schools are also part of the religious school sector.

In addition, Episcopal schools make up a substantial proportion of private schools. Episcopal schools nationally are expanding, with a rise from 347 schools and 59,437 students in 1965 to 527 schools with 78,214 students in 1984 (Cooper, 1988a, p. 27).

Episcopal schools are seen to offer high-quality schooling for people of all denominations, with an emphasis on college preparation. Episcopaleans started some of the nation's most prestigious private schools, "such as St. Paul's and Groton, though the church leadership nationwide has put little money or energy into schools. Today, in a number of communities, church clergy and laypeople have cooperated in starting elementary Episcopal schools, often growing from a church kindergarten or preschool" (Cooper, 1988a, p. 27). This was, as you will recall, how St. Catherine's was founded in 1955. Local clergy and interested parents opened the school in response to local interest. A similarly dramatic increase can be seen in enrollments at St. Catherine's, which is discussed here with Episcopal schools because of its roots, even though it has recast itself in different terms as nondenominational and college-preparatory.

College-preparatory schools are known for their academic excellence, elite clientele, and reputation for getting their students into prestigious colleges. St. Catherine's, like other college-preparatory schools, belongs to the National Association of Independent Schools (NAIS). Boarding schools (23 %) and day schools (77%) comprise the membership of NAIS. There has been an increased demand for NAIS schools, and they are changing in structure from boarding to day schools, from single-sex to coeducational, and from more secondary to more elementary schools (Cooper, 1988a, p. 27). The trend is one of making what was once the preserve of boarding schools, usually church affiliated, available in the form of local, elite, coeducational, independent schools, often parent controlled and with very high standards. Some of these schools have a secular thrust; others emphasize character development, spirituality, and social values, such as St Catherine's.

Social Values Schools

Social values schools, as the name suggests, provide a set of social values for students and an alternative form of community to public schools, although in very different ways. One example is the "progressive," "free," or "open" schools, that is, those that are child centered and noncompetitive, which flourished in the 1960s. While many have closed, a number still exist in various guises and some have even joined the public school system as alternative or magnet schools. Others continue to be founded.

Togetherness School in Southville (Grades 4 through 12) was established in 1970 as an alternative academic school. The school is located in a lovely Southern mansion amidst tall trees and rolling meadows. It has a college-preparatory goal but sets itself up as "not like St. Catherine's." St. Catherine's is more socially prestigious, while Togetherness takes on an arty and liberal stance. Togetherness School was founded by two traditional prep school administrators who believed in the academic mission but felt it could be more humanely and better achieved through a liberal approach. Togetherness attracts students who do not quite "fit" into the rigorous style of St. Catherine's, many of them the children of local academics. Togetherness style is suggestive of student centeredness and community, nicely illustrated in the school's fairly relaxed rules and high degree of student involvement and decision making.

Country School (Kindergarten through Grade 5) was also opened in 1984 as an alternative school centered around the notion of community. Parents founded the school and they continue to be highly involved. It is Deweyan and progressive in its thrust. The school building itself was actually constructed by parents: a three classroom log cabin surrounded by playgrounds and pretty countryside. Chintz curtains, the smell of baking brownies, and the friendly interaction of teachers and parents help create an idyllic country homestead atmosphere.

Another school stressing social values in the form of a social-spiritual agenda is Waldorf School. Waldorf School has a "religious," primarily Christian, emphasis, which makes its professed label as an independent school technically correct but misleading. The school's spiritual emphasis may in fact place it closer in kind to Christian schools than other independent schools. As one teacher put it:

Our emphasis is on morality and spiritual growth. Every teacher is concerned with right and wrong. In our zeal to separate church and state in the public schools we have ended up with a situation where it's very difficult to teach values because it's a euphemism to think you can teach values, divorced from religious ethics. (Interview, teacher)

That a group of parents who wanted this type of schooling for their children founded the school and have continued to support it means that there is also considerable overlap between school and family.

Other social values schools, often called *alternative*, are those that emphasize cultural, ethnic, or other different values emphases. Minority neighborhood private schools are an example, of which there are 75 such schools around the country (U.S. Department of Education, 1989, p. 5). They are typically locally run and aim to provide minority culture-based schooling for their communities. Southville does not have any of these schools to date.

Technical Values Schools

Technical values schools adopt a scientific and behaviorist approach to teaching and learning. They are concerned with control and efficiency. One of the schools we studied, Dyslexia Center, is strongly technical. Montessori School attempts to bridge the gap between the social and technical approaches, and Genius School is a blend of both religious and technical. St. Catherine's, in turn, is the only school to utilize all three approaches, religious, social, and technical.

Dyslexia Center, founded in 1974, has the strongest technical approach to learning. It deals solely with students who have learning problems but who are considered intelligent in other ways. The school adopts a clinical and individualistic version of science, like medicine or psychiatry. It is located in a substantial two storey house in the city, close to a prestigious university, lending it the air of an expensive private clinic. Fees are set at around $7,800. Students are expected to enroll, be treated, and return to their former schools in due course. The school draws on a well-known method for treating dyslexia, the Orton-Gillingham method. In this method students engage in specific, usually multisensory activities (e.g., tracing letter shapes in the sand), and are tested repeatedly to gauge progress. The school's view of education as a scientific or technical process is revealed in the metaphorical language used in the school. For instance, teachers refer to "processing problems," "competencies," "gross-motor skills," "exit skills," "outcomes," "behaviors," "tactile-kinesthetic methods," and student as "product."

Montessori School, which opened its doors in 1982, also has a scientific and technical value orientation, but this is balanced by a more humane, social community outlook. The teacher adopts the role of a kindly manager or advisor, and students work on individual, carefully structured activities: "All of our tasks are discrete units in the scientific tradition . . . . We emphasize quality work, not just quantity, and that means allowing self-choice and working through the various stages at a pace suited to the individual's development" (Interview, teacher). The curriculum is heavily math/science oriented, and even language is taught as a set of discrete skills.

On the other hand, Genius School attempts to combine technical and religious goals. The school was founded in 1980 by a former prep school teacher and his wife. They named it after a famous scientist, whose photographs serve as inspiring symbols on the school walls alongside pictures of Jesus. Students who come to this school are considered intelligent though they have been experiencing difficulty in other schools. In this sense the school is similar to the Dyslexia Center, functioning as a remedial clinic, although Genius's fees are considerably lower, set at around $3,000. The main teaching technique used here is that of individualized tutoring and the use of standardized materials. Testing occurs regularly. Prayer is practiced daily, and the school has an emphasis on thinking good thoughts, kindness, faith, and hope, which lends it a religious air.

Another group of schools in the technical category are those characterized as "military." Most military schools disappeared during the antimilitary 1960s and 1970s, a period of serious societal conflict over Vietnam and the military in general. However, some 36 of these remain in the South and Midwest, with an enrollment of approximately 10,000 students (Cooper, 1988a, p. 30). In the immediate countryside surrounding Southville, one of these military academies can be found. Such schooling is based on discipline, drill, and recitation, and is concerned with instilling conservative values and U.S. patriotism.

A NICHE FOR THE SCHOOLS

St. Catherine's and Waldorf School are independent schools. Both schools are free of sectarian control, although they have religious/spiritual leanings. St. Catherine's has Episcopal religious roots, which, though dissolved to a large extent, continue to exert some influence in the affective realm. The school endorses religious freedom, but it is not secularist like the public schools. Waldorf School also has a spiritual basis in its anthroposophy belief system. Some teachers and parents claim this to be the most important aspect of the school: "Independent thinking is very important and spirituality, the coming together of the whole person. We want the children to develop an appreciation for what exists in the world beyond just the material aspects of life" (Interview, teacher). Waldorf School's social emphasis on community, and the children's inner unfolding as part of a developmental model of teaching and learning, places it in the overlap area between social and religious values.

St. Catherine's draws on all three traditions: religious, social, and technical. Its religious practices are largely restricted now to weekly chapel and daily prayers to begin class each day, but the school nevertheless attends to the "spiritual needs" of students. The school also has a social tradition in its strong community bonds and, surprisingly at times, progressive values. The school is steeped in tradition yet also attempts to keep up with the times and respond to modern social problems. Character development and social responsibility are seen as critical to a child's education. The technical focus in the school is evidenced in its rigorous math-science program, subject specialization, standardized curricula, and the constant testing regimen that is at the core of the school's organization. The school intends to produce only top graduates who will have their choice of colleges to attend. However, it does not just have a technical orientation. The liberal arts are equally important. Expectations for students are high in all areas, including math/science, the arts, character development, sporting skills, and ethics. The school has confidence in its ability to deliver on all counts. "We're the IBM of schools," states the Director of the Lower School.

The other significant issue in terms of the schools' fit in the ecology of schools is that they were founded in the last few decades. Waldorf School was founded in 1982 as an alternative school, a structured form of schooling that was unlike public schools. St. Catherine's elementary school was founded in 1955; in 1970 St. Catherine's merged with a well-established elite college-preparatory school originally founded in 1910 as a girls' boarding school. Thus, St. Catherine's can be seen as wedded to the tradition of college-preparatory and boarding schools.

Both schools have disproportionately low minority enrollments. Only one minority student attends Waldorf School, while St. Catherine's has an 8% minority enrolment. There is also some social class differentiation between the two schools. At Waldorf School the bulk of parents have an estimated combined parental income of $25,00–$50,000, and at St. Catherine's average combined parental incomes are in the order of $80,000–$120,000. While both schools have representatives in the student body from all social class backgrounds, St. Catherine's remains an elite school, and Waldorf School primarily serves the middle- and upper class social strata. Mostly its clientele are college educated people who are interested in "new age" ideas.

Waldorf School, founded in opposition to public schools, offers a critique of mainstream schooling. Public institutions including governments and education are seen as inadequate and, in many cases, corrupt. Public schooling is seen as too large and impersonal. In this view the individual does not receive the attention that he or she needs to become educated as a whole person. St. Catherine's, founded in the tradition of college prep schools is concerned also to provide an education that is different to that of the public schools. Traditional beliefs and values, and a Christian spirit, serve as the preferred basis for interpreting value problems in the school. Character building through religion, without dogma, is thought to develop an awareness of social responsibility in children. Teachers in both St. Catherine's and Waldorf School are clearly visible moral standard setters of their communities, as well as attending to students' intellectual development. This is an important point, for the trend toward different varieties of schooling is not just a bid for schooling with a desired content. Parents are also seeking schooling that most nearly represents the kind of cultural experience that they want for their children. In the next chapter we will begin to explore the stories and myths that schools use to validate their cultures and to create a place for themselves within an ecology of schools.

4

MYTHICAL AND PHILOSOPHICAL FOUNDATIONS

The telling of stories, and the creation of myths, are done by all peoples to help order their world. Schools do this, too. The making of a school philosophy grounded in myths is an important part of school culture. Schools create and present a story about themselves to attract a clientele and carve out a niche for themselves within an ecology of schools. Tyack and Hansot (1982, p. 8) write, "Organizational myths are a way of making vivid a sense of what institutions can be; by elaborating a heroic past, they direct people toward an equally potent future. Embedded in myths are images of potentiality." A school's past is embellished and reshaped to help define an idealized "face."

Lesko (1988, p. 24) uses the example of the failure of the U.S. space shuttle Challenger in Spring 1986 to show how quickly myths can be formed. The event reduced to its bare elements was that the Challenger exploded minutes after liftoff. The myth created by the media was that the astronauts who gave their lives in the venture were American heroes and heroines like the Wright brothers and Amelia Earhart. They were seen as "trailblazers, whose curiosity, commitment to the space program and personal strength impelled them to accept great danger as part of the adventure" (Lesko, 1988, pp. 24–25). The story became a story about America and its values—a belief in progress through courage and effort. Without discrediting this view, for the astronauts may well have possessed those traits, it is a myth, nevertheless, because of the value-laden embellishments that allow the story to legitimize a particular ordering of the people and situation.

In schools no less than in other situations, the traditions of the past, the heroes and heroines, glorious deeds and ideals, guide the creation of myths. The local history of schools, and the people, events, and networks that have informed and inspired them, are critical in understanding a school's culture. As an example, the schools may associate with like-minded schools, which helps bond them together and create an identity. I want to emphasize at this point that the use of the word *myth* in connection with culture is not pejorative. This is not to say that schools create an artificial rhetoric in the vulgar use of the term, but that all social interaction is grounded in the interpretation of people and events from different vantage points. As humans we speak metaphorically in narrative form. We use rituals and metalanguage that say more than they appear to do. We are continually interpreting a social world that is always in a state of flux. Neither are schools a single, coherent entity with a fixed view of the world. Instead, they struggle with their internal contradictions and individual experiences to interpret their worlds in certain ways. For example, both St. Catherine's and Waldorf School share some traditions as private schools, but they are also particular schools in process, created by serendipity and by design.

School culture is a complex web of overt purposes and covert meanings, constantly fashioned by myth making. These myths have to do with: (a) the school's original and changing mission, (b) the people or groups who have had an inspirational effect on the school, and (c) the connections that the school may have locally, nationally, or internationally. By looking closely at these foundations we can begin to understand the role of myths in the creation and maintenance of school culture.

WALDORF SCHOOL

Déja Vu: Waldorf in Australia and the U.S.

In New South Wales, Australia, I visited a Waldorf school, attending festivals and open days. A friend who was on the school board had invited me to these events in his school. Remembered well were the unusual children's paintings, watercolors in soft pastel shades and often with diffuse circular shapes enclosed by a contrasting color. I wondered: Why are the children's paintings so similar? Also remembered from those visits were the beautiful wooden desks, chairs, and other furniture that reminded me of my childhood in the late 1950s and early 1960s. Then natural timbers were the norm, rather than the plastic, metal, and synthetic materials found in schools today. And the kindergarten rooms were soft in shape and texture, draped with muslin in pastel shades that I later came to think of as Waldorf colors. The school was set in woodlands on the edge of a university town and educational center. Originally, the school site had been a regionally famous art gallery that had since relocated. I admired the setting, having been there many times during its life as an art gallery. It seemed like a perfect place for a school. Children were growing up surrounded by beauty, close to nature.

Once I began to study Waldorf School in Southville, a U.S. university town, I was surprised to see those same paintings, the muslin drapes and wooden furniture, the setting in the woods. This raised the issue of whether such features were part of a Waldorf code of ethics, and if so, how was it imparted? I learned that there are Waldorf training colleges and anthroposophical training centers on an international scale, from New York to Sussex, England, which could be one way of insuring uniformity. But it left unanswered the question of how such consistency had been maintained internationally. The schools were, after all, selected at random, or rather, by chance. Children would not paint blue moons on a yellow background, the whole class, in watercolor, in both the school in Australia and the one in Southville, without some guidance. And these events were separated by cultures, distance, and a time period of 3 years.

A home video made by an anthroposophist in the U.S. provided more points of similarity and raised more questions. On the video were nine Waldorf schools on the East Coast. Two of the schools were in Vermont, three in New Hampshire, two in Massachusetts, one in Colorado, and one in New York. In common with Waldorf School in Southville were a number of features. All the schools were located in natural settings of considerable beauty. Trees, lakes, and mountains surrounded the classrooms. In all the kindergartens and younger grades were the tell-tale signs of a Waldorf approach: beeswax figurines that the children had made, a madonna and child painting on the wall, simple wooden dolls, the children's watercolor paintings, wool in a large cane basket. Missing were books, technology, Lego and construction, educational toys, and so on, that one usually finds in public school kindergartens. I was impressed by the consistency across Waldorf schools, something I was later to learn is viewed as "integrity" by Waldorf educators. Similarly, the grade school classrooms were alike in their natural simplicity and the dominant presence of natural timbers for flooring and furniture. In one, high school students were making wooden flutes in the woodworking room. In another school, a large building for eurythmy was under construction. To be a Waldorf school implied a certain set of principles.

The Mission of Waldorf School

The Waldorf school studied here is a *federated* school. Federated schools are those "which are not yet ready to assume the responsibilities of sponsored schools because of their youth and size, yet which wish to establish and strengthen their ties with the main stream of Waldorf education through their on-going relationship with the regional committees" (AWSNA, 1988, p. 14). Waldorf School sees its mission as connected with the worldwide Waldorf school movement, but it is not yet a full member of the Association of Waldorf Schools of North America. It has, however, taken steps to attain full membership by developing links with neighboring Waldorf schools, hoping for an official "sponsorship." The proposed sponsoring school faculty regularly visits Waldorf School. They evaluate classes and hold workshops in areas of interest, such as eurythmy. These sessions are always well attended, providing a boost to local morale. Once sponsored or adopted by the older established school, there is then normally a 3-year period in which the member school virtually acts as a mentor, advising and acting as a consultant to the newer school.

Many of the parents and grandparents who were instrumental in getting the school started in 1982 are still active in the school. For 2 years prior to the school's opening this small group of dedicated people met to study the Waldorf philosophy, discuss their ideas for the school, and plan its birth. What they envisaged is in many ways still a part of the school's ideals.

> In our vision, our children and the children yet to come deserve the quality education and the opportunities to grow that Waldorf School provides. We are aware that the times we live in are changing and often confusing, with powerful social forces at work to suppress individuality and intellectual growth. As Waldorf School succeeds in its teaching, the children who attend will become prepared as adults to respond in powerful and positive ways to whatever challenges to freedom and demands for conformity are placed on them. (*Handbook*)

The parents' aim was to counteract what they saw as "powerful social forces at work to suppress individuality and intellectual growth." Schooling was to be an enriching process that attended to the *whole* child, not just the intellect. They saw the public schools' emphasis on the intellect as deficient, and neglectful of spiritual, emotional, and social growth. Instead, education was to be beautiful, harmonious, and challenging, a notion voiced in John Milton's classic verse.

> I will point ye out the right path of a virtuous and noble education; laborious indeed at the first ascent, but else so smooth, so green, so full of goodly prospect, and melodious sounds on every side, that the harp of Orpheus was not more charming. (Milton, 1967/1644, p/ 232, quoted in *Handbook*)

It is Milton, a British scholar and artist, along with Blake, the romantic poet, and more importantly, Rudolf Steiner, the Austrian founder of Waldorf schooling, who are inspirational "mentors" to the school.

When asked about Rudolf Steiner and anthroposophy, students, teachers, and parents have different responses. Some have only a scant knowledge of this key aspect of the school's heritage, while others are committed anthroposophists. For students a typical response was "Steiner? He was the guy who started this school, wasn't he?" A similar disparity between those who are committed anthroposophists, and those who are not, was found by Dugan (1990) in his survey of San Francisco

Waldorf parents. He found that many of the nonanthroposophists were attracted to the school by such things as the dedication of teachers and the integration of art. Dugan himself was sympathetic to popular "new age" beliefs one finds in Waldorf schools. But once he knew more about the school, as a parent, Dugan wrote that "students were being taught lunatic fringe beliefs that are completely unacceptable as science outside a cult of believers" (1990, p. 1). More specifically he objected to the "dumbing-down" of the science curriculum to avoid conflict with anthroposophical doctrine: "this meant teaching mainly observation of nature, without the essential theories that tie it all together and lead to useful application of the knowledge" (1990, p. 2). Dugan seems to be a disenchanted parent who set out to discredit a particular school. His report does not show sensitivity to the philosophy behind Waldorf schooling. However, he raises an important point that I also found in the present study, which is that some Waldorf parents know little about anthroposophy, and that this creates a divide between those who are fully "in" and those who are not (also see McDermott, 1984, pp. 295-296).

Teachers in the Waldorf School argued that it used Steiner's method of education, but did not teach the content of anthroposophy. To an extent this is true, but anthroposophical underpinnings guide much of what goes on in the school, making the school like a private religious school, and not all parents realize this. Anthroposophy is an esoteric belief system created by Rudolf Steiner. Rudolf Steiner thus has a profound effect on the school, and to understand its culture we need to study the myths surrounding the man, his anthroposophy movement, his "threefold" vision for society, and his methods of schooling.

Rudolf Steiner (1861-1925)

For the romantic that he was, Steiner did not mince words: "we do not want to believe anymore . . . we want to know" (Steiner, 1967, quoted in Oswald, 1988, p. 17). Knowing was possible in his view. Even spiritual experiences could be known, not merely felt or believed. Steiner takes terms from the Christian tradition—original sin, the Christ, Calvary, redemption—and uses them in his own way. According to Steiner, humans possess original sin because they embody a material being, when in the beginning there was only a spiritual being (Steiner, 1972, quoted in Oswald, 1988, p. 17). Redemption, then, consists in returning from material being to the pure spirit. This was made possible, he argued, by Calvary, and also the ability humans have of engaging actively in their own redemption effort by thinking. So it is not blind faith, but knowledge, in Steiner's theory, that is humankind's redeemer.

The theme of modern society's loss of spirituality and the degeneration into materialism is a familiar one at Waldorf School. The aim is to:

> give the children a chance to choose in their lives beyond what is fed in the general culture. The hope certainly for me is not that the choices that I've given them at this point are what they'd choose but that something that I'm doing will allow them to choose for themselves and that it'll make possible the idea that there are aspects of reality that are not touchable, are not fed to us in the way the media and consumerism feeds our lives—that there is another possibility there for them. (Interview, teacher)

These ideas are consistent with Steiner's. He was an intensely spiritual man, having first made contact with the spirit world when he was 8 years old and saw an apparition of a recently deceased relative (McDermott, 1984, p. 7). Steiner believed that he held the gift of being able to "converse with the spirits of nature," but he did not go on to study literature or history, as one might expect of someone with heightened sensibilities, because he said "they had [in the German academic world of that time] no definite method and no significant prospects" (Steiner, 1907, quoted in McDermott, 1984, p. 14). Instead, he studied mathematics, chemistry, physics, zoology, botany, mineralogy, and geology. The hard sciences, he believed, would better prepare him for gaining a thorough spiritual conception of the world, to render objective and "know" religious experiences.

For inspiration Steiner studied Goethe, who became his "mentor." Steiner also was mentored by an unknown "master" whom Steiner first met when he was 19 years old and whose identity was never disclosed (McDermott, 1984, p. 11). The "master"

was Steiner's initiator into the spirit world. He advised Steiner
to study Fichte so that he would "gain an understanding of the
materialism which it was Steiner's life task to transform"
(McDermott, 1984, p. 10).

Goethe (1749–1832), like Steiner, affirmed the positive role of
subjectivity and individuality in gaining knowledge of the world
beyond a materialistic conception. Steiner worked for many
years, 1880s onwards, on Goethe's studies in natural science,
edited Goethe's collection of scientific writings, and wrote his
own interpretation of Goethe. In 1891 Steiner received his Ph.D.
from the University of Rostock—his thesis, "The Fundamentals
of a Theory of Cognition" was published as *Truth and Knowledge* (1981/1892). However, it was not knowledge per se in
which Steiner was interested. He sought a deeper understanding
of the interface between cognition and spirituality. Steiner was
concerned with exhibiting and teaching "a knowledge which
presupposes disciplined surrender, dedication and love" (Mc-
Dermott, 1984, p. 11).

Steiner's work thus consisted of searching for a "scientific"
explanation for the religious and emotional side of human existence. Steiner believed in the scientific method as the answer
to all aspects of existence: "faith is now replaced by full knowledge and unshakable insight" (Steiner, 1947a: quoted in Oswald,
1988, p. 17). Religion and science were not seen as incompatible.
Steiner felt that, while Western peoples had lost a sense for the
esoteric, Eastern people still held an esoteric wisdom that was
behind the harmony of religion and science (McDermott, 1984,
pp. 22, 97). Such romanticism would seem to be incompatible
with modern-day scientific ideology. But conventional ideas of
what science is differ from Steiner's writings on the subject. In
Waldorf School it is romantic, emotional, aesthetic, or creative
science, not rational, objective, empirical science, that is the chief
vehicle for learning. "Objective" knowledge, mathematics, and
science are not neglected, but approached in a different way,
through an imaginative, storytelling mode.[1]

---

[1] A storytelling mode, with its emphasis on relationships and contextual
detail, has been characterized, in contemporary literature at least, as "women's
ways of knowing" (see Belenky, Clinchy, Goldberger, & Tarule, 1985). As an
example of research in this mode, Buerk (1986) studied bright women who

Anthroposophy

Anthroposophy or the spiritual science movement was created by Rudolf Steiner. He founded anthroposophical societies in Germany, then they became established in England, other European countries, and the United States. The word *anthroposophy* comes from a combination of the Greek *anthropos* : man, and *sophia* : wisdom (Pouderoyen, 1980, p. 4). Human wisdom is believed to come from a knowledge of the spiritual as well as the material world. Steiner wrote on the material world, about such things as beekeeping and farming, as well as on the higher plane of spirituality. His spiritual works included *The Philosophy of Freedom* (1970); *Occult Science* (1972); and *Knowledge of the Higher Worlds and its Attainment* (1947a). (See McDermott, 1984, for a comprehensive bibliography on anthroposophy.)

Steiner aimed for cultural renewal through anthroposophy expressed in different fields. In the social arena he established the first Waldorf school in Stuttgart, which flourished. At the time of Steiner's death in 1925 there were nearly 900 children in the school. In the scientific field Steiner inspired a medical movement and research laboratories. Doctors founded their own pharmaceutical company and a hospital in an effort to break with established practices and create a new, holistic approach to medicine. In the artistic field, the Goetheanum, an artistic building made of two large domes, was built in Dornach, Switzerland, in 1920. Inside the building were pictures of world creation, colorful glass windows, carved wooden walls, and doors. It was an avant-garde center for the expressive and dramatic arts.

These activities meant that Steiner made enemies as well as followers, for he was proclaiming an antistatist stance, a position that was a direct threat to many of his countrymen: In Munich and Elberfeld in 1922 agitators at a meeting endangered Steiner's life—"the instigators, the kind of people who later

---

avoided mathematics because of its abstract form and emphasis on decontextualized, objective, independent thinking. When the women were taught using, instead, a focus on group achievement and contextualized, intuitive, and relational ideas, their performance improved. Storytelling as a means of learning serves a similar function.

adopted National-Socialist ideas, saw in Rudolf Steiner a deci-
sive threat because of his cosmopolitan social ideas, and his
attitude toward establishing the freedom of the spirit of man. On
New Year's night 1922–23, the wooden structure of the Goetheanum was destroyed by arson" (Carlgren, 1972, p. 19).
However, such opposition did not kill the anthroposophical
movement. Steiner immediately designed a new Goetheanum in
Dornach as the center for the Anthroposophical Society. It was
built in 1928 to Steiner's specifications and continues to be used
today. He also made preparation for the reorganization of the
society in many countries, including Germany, Switzerland,
Austria, Norway, England, and the Netherlands (McDermott,
1984, pp. 32, 288). Anthroposophy is, like its child the Waldorf
school movement, a fast growing international phenomenon.

In communities where there are Waldorf schools people can
often choose professional care offered by anthroposophists. In
Southville, anthroposophically trained doctors offer holistic
medicine and the healing arts. Moreover, in Waldorf School itself, homeopathic and other natural remedies are used for any
minor illnesses that the children may have. In emergencies conventional medicine is accepted, but the tendency is toward natural methods of healing. Anthroposophically based businesses in
health foods and herbal medicines are also thriving in the area.
Anthroposophy has thus translated traditional medicine, the arts,
science, and education into quite different entities.

> Anthroposophy deals with the idea that in the course of human
> evolution that human beings have become separated from the
> spiritual aspects of their lives. Way way back their initial and
> primal connection was with the spirit world, the cosmos. Now we
> need to reconnect, but this time consciously and with our
> intellect. It's like a baby inside the mother who is completely
> connected to the mother, but doesn't know the mother at all. Then
> the child goes through adolescence and rejects the mother and
> pushes apart. And it's only when they're finished that process
> that they can really come back and develop a relationship. That
> lives very much in me. Questioning is very much a part of the
> belief system. And so I am on the path of anthroposophy. That's
> what I use as my context to understand things in the world.
> (Interview, teacher)

Anthroposophy is an organic and evolving concept which means different things to different people. As one of the teachers pointed out, Steiner argued that the word anthroposophy would change every day if it were to describe reality (Interview, teacher).

Steiner's Threefold Society

Rudolf Steiner's worldview was developed in a context quite different from the contemporary U.S. society in which his ideas have been taken up. At the close of World War I, in Spring 1919, Germany was being threatened by civil war. The German economy was collapsing. Unemployment was high. Demonstrations and riots were commonplace. People joined radical cultural and political movements seeking answers to the current social decay. Different voices expressed opinions about the future of Germany and the world. Rudolf Steiner, at the request of scientists, politicians, and industrialists who were acquainted with anthroposophy, presented to the public his concept of a new social order. He gave lectures and talks and published a book, *The Threefold Commonwealth* (*Die Kernpunkte der sozialen Frage*) (Carlgren, 1972, pp. 12-13). The bridging of class differences was one of the aims of the new "threefold" social movement. Steiner had had humble beginnings as the son of a minor railway official and a peasant woman. Class differences were thus problematic and able to be overcome through a new conception of the world.[2] It is also interesting that Steiner talks about the "civilized world," consistent with his view of cultural evolution. At our present stage in "cultural evolution," Steiner believed "civilization" was no longer healthy, and education in its "noblest form" was needed to heal the ills created by modern society (Steiner, 1937, pp. 127-128).

---

[2]Ironically, today we see a middle/upper middle-class dominance in Waldorf schools. Among the college educated and reasonably affluent, interest in alternatives and new social forms and ideals is more likely to be entertained than by those whose primary concern is eking out a daily living. Waldorf schools are now criticized for neglecting egalitarian concerns, and for their apolitical stance with regard to gender, racial, and socioeconomic class issues (see Uhrmacher, 1991, pp. 258, 264).

Steiner's new social order or "threefold society" was to be made up of the spiritual-cultural sphere, the economic sphere, and the legal-political sphere. Steiner was against centralization of power in all three spheres by the state. Instead, he proposed decentralization of social life. Steiner argued that the spiritual-cultural or humanistic sphere, not economics or politics, should guide education. He did not want the state governing education or science. He believed in independent schools and independent scientific research, so that they would not be influenced or contaminated by influential circles of politicians or business-men. Those politicians and businessmen whose help Steiner enlisted were presumably a minority of free and independent thinkers who were against the misuse of power by governments and industry. Also, while Steiner referred to national bound-aries (e.g., the "German people"), he saw a decentralization of power as leading to the crossing of national and cultural bound-aries: "one consequence of this independence would be that the institutions of education and research throughout the world would be free to interact and collaborate without regard for political boundaries" (Carlgren, 1972, p. 14). In addition, au-tonomy in spiritual life and the growth of religious communities and cultural institutions, would result. It was important for Steiner that people would learn to respect one another and live in harmony with their environment (Steiner, 1937, p. 31).

In the economic sphere, Steiner proposed a social order that would be a middle road between capitalism and communism. He lauded individual initiative and criticized government con-trol and bureaucracy, yet did not hold to the birthright and inheritance principle. Steiner argued that only people who are capable and worthy ought to be given the chance to run business and other enterprises: "administration of law directed in this way renders it impossible for rich economic enterprises to be handed down through inheritance into unproductive hands" (Carlgren, 1972, p. 15). However, in the legal-political sphere Steiner upheld the principle of equality to be enforced by the state. He did not want a concentration of power in the hands of a privileged few. The judicial system of the state could be used, argued Steiner, to help overcome social disparities and conflicts. The social order that Steiner envisaged would ensure equal rights for all before the law, and at the same time would not dampen individual initiative and enterprise. Once again Steiner was adamant that government and business ought not place restrictions on education and research. Particularly important was the establishment of conditions for a free spiritual life.

Like all new social visions, Steiner's required education to recruit and train supporters. Through a so-called "free education," that is, independent schooling free from state control, students would learn in a manner which would give rise to their own impulse to someday reform the existing society. In an outline of his views, "Education for the People," a course given in 1919, Steiner argued that all teaching should be done: "in such a way as to be always related to man, so that man meets and recognizes man as a being belonging to the universe." Much of what Steiner advocated for the new school was highly prescriptive. To outsiders it may resemble dogma (also see Uhrmacher, 1991, p. 259). Yet this is what Steiner denied. He claimed that Waldorf schools are founded on the principles of anthroposophically oriented spiritual science, but that this was not done with the intention of establishing its outlook or *weltanschauung* (Carlgren, 1972, p. 17).

The Roots of the Waldorf School Movement

The Waldorf school movement was an educational reform effort aimed at fostering the notion of control over one's destiny among the socially and economically oppressed working class. The first Waldorf school was started by an industrialist, Emil Molt, owner of the Waldorf-Astoria cigarette factory in Stuttgart, Southern Germany. Molt had asked Rudolf Steiner to create a new type of school. It was the aftermath of World War I, 1919, and Molt considered that the decay of social and economic life in Germany needed to be attacked through a change in attitude of the people, not through a change in government (Barnes, 1988). Steiner took on this task, recognizing needs in education that others had neglected. He believed in attending to the individuality of students and nurturing their spiritual needs. Schools at that time followed the industrialized pattern that had been established in factories. They gave tests, treated students as little more than a number (reminiscent of "girl number twenty" in Dickens's *Hard Times*), and neglected aspects of development that could not be scored and measured on tests. Schools were becoming a means of production, and the products, the students, were to be produced as quickly and efficiently as possible. Steiner posed an alternative view: "the less we need to use books the better. It is only when the children have to take public examinations that we need printed books at all . . . ideally we should have no examinations at all" (Steiner, 1967, p. 23). No exams and few books being advocated by a learned man was a welcome proposal. At a time when schools were becoming more and more impersonal and bureaucratic, Steiner offered people an education that was built around the concept of humanity and spirituality. Humans were perceived as made up of body, soul, and spirit, unlike in other schools where one or another aspect was neglected.

The first program that Steiner instituted was an adult education program. The program was so successful that it was extended to a full scale school for the children of Molt's employees. Steiner founded his school on a number of principles that echoed his "threefold society" plan. The school had to be open to all children, regardless of class, race, or religious background. The school was to be coeducational and independent of economic and political control. Steiner was strongly opposed to state and business control of education. Also, the school would offer a full 12-year curriculum, thus opposing the 11-plus exams in European schools that sorted students into academic and vocational streams. Finally, teachers were to be given administrative responsibility (Barnes, 1988, p. 2).

During the early days of the school in Stuttgart, Rudolf Steiner took an active role (McDermott, 1984, p. 31). Schools soon sprang up in other parts of Europe. But Steiner died in his studio in Dornach, Switzerland, in 1925, and did not witness the first American school, which was founded in 1928, although he had talked about it before his death. The Waldorf school movement continued to make slow gains on an international level. Then it faced a setback. Immediately prior to the onset of World War II, in 1938, the Nationalist Socialist Party closed down most of the Waldorf schools in Germany. Hitler's regime had no tolerance for schooling that aimed to socialize children towards freedom, independent thought, and antistatist ideals. At the close of the war, in 1945, the schools were once again reopened under the protection of British and American military governments (Barnes, 1988, p. 3). And by 1972 there were 43 schools in Germany, with around 18,000 students. Most of them had a class thirteen for those students taking the state school examination, and many also had a kindergarten (Carlgren, 1972, p. 200). In other European countries, the post-World War II growth of Waldorf schools was sporadic yet undaunted, and in each country the schools assumed some of the traditions and cultural flavor of that country. For instance, in Britain the Waldorf schools "kept to the English tradition of the boarding school, to which belong a country atmosphere, participation in sports, a smaller number of day pupils, and so on" (Carlgren, 1972, p. 201). Other countries with a European heritage (e.g., Australia, New Zealand, and South Africa) or with a German influence (e.g., Argentina and Brazil) also founded new Waldorf schools.

The Waldorf school alternative is still very much alive in all Western industrialized nations. Its appeal lies in its attention to teaching as a human activity and an art form. Waldorf schools do not rely on "detached and alienating forms of instruction" such as textbooks, teaching machines, videotapes, or computers (Interview, teacher). Instead, the focus is on the teacher as a warm, live, thinking, feeling human being who is there to help and guide students' growth, including spiritual growth. Steiner held that, "in this materialistic age," people had become alienated from the spirit of the universe, and that they needed to be reunited with this spirit world (Steiner, 1937). The teacher works with students over an 8-year period (from first through eighth grade), and ideally a cooperative, organic community is born. Bureaucracy, centralization, or heavy administrative machinery, found in schooling formed on an industrialized model, is rejected. Waldorf advocates point to the 1960s hippie movement, not just as a revolt against vulgar and excessive materialism, or as a movement towards the left, or as evidence of an abrasive generation gap, but rather as dissatisfaction with the industrialized form of education one finds in Western nations. The industrial model is seen to permeate all levels of education, giving rise to resistance. The Waldorf alternative is an educational system independent of industry and independent of the state. Its functions are to provide parents with real opportunities to participate in their children's schooling, to allow teachers to enjoy a rewarding if demanding profession, and to offer students the human contact they are perceived to need.

There are costs involved. With involvement and independence parents and teachers also take on responsibilities that in public schools are undertaken by the state. Students face potential problems of being different from their peers on transferring to a regular school, or, upon leaving school, because of their different socialization experience. Yet the gains of independence, autonomy, and freedom for the child cultivated through attention to human aspects of life are considered to far outweigh any disadvantages. Just how well Waldorf students "do" in comparison with other schools is unclear. Few statistics or even qualitative reports are available, because the testing notion is antithetical to Waldorf ideals, and research on Waldorf schools that is not merely promotional writing is rare. One thing is clear, though, and that is that, for insiders, there is a strong commitment to Steiner's view of education; they believe that Waldorf graduates are prepared to "be whatever they want to be in life, whether professional, technical or in the artistic arenas" (Interview, teacher).

Steiner's Views on Education

Steiner repeatedly gave thanks in public lectures to the higher powers who had sent children down to earth. He believed every child was a gift from these higher powers, and that, therefore, no one can claim ownership of any child. All parents can do, argued Steiner, is guide and care for children so that they will be equipped to make their own decisions.

Intuition and spiritual knowledge were held to be the key to good teaching. Steiner wrote: "All education, all instruction, must flow out of a true knowledge of the human being. It is the *Art of Education*, founded on a real knowledge of the human being, that we are trying to develop in the Waldorf school" (Steiner, 1926, p. 9). One of the essentials of education, he said, included having a teacher who understood his or her own temperament and those of the students (Steiner, 1926, 1967). Through "self-knowledge" and "self-education" teachers were thought to be able to learn to control the negative aspects of their own temperaments (Steiner, 1926, p. 7).

Steiner had developed a "psychology" that mapped out different types of temperaments in students and teachers. He advocated seating children with like temperaments together in the classroom on the grounds that this reduced their temperamental tendencies (Steiner, 1967, p. 18). In his view there were four main types of temperament—the melancholic, phlegmatic, sanguine, and choleric. This is an important idea, though outdated, because teachers at Waldorf School today still use Steiner's turn-of-the-century terms in describing students.

The two strong temperaments, in Steiner's view, are cholerics and melancholics. Cholerics are considered to be the strongest, people who have the greatest attention (Steiner, 1967, pp. 17-20). They are sturdy and vigorous people who tend to express their will with passion (Steiner, 1967, p. 13). Melancholic people are also strong, but more placid. Their attention is not so easily aroused, and they are seen to brood quietly (Steiner, 1967, p. 13). The weak temperaments are those of the sanguine person and the phlegmatic. Sanguines are impressionable people, typically delicate and graceful, but easily distracted (Steiner, 1967, p. 20). Finally, phlegmatics have the least strength of all and the least attention. They are low energy people with little or no interest in the world (Carlgren, 1972, pp. 61–62; Steiner, 1967, p. 17).

Temperaments were held to exist because of the predominance of one of the human "bodies"—the main ones being the ego, astral body, etheric body, and physical body (Steiner, 1967, p. 12). Those for whom the astral body, or inspiration and sensitivity, was dominant were considered to be cholerics. Those who had a strong ego, or intuition, were melancholics. Those for whom the etheric body, or imagination, was dominant were sanguines. And people whose physical body was dominant were phlegmatics (see Steiner, 1967, pp. 12–17, 50). Steiner's own words (1967, p. 112) best convey these ideas: "You walk through a wood and see mushrooms or fungi and you ask yourselves: what sort of temperament is revealed here? Why are they not growing in the sunlight? These are the phlegmatics, these mushrooms and fungi." He saw human spirituality and development as similar to the plant world. In thus likening the child's soul to a plant, Steiner keeps company with the psychologist Gesell (1977), who described the child's psyche as a plant that receives its form from within. The plant is seen to grow in response to its own inner forces of growth, unlike a lump of clay which is fashioned from without.

Steiner also subscribed to a stage theory somewhat similar to Gesell's and Piaget's. Steiner described the first 3 years of life as the period when the child was almost wholly a "sense organ" (Steiner, 1968, p.19). This period was seen as critical for soul development. Steiner argued that a child needed the comfort and security of a stable mother–child relationship for spiritual nourishment. Such a policy is somewhat out of touch with modern day life, where many children are nurtured by other caregivers. However, Steiner supporters insist his claim is valid and invoke other research to add weight to the legitimacy of this maxim for present day parents: "When Bowlby and other researchers investigated the reaction of children to various forms of spiritual undernourishment, and the change from one 'mother-figure' to another, they found . . . that at this age (0–3 years) the deepest of all the child's spiritual needs is to be cared for by one and the same mother" (Carlgren, 1972, p. 29). Uhrmacher (1991, p. 257) points out that mothers in the 1990s who are financially able and wish to stay home full time with their young children are pleased to find a school movement that legitimizes their belief.

Steiner's view of stages of development in the child was that the first stage, *willing* (0–7 years), was followed by the *feeling* stage (7–14 years) and the *thinking* stage (14–21 years). At the age of 7 the child gains, in his view, new inner faculties to do with intelligence, social skills, and/or individuality, and these skills and inner faculties continue to develop over the years. Humans are seen as evolving from a lower level or primitive form in much the same way that cultures evolve.

Steiner's ideas were unusual even at the time of his writing. His science was not that of conventional scientists or physicians. Steiner used "ancient science" as the basis for his "spiritual science" or anthroposophy. Steiner's science, as practiced by anthroposophists, claims the existence of a natural science of the human species that must be accepted on faith. Steiner believed that modern science had failed: "Man does not to-day observe himself with such nearness and intimacy as he did during earlier epochs of civilization. For that which this all-pervading Natural Science has brought to mankind cannot be directly applied to the innermost being of man" (Steiner, 1926, p. 8). What science had done, he believed, was neglect humans' inner being. Everything had become quantified and measured. Steiner railed against this. "Outer standards or measurements" (p. 8) and the "observation of external sheaths" (p. 9) were seen to be alienating humans from "what is human." He argued that, as a result of this overattention to the external and directly observable, education and the teaching of children had suffered.

Are Waldorf schools thus part of a counterculture or scientific-romantic cult seeking worldwide expansion? Certainly anthroposophists are committed to the idea of a new social order based on Steiner's threefold plan. They are committed to spiritual growth, rejecting base materialism and seeking a higher and purer form of existence. And they urge parents to form a "unified international opinion" that could put pressure on governments to provide financial support without strings attached for Waldorf schools. The school movement wants freedom to express its philosophical convictions without the constraints of government dictates. Moreover, each Waldorf school claims to be "completely autonomous." Nevertheless, ties exist between schools: cultural, emotional and philosophical, rather than administrative or economic (although membership to AWSNA must be approved, resources are sometimes shared and support for schools is given in the form of mentorships). Thus, while there is no centralization of power, values, ideals, and beliefs are shared. What Waldorf schools share are cultural beliefs set down by Rudolf Steiner and translated over the years by his followers. Just as I recognized the pastel watercolor "swirl" paintings in the Australian Waldorf school as very similar to the ones in the U.S. Waldorf School under study, so too are there many features held in common. Myths in the form of the school's mission of spiritually based schooling, reverence for Rudolf Steiner, and a worldwide commitment to a network of schools give the two Waldorf schools special bonds while allowing them to retain their own distinctiveness.

ST. CATHERINE'S

In the Company of Elite Schools

Within the context of Southville community, St. Catherine's is the elite school. Its status is recognized by those within the school and from without. At the same time, in a larger context St. Catherine's has less of an elite status. Some "prep" schools on the East Coast were founded as far back as the late 1700s and early 1800s, for example, Episcopal High, founded in 1839, a time when "Jefferson had been dead only 13 years, and Napoleon and Beethoven dead for less than 20" (Ringle, 1989). Such schools (Episcopal High, Phillips Academy, etc.) are part of a tradition of prep boarding schools that places them among the elite of the elite. St. Catherine's does not have the reputation of the older and more prestigious schools. As one informant noted:

> The Association of Independent Schools publishes a book which lists grade point average, SAT scores, endowments, number of acres, etc., and St. Catherine's doesn't score well at all. (Interview, teacher)

Pedigree is thus paraded and shows up St. Catherine's in a less than favorable light for those who would like to see the school regarded as highly prestigious.

Yet St. Catherine's is a boarding school in its middle and upper division, and its tradition goes back to 1910, when it was a girls' Episcopal boarding school, which qualifies the school as elite within the context of American private schools. Less than 1% of all high school students in the U.S. attend a secondary boarding school (Persell & Cookson, 1989, p. 33). The lower (elementary) division of the school, founded in 1955 and thus a recent phenomenon, earns its high status by association with its parent boarding school.

To be among the elite, a school needs a fair degree of wealth in the form of endowments and property. St. Catherine's boasts assets of a $7,543,000 plant, which includes 60 acres of prime real estate on which the school is located, and an endowment of $1,320,513. One also needs an exclusive clientele and prominent alumni. This helps, not only with reputation, but also endowment. George Bush's attendance at Phillips Academy, founded in 1778, and Theodore Roosevelt's son's at Episcopal High, founded in 1883, for example, gives those schools a boost in their "prestige level." For the Southville community the alumni and student body of St. Catherine's are also impressive. Wealthy businessmen, famous actors and actresses, those in the arts and sciences, are "old boys and girls," parents, and patrons of the school.

The Mission of St. Catherine's

St. Catherine's claims a dual goal of academic excellence and the development of character. Academic excellence is touted, but in a way that sees academics as part of the overall moral development of the individual:

> We at St. Catherine's believe that the transmission of knowledge, encouragement of curiosity, and the development of responsible, honorable behavior are the great ends of education. In asking students to master a specific body of knowledge we seek not to impart knowledge alone, but to instill the lifelong habit of learning. Although we expect our graduates to be prepared for the nation's finest colleges and universities, our true purpose is to create a challenging yet charitable atmosphere where students gain skills necessary for both creative and disciplined thought, where they have opportunities to achieve in athletic and artistic endeavors, where they understand their responsibility as members of a community, and where high expectations for both their personal and intellectual lives are complemented by the School's commitment to nurturing students in the spiritual dimension of life. (Student handbook)

The aim of preparation of students for the nation's finest colleges and universities, and high expectations for students' personal and intellectual lives, is counterbalanced by concerns for the social good. The school has, however, a strong academic thrust. Achievement is emphasized and an appreciation for the work ethic. Students are academically oriented, highly competitive, and from an early age preparing for college. They say they like best those teachers who stress academics and achieve high-level results.

For the development of character, the other main aim of St. Catherine's, the teaching of values is regarded as important. Values are touted as important in an "age of declining values." At St. Catherine's two types of values are expressed, those to do with manners and conventions, and those that are moral values, including fairness, objectivity, honesty, openness, and independence.

The first type of values has to do with learning how to fit in with social conventions befitting a prep-school graduate. The old truism that "manners maketh the man" is taken seriously at St. Catherine's. Students are socialized into appropriate dress and other behavior. Teachers model by example, but rules are also clearly specified. To give a flavor of the prescriptive detail that is given in this regard, the handbook states:

1. No T-shirts are to be worn during schools hours. Shirts with collars are preferable for boys.
2. Shirt tails must be tucked in.
3. Athletic clothing such as sweat pants and gym shorts is not appropriate school attire.
4. No hats are to be worn in the school building.
5. Inappropriate dress includes, but is not limited to the following: oversized, faded, or ragged clothing or shoes, flip-flops; shoes without socks and/or laces (boys); cut-off shorts; clothes with inappropriate writing; undergarments hanging out of shirts and shorts. (Student handbook)

Boys sometimes violated the dress code by wearing their shirt tails out. Mostly this occurred as a result of vigorous activity during play, but sometimes I suspect it was also done deliberately to defy the code. Teachers across the school could be heard reminding boys to "tuck in your shirt." By and large, however, students and teachers alike dressed well. On chapel days in particular the standard of dress was high and rather formal.

The second values emphasis has to do with morality. Much is said about honor, which is seen to encompass all the principal values of goodness:

"Honor is excellence in character, integrity, and uprightness." With these words the Honor Code of the [original boarding school] began. From our [lower school] tradition comes these words: "If you can honestly say to yourself in any situation, 'to the best of my knowledge, I have acted honorably and there is no trace of deceit in what I have done,' then you need never be

concerned that you are falling short of what the School expects.''
From the great traditions of these two schools, the Honor Code of
St. Catherine's was forged. This sense of excellence in all things,
and the thorough notion of self-honesty, form the basis of our
educational philosophy and shape the values of our community.
(Student handbook)

The Honor Code is put forward as one of the most sacred
traditions of the school. The school's maxim is no lying,
cheating, or stealing, upheld by social pressure to be honorable:
''it remains up to students to ensure that honorable behavior is
encouraged and nurtured and that dishonorable behavior is not
tolerated.'' Nearby Southern University also has a similar Honor
Code.

St. Catherine's is not a religious school as such, but rather
claims to be a ''nondenominational college-preparatory'' school.
However, it has a religious emphasis through its Episcopal roots,
and supported by school tradition:

the School philosophy states that we attempt to nurture the
spiritual growth of the members of the student body. The religious life at St. Catherine's is reinforced by weekly Chapel
services . . . The Headmaster conducts Chapel on a regular basis
in each division . . . Our Chapel program is a vital part of the
School's tradition and is understood to be an integral part of the
life of the School. (Student handbook)

Spiritual growth that is not limited to any one religious category,
is emphasized. ''There is not a specific religious doctrine, but
being kind to one another, having good manners and giving to
each other are important here'' (Interview, teacher). Jews, Catholics, and Protestants of all kinds join together in weekly chapel
to think about ''moral issues that apply everywhere.'' At times
though, the school's Episcopal roots assert themselves more
directly, and chapel becomes ''distinctly more baby Jesus''
(teacher's words) than one might expect in a school claiming a
nondenominational thrust.

Episcopal Themes

It was an Episcopal rector in Southville who founded the school.
The land on which the school was built was diocesan property.

And even though the school is no longer a church school, a number of modern day Episcopal concerns can be seen in the fabric of school life. These concerns have an impact on the present school, however subtle and far removed they are from their original source.

First, it is noteworthy that St. Catherine's draws on a wealthy clientele and the traditions of the English prep school. Similarly, the Episcopal Church has traditionally been associated with wealth and gentility, and Episcopaleanism also has English origins. The Episcopal Church was once the Church of England in the colonies. Indeed, the state in which St. Catherine's is located was one of the two states in which the Church of England was fully and effectively established, so that emigrants "were to enjoy all the liberties and privileges of Englishmen in the homeland. Part of this heritage, of course, was the established church" (Addison, 1969, p. 28). Southville and its environs are an area that historically had a strong English, and Episcopal, influence. Traditions such as Southville's annual steeple chase stand as testimony to the community's English heritage. British prep schools and "public" (i.e., private) schools in general have always been for the children of the well-to-do. Even Anglican priests cannot afford to send their children to these schools (Sisson, 1983, p. 68). Prep schools are also successful in steering "their pupils towards the best university places and the best jobs. This valuable characteristic is what parents are really willing to pay for" (Sisson, 1983, p. 70). St. Catherine's, too, prides itself on its mission and track record in preparing students for the best schools in the nation.

Second, the Episcopal Church is essentially a tradition bound, hierarchical institution. We can see this is the Church's structure and in the language that it uses. Patriarchal and kingly language, referring to "God the Father," "the Almighty," "the Kingdom of God," is used in the Episcopal Church. St. Catherine's also values tradition and hierarchy. The school hierarchy places the headmaster at the top, followed by the Directors of each school division, Curriculum Advisors, Subject Masters, Grade Supervisors, then teachers. School traditions are also celebrated and protected: "traditions foster a sense of community and provide a historic continuity for the school" (School prospectus). Tradition, however, is not immutable. The school wants to remain abreast of new ideas and to use logic and reason, as in secular life, to understand the world. Tradition has an authority, but this must be checked against the authority of reason. The Episcopal Church, likewise, emphasizes tradition, but in combination with scripture and the use of reason (Mathus, 1989).

A third Episcopal theme evident at St. Catherine's is that of the usefulness and value of the scientific method. The church does not have any quarrel with the teaching of science or with the teaching of evolution or biological process; it simply insists that science not be made a primary goal or an ultimate value. Science is considered one important way to know, but not the only way; spiritual ways of knowing are also possible. The use of science is to be done in the context of a belief in God. The Episcopal Church seeks to find out what it "means to be human," from the position that human life cannot be defined simply by concentration on science and rationality, for there is a spiritual side of human nature (Mathus, 1989). The school, too, emphasizes science and a scientific view of the world, but in conjunction with the spiritual dimension.

A fourth important theme in the Episcopal Church and at St. Catherine's is the engagement in complex ritualism. Episcopaleanism teaches that we must *experience God* through worship. The liturgy and the sacrament are experienced through the senses of sight, hearing, smell, and so on, thus lifting the worshipper out of the material world and into the spiritual world (Mathus, 1989). The colors and candles, flowers on the altar, hymns, and movements of participants create a situation for spirituality. The liturgy complements sermons and instruction, providing a context for experiencing God. At St. Catherine's chapel, too, the liturgy, the display of religion, and invoking feelings of spirituality are at least as important as any sermonizing that occurs.

The importance of education is another theme that can be seen in St. Catherine's philosophy. The idea is upheld in Episcopaleanism that, to approach full humanity, we must be educated (Mathus, 1989). Human nature is held to be the creation of God and not a result of a person's own will or development, although people are urged to improve themselves through education and worship. Nevertheless, life is not seen as predetermined or predestined. Rather, the individual must determine the propriety of his or her own life and work towards becoming most fully human. Education is seen as important in enabling the individual to develop a sense of objectivity, openness, imagination, and fairness. The Church does not hand down pronouncements or teach by imposition, but aims to cultivate the individual's knowledge and virtue. At St. Catherine's the school also does not act as an immutable authority. Teachers try to engage students in dialogue, to encourage them to make their own decisions.

An orientation toward the individual is thus a sixth Episcopal theme evidenced at St. Catherine's. The individual is seen to be engaged in a continual process of life choices. Teachers seek, not to force or compel a child's growth, but to model the educated person and to teach students a love of learning through the sciences, arts, and religion. Education is revered, along with spiritual growth and development, with an emphasis on the individual. Education is about "transmitting knowledge," "teaching skills," and bringing each person toward a discovery of his or her own unique identity (Handbook). Humans are viewed as both social and rational beings who are able to make intelligent decisions. In Episcopaleanism there is none of the hellfire and brimstone or "one-right-way" to God that one finds in some other protestant religions. The Episcopal God is a benevolent and loving God. Humans and the rest of creation are also seen as intrinsically good, not lowly "worms" of fundamentalist Christians, or possessing the original sin of Roman Catholicism. In Episcopal theology the soul is united with the physical body before birth, and therefore humans are not just material or physical in nature at birth. They are also spiritual beings and inherently good like the rest of creation. Holiness is seen as innate in human nature (Mathus, 1989). To find God in the Episcopal view, the individual searches for his or her own way. There is not just one way to God, for every human being is unique.

Finally, the Church and St. Catherine's teaches that, while humans are a unique part of nature, we are also discontinuous with the rest of nature. It is humans' rationality, intelligence, and spirituality that is believed to set us apart from the rest of nature, for we are "made in the image of God." Humans are seen to have both an ordinary human nature *and* a divine nature as a result of God's intervention. Clearly we cannot easily "ring down the curtain" on a school's past. These themes, of tradition, wealth and gentility, hierarchy, the scientific method *and* spirituality, ritualism, a high value on education, individuality, and humans' discontinuity with nature, are a constant reminder of the school's heritage. They serve to reinforce the emphasis on spiritual, as well as academic, growth in students.

Memberships and Affiliations

St. Catherine's is an accredited member of the state's Association for Independent Schools, which has some 66 member schools of varying size and status. The school is also a member of the Cum Laude Society, the Council for Religion in Independent Schools, the Educational Records Bureau, the Council for the Advancement and Support of Education, the National Association of Episcopal Schools, the Secondary School Admission Test Board, and the National Association of Independent Schools. Although it has no official church affiliation, St. Catherine's nevertheless continues its membership to the National Association of Episcopal Schools (NAES). The various associations with which St. Catherine's is accredited or affiliated by no means provide the school with a unifying infrastructure. The school is completely autonomous. The advantage that it gains from these affiliations is the moral and social support that ensues from membership in elite organizations.

A key membership for the school is the state association of independent schools. Within the association there is a hierarchy of schools based primarily on size. Schools with a comparable size to St. Catherine's (c. 365 students in the elementary level) and range of grades (Preschool–grade 12) are considered peer schools. Also, collegiate status and the quality of the student body are standards that the school uses to define itself and other schools.

> To measure ourselves and see what we're doing, we probably look more at Collegiate in Richmond or St. Catherine's in Richmond or St. Christopher's or Woodberry Forest in Orange County. I'm sure that's true of all the schools in the association. (Interview, teacher)

By associating her school with Woodberry, the teacher has selected a school that has been named among the 16 most

socially elite prep schools in the U.S. (Baltzell, 1964). Woodberry, along with 15 schools including Taft, Hotchkiss, Kent,
Groton, and Episcopal High, is described as "old, eastern,
patrician, aristocratic and English" (McLachlan, 1970, p. 6;
Persell & Cookson, 1989, p. 335).

Association with like-minded schools is done, not just for the
purpose of having a sensible peer, but also to hold to shared
ideals that can sometimes lead to a kind of rivalry: "we just
don't measure ourselves by association schools. We look to any
independent school that we think is good" (Interview, teacher).
Peer-referenced norms can apply to schools, not just students.
Comparing the school against others is one of the ways St.
Catherine's keeps abreast of new ideas and monitors itself
against competitors. Within Southville the school sees itself as
in a class of its own "we're the IBM of schools, if you want a
cultural metaphor" (Interview, Director of Lower School). In the
larger scene, at a state level, the school then seeks out those
schools it considers its peers.

Another aspect of a school's networks and connections is its
relation to other institutions and organizations that are not its
peer schools, but important in other ways. St. Catherine's
considers it also helpful to stay in touch to a degree with the
public sector. Teachers attend public conferences: National
Council for Teachers of English (NCTE) and National Council for
Teachers of Mathematics (NCTM), as well as private conferences: National Association of Independent Schools (NAIS). In
addition, St. Catherine's faculty consider it important to stay in
touch with what the "good" public schools are doing. In making
the recent decision to move the fifth graders up to the middle
school, in order to make room for a burgeoning lower school
growth pattern, public and private schools that were considered
"good" were consulted:

> We picked schools that we knew were good [in and outside the
> state] and then just called them to see what they were doing. Plus
> we looked at any literature, any research that we could find on the
> topic. (Interview, teacher)

Professional journals and research, as well as contact with
Southern University and the university community in general,
are important affiliations for St. Catherine's.

Inspiration of the English Prep School

College-prep schools in the U.S. have their roots in the tradition of the English prep schools. While it is apparent that St. Catherine's is not just a replica of an English prep school, these roots deserve some consideration, because the school sees itself as a private prep school.

English preparatory schools are an integral part of the "public" school system, for they serve to feed it. In the 1800s *preparatory* was used interchangably with *private*. It meant both schools educating young students before they went to public school (the present English definition) and schools preparing students for university (the present American definition) (Leinster-Mackay, 1984, p. 2). Eventually, public and preparatory schools became an integrated system with the prep school *the* recognized avenue to the public school. These schools were, and are, academic, with an additional emphasis on team sports, known as athletics. Athletics plays, and has played since the 19th century, a key role in English prep schools, based on the age-old premise that "the boy who learns to play for his side at school will do good work for his country as a man" (p. 196). Goals of patriotism and the development of team-spirit, considered so necessary for the formation of character, insured the establishment of athletics, mostly in the form of cricket and football, in the English prep schools.

At St. Catherine's today athletics (la crosse, volleyball, football) is an integral part of the school. Side by side with academics the athletics tradition competes for attention, which sometimes creates a problem:

> I guess I see quite a contradiction at this school, because academics is highly rated here. It has to be Latin, Science, English, History, and so on, and academics comes first. And yet we disrupt our classes to take kids out and put them on buses so that they can go play interscholastic sport. . . . We spend a lot of money at this school on our athletic program. (Interview, parent)

Moreover, the reasoning behind the English prep school's insistence on athletics is also voiced at St. Catherine's: "sport is building morale and team-spirit."

You hear of presidents going to war and building leadership and character, and sport is often regarded as a lesser activity that's less harmful but does the same thing. Sport is regarded as building leadership and character. (Interview, parent)

Girls and boys at St. Catherine's learn in the elementary school to play football and volleyball and la crosse. The argument is put forward that all children, not just the boys, are learning valuable moral lessons about teamwork and commitment through such athletic involvement.

The other main feature of the English prep school is its academic thrust. They existed to get boys into public schools, and in order to do so the boys had to pass rigorous entrance examinations. The importance of getting into a good school is no less a concern for St. Catherine's than it was for the English preps at Summer Fields (1964), Parkside (1879), Sunningdale (1874), and Cheam (1645), all of whom sent large numbers of boys to prestigious Eton (Leinster-Mackay, 1984, p. 114). From an early age students at St. Catherine's focus their attention on academics and academic activities.

It is also important that the prep school curriculum has changed over the years from a core curriculum of Latin to that of the English language, which was seen as more relevant to modern day needs (Leinster-Mackay, 1984, p. 228). Nevertheless, Latin (not English) continued to be considered by traditionalists as a pillar of the preparatory school curriculum (Leinster-Mackay, 1984, p. 230). At St. Catherine's in the lower school the curriculum focuses on English (Reading and Language Arts), mathematics, science and social studies with additional instruction in French, computers, art, music, drama and P.E. (Curriculum Guide). At the middle school level, however, all seventh and eighth graders are required to take Latin. The emphasis on Latin would seem to be a carry-over, prevalent in the South, from the days when to be properly educated meant to be classically educated. The upper school's requirements for graduation include 2 years each of two foreign languages (French, Latin, or Spanish) or 3 years of one foreign language. Also stipulated at this level is one year of Religion, one semester of Computer, one semester of Fine Arts, and satisfactory completion of 60 hours of community service, among other requirements. Such requirements are considered an essential part of the prep school tradition.

If prep schools see themselves as much more than academic hothouses, and they do, then the fact remains that they are concerned with the goal of getting students into good colleges, and this infiltrates all levels of the school. The cycle is somewhat self-perpetuating, since St. Catherine's parents are predominantly professionals who have been competitively successful:

> There's no doubt that competition exists. Most of them are born with it and bring it to school from home. Many of our parents are overachievers themselves. And of course there is always the quest to get into a good college. (Interview, teacher)

It is also suggested that St. Catherine's location in the South is "just enough South to keep that down," thus drawing attention to the age-old distinction between Northern industrial-style aggessiveness and a more placid Southern gentility.

Such myths, the idea of athletics as preparing children's characters, the academic emphasis, the Episcopal influence, the goal of classic education in the best British tradition, the school's relation to other schools in Southville as the "IBM," help define St. Catherine's school culture. The project of the school is set against this backdrop, for what the school believes it is about then plays into its daily processes.

CONCLUSIONS

Schools are clearly not the same when it comes to defining themselves. Images of society, values, and assumptions of Waldorf School differ from those of St. Catherine's. In the first case, "myths" about Rudolf Steiner and his vision of and for society underpin that school's particular order. The belief in schooling "free" of the state, the belief in humans as part of the universe or cosmos, a spiritual emphasis, the belief in the value of few printed books and no exams, an antimaterialist stance, a view of human development occuring in 7-year stages, and a commitment to the art of education through attention to the aesthetic are guiding principles of Waldorf School.

Waldorf School endorses a set of beliefs and values apart from the dominant culture of our society. An alternative is proposed. While the members of the community do not drop out of society, there is clearly a desire to promote new cultural values or impulses. Change is one of the key values of the school, ironically held in conjunction with a Puritan-like emphasis on discipline and restraint.

Steiner, the school's "guru," talks about the present age being the beginning of a new epoch, the Fifth Post-Atlantean Period, a time for the imminent transformation of the world. The story goes something like this: 500 years ago, with the advent of modern consciousness and the Enlightenment, people came to believe in progress and science. They replaced religion with science as the guide for human action. People came to believe that science would solve human problems and provide a better life. Humankind's duty became that of conquering and dominating nature through scientific advances and technology. The exploitation of natural resources was considered proper for the attainment of human happiness. Air and water, for instance, were free for the taking. The main goal became materialistic wealth and comfort. Rational logic and reason replaced feeling and intuition as the means to understand the world and make decisions. In Steiner's view contemporary society became plagued by the resultant anomie, aimlessness, and spiritual void. Logic, not feelings, have come to govern our personal and professional lives. Waldorf School is opposed to such a view.

Waldorf education is to play an important role in changing the individual and society. Steiner proposed the threefold social order which was a radically *new* social conception, although he also claimed to be taking into account the conditions of the society in which people were living, for children begin as a product of a social order and they must also return to the social order when their education is complete (Steiner, 1947b, p. 92). People in Waldorf School believe they must change themselves first, by developing spiritually and growing through contemplation; then this is seen to have a broader effect. Spirituality is thus a predominant school theme. Modern society is seen as inherently secular, which does not satisfy people's desire for a meaningful existence. People are seen as lost in a void of meaninglessness. Steiner's "new age" beliefs and practices are thought to allay the void and bring people much closer to God. What Steiner means by God is a closeness with all of humankind and nature, a feeling of connectedness with the other beings in the universe.

Another Waldorf School myth or cultural theme is that of anticonsumption. Western society is seen as built on excess and spiritually deadening materialism. In this view we have accepted the marketplace as the arbiter of values. People think that the way to solve all life's problems is to go to the marketplace. In the Waldorf School view these are misguided values. Instead, growth and wisdom is seen to come through "inner work" and reflectiveness based on an harmonious relationship with the world, others, and oneself.

St. Catherine's, on the other hand, draws its mythmaking from a representation of schooling that is more traditional. The school defines itself as a serious and professional enterprise with a task of preparing students intellectually through academic activities in the tradition of the English prep schools. Academics means rigor to be measured through tests. Students are tested to see whether they have acquired the requisite body of knowledge and skills, and the school measures itself against other schools it considers to be "good," that is, like St. Catherine's. The organizing principle guiding the academic and extracurricular (particularly sporting) enterprise is one of competition and individual achievement tempered by a concern for character building and self-esteem. Waldorf School myths relate to a vision of an organic world, whereas St. Catherine's myths have to do with a rational, tradition-bound and hierarchical world.

The schools are both "religious" in orientation, but with very different messages. Waldorf School has a subjective, aesthetic, contemplative, and mystical approach to spirituality. St. Catherine's, in contrast, utilizes an intellectual and questioning approach. St. Catherine's does not accept a literal interpretation of the scripture and creeds, but one which is academic and analytical in its search for meaning. In the next chapter we will turn to the manifestation of these beliefs in the school's curriculum. The philosophical and mythical foundations of school culture are perhaps expressed most clearly in the content that the school selects, the process it uses to impart the content, and the means created or selected to define student progress.

5

CULTURE IN THE CURRICULUM

Knowledge in school isn't only representational. Knowledge also embodies a certain world view. Messages of value are embedded in everything that is taught. Ideas about the world, relations to others, and the individual's place in the world are expressed in the curriculum. Particular social meanings and not others are encoded. The curriculum contains cultural beliefs and assumptions about such things as authority, hierarchy, or equality. When Waldorf School allocates an important resource, time, to eurythmy, and St. Catherine's does not even recognize eurythmy as a subject, this is an important difference in the content and meaning of schooling. When Waldorf School keeps its communications about what is to be taught primarily at the level of an oral "text," whereas St. Catherine's carefully defines and articulates its curriculum in an abstract and rational document, this is another example of the school's view of knowledge and the world. The curriculum at St. Catherine's is traditional, competitive, and academic, teaching children about a world quite different to the one Waldorf School envisages, with its attention to noncompetitive and aesthetic modes of thinking and learning. Like myths, ritual and other forms of collective communications, the school curriculum is not simply expressive. It has a socializing function.

AN ORAL CURRICULUM: WALDORF SCHOOL

The curriculum at Waldorf School is primarily an oral narrative shared by faculty, not a written or technical document.

> You won't really find the curriculum printed anywhere. There's one book with Steiner's quotes [Stockmeyer, 1982], but it's very difficult to read. And the one page outline that we have is pretty much what we teach. It's really up to the teacher to study and do the *inner work* and to bring it from that inner work. The study and the understanding that man is a spiritual being and what this means and the stages that we go through in life is what it's all about. But we don't have clear materials laying it all out. (Interview, teacher)

However, although the curriculum has been mainly developed and maintained through oral means, its underpinning conceptual work is clear and explicit.

A developmental view of learning is subscribed to at Waldorf School. The three stages of development, *willing* (0–7 years), *feeling* (7–14 years), and *thinking* (14–21 years) are seen to demand particular approaches and particular content and materials. The curriculum is therefore a spiral curriculum with subject matter varying in difficulty and style depending on the child's perceived level of growth. The child's loss of baby teeth at around the age of 8 is taken to signify readiness for a new stage of learning. In addition, the school endorses integration across the subjects. The study of the Bible in grade three is relevant to history and other subject areas; movement and music pervade arithmetic and English lessons. These two aspects, integration and a developmental view, can be seen in the curriculum at each grade level. Moreover, despite Waldorf School teachers' lack of documentation, the curriculum is relatively uniform across Waldorf schools. Perhaps the Waldorf school movement is in a class of its own in this regard; one may find children in grade three Waldorf schools in Germany, England, Australia, South Africa, and the U.S., for instance, all studying old testament Bible stories at the same time.

The Magic of Kindergarten

Teachers at Waldorf School believe that children who are not spoiled by lavish and sophisticated toys develop a much finer imagination and creativity. "Finished" toys are seen as lacking; they leave little to the imagination. What one finds in Waldorf School are "anthroposophically correct toys" that is, simple pine cones, cords of timber, wooden blocks, and handmade primitive dolls made of wood, cloth, and woollen materials. Some parents who are new to Waldorf School worry about the disjunction between the school and the "real world."

> I live in the real world, and I am wondering whether there will be problems in terms of what is stressed in the school conflicting with television and toys in the real world. Do you want parents to adopt some of the ideas and philosophy of the school?

The school's reply is a pragmatic one.

> Yes, ideally that would happen. There would be a meeting of home and school. In my case my children go to Mother's and watch a thousand hours of television. And that's good because then they get to see how it is there and how we have different rules at home. Also, for me I've had to gradually introduce real-world toys for Christmas and birthdays to some extent. There weren't any before. Whereas parents who have given their children all the materialistic toys may move more towards naturalistic toys. (School spokesperson at parents' meeting)

Waldorf School's approach to materialism, television, and toys differs from that found in the so-called real world.

Teachers strive to create an environment composed of all-natural materials. For instance, a "Nature Garden" is a feature of the kindergartens and Grades 1, 2, and 3. In the Nature Garden natural materials, such as stones, sea shells, twigs, and wood, are arranged on a table covered with a white linen cloth. Hanging above and around the table are filmy muslin drapes in pastel shades, giving the Nature Garden centrality in the classroom. At certain times a homemade beeswax candle is lit in the Nature Garden, and verses celebrating nature are recited.

In keeping with the emphasis on simplicity and things natural, strong feelings are held by Waldorf teachers about television. Parents are advised to restrict or eliminate their children's television viewing. The school does not use television, videotapes, or any other electronic equipment. Television is believed to spoil children's ability to fantasize in a healthy way. Instead, the curriculum is designed to develop children's natural abilities through music, cooking, painting, modelling, and the imaginative acting out of stories of fantasy characters, giants, and dragons. Academic activities, such as reading, are not taught in kindergarten. One finds instead an attempt to preserve the "magic of childhood" and avoid the pressures of "fast-track" approaches to schooling.

Kindergarten teachers adopt a mothering and nurturing style. Even the shape of classrooms is altered and rounded, using colored drapes of muslin to make them "womblike." Certain colors (peach-pink tones) are used to enhance this feeling:

> The peach color is supposed to be warm and womblike. That's the reason for it. When I was teaching, I didn't want it to be too pink, and so I added brown and people warned me against going too brown. The peachy-pink is chosen to be the right color for this age group. (Interview, teacher)

The idea stems from Rudolf Steiner, who had a great deal to say about color and its effect on humans (see Steiner, 1937, pp. 41-57). A Waldorf educator (Carlgren, 1972, p. 34) gives the following advice about teaching kindergarteners through the use of color. "One can interest children in paintings [as an expression of feelings] through fairytales, in which they bring out the humorous, sad, calm or exciting mood of the tale in simple color harmonies."

Another indicator of the "mothering" approach is that kindergarten teachers cut the corners off square pieces of paper on the grounds that paper with corners is "too hard for the little ones" (Interview, teacher). Moreover, play, rather than an academic approach, is selected as the best means of learning at this stage, consistent with the school's belief in natural development and gentle mothering. The madonna and child portrait found on Waldorf School kindergarten walls further symbolizes the maternal approach.

Fairy Tales for First Graders

Waldorf School's Grade 1 curriculum is centered around the teaching of fairy tales. During main lesson the teacher narrates a

fairy tale, and subsequent activities of the day are built around it.
The events of nature, for example, are experienced in nature
walks and explained by the teacher through fairy tales. Children
are also gradually introduced to the alphabet through fairy tales.
During one of the lessons I observed, the teacher told a story
about a princess to introduce the letter p. She had drawn an
elaborate picture of a princess on the chalkboard, with the letter
shape drawn over and next to it to show the connection. The
story served to heighten interest in the new letter and provided
a useful device for remembering the shape of the letter. Children
learned the letter as a picture first, then as an abstract symbol.
Steiner felt that the teaching of reading should "recapitulate the
same process that is to be found in the old Egyptian, Babylonian
and Chinese cultures, namely the transition from the picture-
element to the sign" (Carlgren, 1972, p. 81). Moreover, the aim
of using fairy tales is to combine the technical skills of prereading and writing with the teaching of values or morals.

Waldorf teachers believe that the dramatic vividness of fairy
tales allows children to reflect on the human condition and their
own inner selves. Fairy tales are said to be full of the poetry that
is seen as critical for self growth. They contain wisdom about
human nature and the social world, represented symbolically in
fairies, gnomes, and other creatures. Teachers try not to engage
in detailed intellectual moralizing. Rather, the stories are
thought to speak for themselves. Teachers see these stories as
preparing the child to cope with the modern world with all its
problems, such as competitiveness, materialism, and violence.
Through an extended exposure to fairy tale witches, trolls,
wicked princesses, and bad kings, as well as good kings,
beautiful and kind princesses, and the like, children's characters
are believed to be developed.

Fables and Saint Legends in Grade 2

In the second grade students are taught fables and legends about
saints. The values emphasis continues in the curriculum. Literature is used again to heighten aesthetic sensitivity in children.
Fables are chosen because they depict human weaknesses in
animal form. The children are led to recognize the human
potential to give in to their "animal" nature. They can see how

animals deceive, manipulate, and exploit one another, and this is thought to evoke feelings of tolerance and humor in the children. Fables are selected for their moral messages.[1] Legends are said to show the opposite. In contrast to fables (which depict characters who are animals) "legends show characters who can control animals and their own animal instincts and who are larger than life" (Interview, teacher).

> Fables and legends are used because the children have gone one level more into living on the earth than they had in the first grade, when you told fairy tales and there was very little real human element. They were archetypal symbols that were being told. Then in the second grade they're starting to become more aware of themselves as individuals separated from the world, from their parents, from the social group, and that's when you start giving them stories of earthly beings, not fairies and gnomes, who are still connected though with the cosmos, and who in some ways go beyond one's usual destiny and reach towards something greater than what you can see. (Interview, teacher)

The saints in legends are thought to serve as examples of the perfection towards which humans may aspire. For instance, children are taught that "Saint Francis fasts to understand better the hunger felt by animals. He is then able to tame wild animals because of his understanding of them." In conjunction with fables and legends the emphasis on nature and the study of nature through nature walks and observation is continued.

Reading is now taught, having been delayed until the second grade. Readers are used.

> I've now read the reader to the children as a story, and with the main lesson block that begins next week we'll read them as a class. The children are just bursting over now ready for reading,

---

[1] At St. Catherine's, in contrast, moralizing through fables is seen as too simplistic: "I'm all for any kind of moral behavior, but there's a moralism in those fable stories in the basals that rubs me the wrong way. There's something too simplistic, too packaged, too like the McGuffy readers that some of us have been through. There's too much emphasis on trying to make sure the Eskimo gets there in the end. Yes, these things are important, but not to the point of being mechanically homogenized. I found that irritating" (Interview, Director of Lower School).

so one of the options they now have when they are done with their
work is that they can read those books. (Interview, teacher)

The reasoning behind this is that the children are not ready to
read until they have reached a certain stage, around the age of 8,
when they receive their second set of teeth. This is regarded as
a *rite de passage* into a more complex mode of thinking and
acting in the world. The bodily "hardening" or development of
teeth and bones is held to parallel intellectual growth.

Bible Stories to Build Character in Grade 3

Biblical stories are introduced in Grade 3 to broaden children's
understanding of the historic roots of Western civilization, and
Waldorf schooling is, after all, a Western form of schooling. The
story of Creation, the Fall from the Garden of Eden, the Tower of
Babel, and so on are considered moral stories that are part of
Western heritage, even for children who are not religious. The
early experiences of humankind placed in the context of moral
and spiritual backgrounds are seen as important. The Bible is
also used because it teaches about authority, defiance of authority, and its outcome. At around 9 years of age, the child is
believed to be going through a period of defiance of authority.
The great stories of the Bible are thought to provide children
with images to help them resolve their own inner struggle
between exerting their will and being obedient to authority,
between resenting adult control and being respectful to their
elders.

> The first inner awakening of the individual, of the future of that
> child, the past stream and the future stream, come together for the
> first time. The past stream is what we've inherited from our
> parents, our physical bodies, our gestures, and the future stream,
> in anthroposophy it's called the ego, is coming to the child. It's
> something that is just his alone. And that can be a very fright-
> ening time, because the child realizes that he or she is really
> separate. Children begin to form groups and look out from
> themselves. They have a new objective sense of the world. Adam
> and Eve were thrown out of the Garden. It's like their experience.
> They're leaving the Garden. They're waking up to the world.
> (Interview, teacher)

The child's spiritual growth is believed to be helped by the biblical example. Once again stage theory governs the decision to introduce biblical stories at this point.

Nature study continues to be important. Through constant exposure to nature, children are seen to grow in their understanding of nature's patterns and forces, strengthening and confirming their own sense of self. Also important is a sense of the environment of the past, before the age of advanced technology. For this purpose students in Grade 3 learn how to make a building, grow crops and engage in many other farming experiences. During the farming unit of work, called a "block," the children stay on a Waldorf farm for a week. They learn about soils and how to care for the earth; they learn about different grasses. They plant wheat and rye and thresh it and make bread. The theory is that, through contact with the primitive things of life, food, clothing and shelter, the children will grow in their knowledge of the world in a spiritual sense. By learning these basic skills and crafts, children are thought to grow to better appreciate more complicated technical processes at a later stage.

Norse Tales, the Greeks and Romans for Seniors

Fantasy is continued in the senior grades through the reading of tales and myths, and through learning about actual historical events. Fourth graders study local history and their immediate environment from a geographical perspective. Significantly, national history is not studied. Such studies would be considered nationalistic and against the spirit of holistic Waldorf education. Instead, students in grades 5–7 study world history. A worldwide perspective is undertaken, so that students can begin to appreciate their place within a world context.

Cultural eras and their different strengths and emphases are examined. In Grade 4 the focus is on Norse Tales. In Grade 5 students study the early nomadic civilizations of India for whom religion was the highest ideal. They then focus on the agriculturalists who "turned towards the earth for inspiration" (Interview, teacher). This is followed by an examination of the artistic cultures of Persia, Mesopotamia, or Egypt. Next comes the study of the Greeks, with their emphasis on government and thinking processes. Greek mythology and civilization are studied, including Plato's "picture wisdom" and Aristotle's "modern conceptual" thinking (Interview, teacher).

By Grade 6 students study an even more "advanced" civilization, the Romans, in conjunction with the study of the Life of Christ. More recent Western history, the Explorers, the Age of Discovery, the Reformation, and the Renaissance, is covered in Grade 7. As students progress to Grade 8 they would also study more recent history, 1700 to the present day. What is studied is seen as parallelling students' own growth and development.

FEATURES OF THE CURRICULUM

Main Lesson

For the first 2 hours of each day students engage in Main Lesson. Main Lesson is the focal "academic" lesson of the day, which may be History, Art Appreciation, Physics, Social Studies, Arithmetic, English, Geometry, or Myths and Legends, for example. A unit of work, or *block*, continues for 3 to 4 weeks, sometimes longer, allowing for a concentrated effort in a particular area. Human interest units, such as History or Literature, are often followed by Arithmetic or Science, allowing for alternation of subject matter, consistent with the rhythmic ritual of the school day. During Main Lesson an unhurried tone is maintained that one of the teachers, who previously taught in public schools, describes as "heavenly." She praises the integrity and wholesomeness of Waldorf School's approach, in comparison with the fragmentation and rigidity she experienced in public schools. Main Lesson is a time when teachers can inspire students through in-depth studies. Teachers review the lesson within the time block and follow up interesting leads that develop. Subjects that require continuous practice, such as German, and Arithmetic and English skills, are then taught as separate regular lessons on a daily basis.

Main Lesson is for "academics," but the material is presented in a way that is fun for the children and engages them. For example, in a second grade Arithmetic lesson, the children made their own ice cream, after purchasing and estimating the prices of the ingredients. Students devised problems to calculate the cost of the ice cream, for example, 4 eggs at 5 cents each is 5c + 5c + 5c + 5c; they added up the list of items and compared the different approaches. Teacher and students sang and chanted the computations. The times tables were worked into an elaborate series of counting, clapping, and movement games that made arithmetic a physical and intellectual exercise. And, as is customary throughout the school, the lesson was recorded in a large blank-paged book using brightly hued crayons.

A Holistic, Experiential, and Developmental Curriculum

Across the curriculum academic learning is combined with physical and emotional activities. Rhythmics, along with music, singing, and crafts provide a strong physical basis to the curriculum. For instance, rhythm is used with whole body movements, such as catching bean bags, stamping feet, clapping, and jumping, to teach mathematical tables and relationships. Concrete, rather than abstract examples, are used in Arithmetic lessons. Thus, Roman numerals, which have a direct visual relationship with the fingers, are taught prior to the introduction of abstract Arabic numbers. So, too, are weights and measures, taught, not in the abstract, but through doing, and through the introductory story that measurements of length were often derived from the human body. Only later do students learn to use modern and more abstract units of measurement. Moreover, the principle of experiencing mathematics without any need to solve problems formally or prove theories is employed. This can be seen particularly in geometry. Students use rulers and compasses to construct elaborate geometrical shapes without attempting to understand the abstract formulations that underpin these shapes. Not until the senior years do students begin to study abstract relations, such as one finds in algebra.

Science, too, is treated in a developmental way. The study of zoology in fourth and fifth grade is undertaken for its potential to teach students about humankind in general, and themselves in particular. Through close investigation of the various skills and abilities of different animals, students are encouraged to see how they are alike and different. Humans' ability to use arms and hands freely, thus employing tools and technology, is "discovered" by the children as a significant difference between humans and animals.

Sixth graders study physics, a subject that continues to be taught in Waldorf high schools. Botany is also taught to fifth and sixth graders to sharpen their powers of observation. But abstract scientific concepts are not used. Students study and report on plant communities, they are made aware of the changing seasons, and they grow plants and trees. The teacher does not set up a laboratory, as happens at St. Catherine's, where students perform scientific experiments. Rather, Waldorf School students are encouraged to *experience* the plant world in its natural context. The use of experiments is thought to teach children that humans can control and manipulate their environment, an idea that is antithetical to Waldorf School beliefs. In contrast, the study of plants and animals as part of a simple, living organism that fits together and is interdependent is intended to teach children respect for the natural world. Waldorf School views humans as one small part in a giant complex web, rather than as instigators and controllers of the world. Environmental problems, such as the covering of the earth's surface with urban developments and desert due to human interference, global warming, the greenhouse effect, acid rain, chemical pollutants, overpopulation, and the destruction of the ozone layer are recognized as human creations and outcomes of an inability to live in harmony with other animals and plants. Waldorf School hopes to teach students to care for the earth and its beings, to celebrate the intimate interplay between nature and self.

World geography is studied in Grades 6–7 to teach further about humans' interactions with their natural environments. Detailed maps are drawn. These maps are done freehand, and are more physical representations than abstract forms. Cultural meanings are tacitly taught. Love of one's fellow human beings, and sympathy for their struggle in different environments is one important lesson. Another lesson is a sense of responsibility for sharing the earth's resources, instead of supporting massive expenditure by major political or economic power groups. Since the U.S. is a major consumer of the earth's resources, there is some self criticism implied here. Students are taught to think about the short- and long-term consequences of an exploitative attitude towards the natural resources of the earth. Such issues are central concerns of the Anthroposophy movement.

Teacher, as an Alternative to the Textbook

A significant feature of the curriculum is the manner in which the material is presented. No textbooks are used. The teacher tells stories, in a dramatic way, for example, of Hannibal or Alexander the Great. Some of the characters are made into heroic figures. Heroes are seen as necessary "food" for a child's intellectual and social development. Historical figures are considered preferable to the "shallow heroes" put forward by the mass media. At the same time, historical heroes are not presented only from one viewpoint. The teacher tries to present the whole person, showing the complexity of the person.

An authoritative form of "text" thus comes from teachers, who get their ideas from any number of sources, including imagination and life experiences. Students then make their own "texts," one book for each block, carefully copying down the teacher's words and illustrating it. Much attention is given to the use of correct color and neatness so that the work is aesthetically pleasing as well as representative of some ideas about a particular content area. The characteristic use of crayons in the younger grades is also reflective of the school's developmental view of learning. Up until the end of fourth grade students use only crayons. At the end of fourth grade, in a special ritual or closing ceremony, teachers present students with their own fountain pens, symbolically marking their passage into the senior grades. By Grades 6 and 7 students have reached a stage where there is more freedom in what they write down, although even here much of the work is dictated or suggested by the teacher. Students' books continue to be an artistic expression, with attention given to illustrations, headings, and good penmanship. It should be noted, however, that the no textbook policy is sometimes broken by teachers who feel the pressure that the absence of textbooks places on the teacher to be an authority on everything. One teacher admits, "I sometimes resort to my old public school textbook routine when I don't seem to have any inspiration" (Interview, teacher).

The emphasis in Waldorf School is therefore on oral culture or the spoken word. Teacher's stories, the "living word" that passes directly from one to another, is considered essential if students are to develop in an holistic way. The grade school years are, after all, considered to be the "feeling" years. Children are thought to learn to empathize and sympathize with others, to experience feelings of joy and sorrow and love as a foundation for community living. They are expected to think for themselves and assert independence, even while having responsibility to the community. Then, in the "thinking" phase of high school, in this view, children further develop their intellects and reasoning powers, ideally to be used for the betterment of humankind.

Specialty Teachers

A number of the specialty teachers in the school are parent volunteers, a situation that is said to be less than ideal. The school would prefer to have specialty teachers who are actually part of the faculty. When teachers come into the school for brief periods, especially if they are not Waldorf-trained teachers, it is thought that the school's "integrity" is diminished. However, the classroom teachers simply cannot do everything. The role of teacher as "text" is a demanding one, and the specialty teachers provide classroom teachers with a much needed break from teaching, as well as bringing their own areas of expertise to the classes.

Physical education varies with grade level. The older children go to the gymnasium and playing fields at Southern University, where they receive instruction from a college student. The younger grades have their own class teacher for physical education, who might take them outside to go sledding in the snow or to play with a soccer ball, or parents come in to give lessons. No organized games, such as hockey, football, or volley ball, are played in this school. Students can be seen kicking a soccer ball around at lunch time, but there is no training in specific rules of the game, and no competition. Waldorf School teachers say they are "morally opposed" to the way that sport and physical education are usually taught in public schools. Exercise for its own sake, such as jogging, is criticized as deprived of any social need and therefore "soul-less." Exercise that is not artistic is also seen as "soul-less." What is proposed instead is Bothmer gymnastics, which is supposed to strengthen "will forces" as well as giving physical exercise. (Bothmer was the gymnastics instructor in the first Waldorf school in Germany. His system of gymnastics was developed at Steiner's request, incorporating the idea of space and geometry to strengthen "will forces.") Waldorf School hopes to be able to offer Bothmer gymnastics in the future.

Handwork and music are taught by parents. Boys and girls do the same handwork. One could interpret this as a far-sighted view of Steiner's. Was he egalitarian and nonsexist in the early 1900s?[2] On closer examination, though, it would seem to be more connected with the holistic and unity emphasis in the school. The class works together as a group doing the same activity, bonding as a community. It is also related to the mothering, nurturing emphasis in Waldorf schools. Students learn to knit, crotchet, sew, and model with beeswax or clay. These are all so-called feminine art forms. Only later in the senior years of grade school are students given the opportunity to do woodwork or metalwork. The introduction of "harder" substances and materials parallels the theory of stage development. As students move from the "feeling" stage towards the "thinking" stage, they are perceived as able to work with "harder" and more challenging materials, such as metals.

German language is taught for its intrinsic value and for its role in the development of the child's whole personality. The

---

[2]Many women clearly influenced Steiner (Rosa Mayreder, Marie Lang, Marie delle Grazie, Gabrielle Reuter, Marie von Sievers, and H. P. Blavatsky) and he did promote women's rights in some ways; for example, in his *Christian Community* women could become priests (see Steiner, 1977; Uhrmacher, 1991, p. 256). Uhrmacher (1991, p. 258) points out, however, and I agree with him, that a number of Waldorf School movement ideas and practices seem sexist and outdated, for example, a major journal called *Child and Man*, and usage in the schools such as *Miss* rather than *Ms*, and *man* rather than *human*. Modern types of feminism, particularly the idea of parity with men, seem to have been rejected in the Waldorf School movement. Anthroposophical feminists emphasize instead the "unique qualities of women" and hold a spiritual belief in "reincarnation (women returning as men and vice versa) and in the wholeness of the soul (masculine and feminine)" (Uhrmacher, 1991, p. 258). Thus, spiritual concerns would seem to take precedence over practical or political ones.

subtleties of speech are seen to enhance the child's inner life.
Eurythmy, the art of movement, is also taught to develop the
child's soul or inner life. Eurythmy is like role play, gymnastics,
or dance, but has spiritual or emotional overtones. The
eurythmist strives to convey visibly speech and music and to
strengthen the "will" in the child. Once again the social aspect
is emphasized. The group attempts to flow together as a harmonious whole, in contrast to competitive and aggressive team
sports. eurythmy is taught by a German woman who was trained
as a Eurythmist in Germany. She comes to the school for the
scheduled lessons only and is not really a full participant in
faculty decision making. Thus, specialty lessons are important,
although the arrangements in this school have been influenced
by financial constraints and the availability of suitable teachers.

Plays and Stories

The performance of plays before an audience of other students
and parents is an integral part of the curriculum. Younger
children's plays are based on fairy tales or myths; older children
perform classical dramas. Plays are seen as a spiritual expression, and important for developing children's aesthetic potential. During the grade school years improving children's appreciation for rhythm, gesture, and movement, and also teaching
them to work together as a community, are accomplished
through drama.

> Building up community is very subtle. It's done through the
> rhythm of the day, that we all fall in tune with one another. It's
> done by the celebrations of the various holidays, and also the
> ways that we come together in meetings as a faculty or as a class.
> With the play everyone has had to learn to co-operate and get
> along well and that's a very important lesson. (Interview, teacher)

For instance, Grades 4–5 performed *Tom Sawyer* to an audience
of parents and friends. The sixth-grade children used their play,
Julius Caesar, to entertain parents and to raise money for a class
trip later in the year. The play was written by their teacher. It
was a variation of Shakespeare's *Julius Caesar,* and the teacher
had written the parts for the children who would act them, thus

seeking to tailor the experience to their individual needs. Just as, in the fairy tales studied in earlier grades, children are led to see and experience social and moral dilemmas and to have contact with a variety of human characters before they would necessarily encounter them in the real world, so are plays used for specific character-building purposes.

Stories and parables are thought to teach problem solving and character development. Problems are approached indirectly. To teach through a didactic tale is one of Steiner's principal methods. Thus, when children are misbehaving, rather than lecture them, the teacher weaves an allegoric element concerning the behavior into a story. The idea is that the children will recognize themselves in the story and be guided towards an appropriate action. Similarly, teachers inform parents about their children in an allegorical fashion. For instance, the teacher may tell a story about the child that portrays his or her character, or the teacher may select or write a poem or verse that is representative of the child. Words and stories, not numerical test scores, are seen to convey most meaningfully a child's growth and development.

TOWARD A VIEW OF THE WHOLE CHILD

In keeping with the integrated curriculum, Waldorf School students are viewed holistically, for their overall development, not for competency in a particular skills. No child fails. A child might be seen as requiring more help in some areas, but there is no concept of failure. The notion of repeating grades is also rare. As the children grow they move up each grade with the same teacher, who has taken great pains to insure that the child is prepared to move ahead.

> Since in the grades you're taking the children with you, you don't leave any behind. It's only in the kindergarten that you might think a child is too young and hold them. I really don't know what we'd do if anyone were falling terribly, terribly behind. I guess it does happen occasionally. This year we had one child who asked to be put back. She was very young for her class and is now blooming. We try to be really careful about placing them in the first place so that children do not experience failure. (Interview, teacher)

With small class sizes, teacher dedication, a holistic approach, and close contact with families, the process is assisted.

In Waldorf School it is not skills that are most important, although these are implicitly taught, but content. The public school emphasis on acquiring skills in a competitive environment designed to sort and differentiate students, for example, learning disabled, gifted, talented, "straight A" student, and so on, is rejected. The content in Waldorf School is that of myths, legends, and stories from Western cultural knowledge (the Bible, Aesop's fables, Shakespeare, botany, Norse tales, and so on), and some Eastern culture, such Indian and Hindu knowledge, for example, Hindu epic poetry. Students learn this body of knowledge and can demonstrate amazing powers of retention. For example, fourth graders recite long passages of John Milton or William Blake. Yet it is the "feeling" engendered and the foundations laid, not the accumulation of facts, that is considered important.

> The poems we study are food for the mind. It's the same reason that in the younger grades the children will imitate. They will draw the picture that the teacher has drawn in the same way. It's the same thing. It's food. It's beautiful language that they have to commit to memory so that it will be there within them. It's a kind of literary nourishment. And they don't even have to understand what they're saying necessarily, but it should be a poem with substance and meaning. (Interview, teacher)

Whereas in public school children are given freedom, usually, to explore and play in their art work and creative writing at the early stages, which later turns into a greater emphasis on memorization, the opposite pattern can be seen at Waldorf School. The school intends that giving children early foundations of rich cultural experiences that are then committed to memory will later give rise to children who are creative, inventive, and able to think for themselves.

One means of keeping parents informed about the curriculum and the child's development is the evening class meetings scheduled throughout the year. Teachers answer any questions parents might have and explain aspects of the curriculum that are new to them, as well as outlining projects in which the class is engaged. I attended a Grade 2 parent meeting where the teacher explained the concept of "form drawing." She gave the rationale behind it, explaining that form drawing is closely aligned with geometry and eurythmy and that the children learn to "feel" the shapes; the symmetry helps balance them in a fundamental way. (For examples of form drawing and a detailed explanation, see Niederhauser & Frohlich, 1984.) We engaged in doing some form drawing, which involved drawing complicated, convoluted, and flowing symmetrical shapes in crayon on large sheets of drawing paper. We were instructed not to take the crayon off the paper. The form (figure 1) was to be drawn in one complete movement:

FIG. 1

The teacher first demonstrated on the board and we copied her movements, which gave an additional perspective on form drawing and is illustrative of the way much is taught in the school.

Teachers also visit children's families at various times throughout the year. Each child's home is visited at least once a year. Friendships are formed, and school–family connections are tight. Parents do not learn about their child through test scores. Standardized testing, or testing of any kind, simply does not happen in Waldorf School. Instead, teachers talk to parents on an almost daily basis. And teachers use their intimate knowledge of individual students to convey more formally to parents a report of their child's progress twice a year. There are no number or letter grades. A teacher explains how this is done:

> We send a little artistic report thing out to parents. I'm picking out poems that have a special message for each child. The other more formal report at the end of the year spells out what the child can and can't do. (Interview, teacher)

The midyear report is generally an artistic and expressive report, a painting, letter, poem, or story about the child, whereas the end of year report is more comprehensive, from one to three pages of written narrative on each child. The report is predominantly for the parents, although it also contains words of encouragement intended for the student. Parent–teacher conferences held in November and February provide a forum for discussion of the reports and any other issues. Thus, even in the evaluation process the central aspects of the curriculum, namely, that a child's growth be much more than simply intellectual, and also notions of community, are apparent. Shared community values are intended to deemphasize hierarchy: "As soon as you take the A, the B, the C mentality out of something it really does alter things. They view one another more equally" (Interview, teacher).

A RATIONAL CURRICULUM: ST. CATHERINE'S

An individualistic and competitive thrust can be seen at St. Catherine's, a school whose self-definition is "traditional academic." St. Catherine's is sought out by parents wanting academic success for their children. Parents anticipate that, in selecting a school with a high level of success as an academic institution, their children will be well prepared. However, the school considers it also has a duty to confer a sense of social responsibility on those it serves. The dual goals of academic excellence and social responsibility create some tension for St. Catherine's. On the one hand, St. Catherine's is a wealthy private school with a somewhat rarefied atmosphere—lavish gym facilities, rolling playing fields, well equipped science laboratory, and so on. On the other hand, St. Catherine's is saying that elitism and exclusivity need to be downplayed, and that fashioning students who do not put themselves selfishly first is important. To examine how this is done, I shall look initially at the achievement and success dimension, which is clearly evident at St. Catherine's through the various grade levels. (Although the study focuses on the Lower Division of the school, where appropriate I shall refer to the whole school context.) Then I shall draw out some of the ways the school attends to social responsibility.

Academic Rigor

St. Catherine's has a traditional academic curriculum. Teachers regard themselves as professionals whose job it is to create a classroom environment where expectations of student performance are high: ''I think achievement more than competition is what we are about. There is an appreciation for the work ethic'' (Interview, teacher). High expectations apply to all students, not just a privileged few. Ability grouping is employed only in Reading. In Math ''horizontal enrichment'' is used, whereby students who have mastered a particular concept or skill proceed to extend that knowledge to a broader base before progressing to the next level. There is no concept of a ''gifted'' program. The student body as a whole is held to be ''gifted'' and capable of a high level of academic success.

These are bright children, and bright children are best served by variety. There's always something going on. As soon as you group children, as we do in Reading, there's always a potential for stigma attached to which group the kids are in. That does not dominate here. I don't see a great deal of exclusivity. They're all bright. (Interview, teacher)

Nevertheless, not all children are academically strong in all areas. The policy of giving preference to siblings, irrespective of entry-level test scores, causes some problems for the school's definition of itself as college-prep. For instance, the few dyslexic students, who do not fit well academically with the vast majority of the school, receive tutoring after school at a nearby private clinic, Dyslexia Center, paid for by parents, in an attempt to bring them up to grade level. Previously, the school was wholly committed to school families and had accepted practically any type of student from a "school family" and then used a resource teacher in a pull-out kind of program to help the children fit into the school. However, St. Catherine's now has a more selective policy. The school suggests to parents of children who have academic problems, for instance, that they would be better placed in another specialized school.

Subject Specialization. Unlike Waldorf School's integrated routine, St. Catherine's subjects are taught by subject specialists in eight 40-minute periods each day. Page (1990, p. 51) refers to the phenomenon of segmenting time and space as "egg-crating." Subject areas at St. Catherine's are distinct, with specialist teachers imparting their expertise in the traditional manner of "chalk and talk" from a basically textbook-oriented curriculum. Content and skills are important, and the texts are seen as providing the necessary structure to insure that students will be challenged and focused in the direction necessary for eventual college placement.

> In asking students to master a specific body of knowledge, we seek, not to impart knowledge alone, but to instill the lifelong habit of learning. (Student handbook)

As well as text-book oriented lessons, students also engage in more active learning experiences, particularly in Science. These lessons are also generally centered around whole class involvement, even if divided into groups, and teacher-directed learning. Specialized classes, taught by specialty teachers, are held in Science, French, Computer, Art, Drama, Physical Education, and Music. Heterogeneous "homeroom" placement is done, which allows for the building of a peer network within the homeroom class, but students also meet in the course of a single day as many as five different teachers.

From the teachers' points of view specialized classes have benefits and limitations. On the positive side, preparation and execution of lessons are simplified. Teachers are able to be expert in their fields, to focus on the subject they are to teach and match the content level to the group of students. On the negative side, teachers often say they can't really "go anywhere" in a subject in the short space of time, of 40-minute lessons. They feel constrained in terms of setting homework: "They have so much homework in all their other classes, I can't really follow up on anything" (Interview, teacher). Also, some teachers feel disunity is created by students having many different teachers.

The school has, then, what is known as a *collection code curriculum* (Bernstein, 1971). Bernstein differentiates between a collection code, where students study discrete subjects (English, Mathematics, Science, History, Athletics), and an integrated code, where there is an emphasis on the permeability or fluidity within and between elements of the curriculum, for example, a foreign language taught through movement and music. St. Catherine's curriculum has very little integration across subjects. Moreover, it is *school knowledge* in bounded disciplines, not everyday knowledge or interdisciplinary knowledge, that is being taught.

The issue of how knowledge is "framed," which Bernstein examines, is also relevant to St. Catherine's curriculum. Strongly framed knowledge is highly stratified, with certain types of knowledge deemed inappropriate. With the strong framing that is practiced at St. Catherine's, teachers have considerable authority over students; students have few or no options in their choice of curricula. The argument is made by the school that a stronger more carefully defined curriculum is necessary to lay a firm educational grounding for university careers and corresponding occupations.

The collection code also means that students are able to develop a clear sense of their ability in, and loyalty to, different subjects, thus fostering identification with, say Mathematics, History, or English. This approach is frequently adopted by college-preparatory schools. Bernstein showed that, in secondary schools in Britain, the less able or working class students were more often exposed to weak framing and integrated codes, (more or less like public schools in the U.S., where the view of knowledge is much broader). Their middle- to upper class counterparts were exposed to strong framing and collection codes. However, an interesting angle on this at St. Catherine's is that the Director of the Lower School suggests that collaboration and interchange across subject lines is now an ideal that the school is working towards. Too much specialization and boundedness between subjects is seen as detrimental. It makes good sense, he says, to reinforce learning by making connections across subjects, so that, for example, "When you're learning percentage in Math you're also studying solutions in Science" (Interview, Director of Lower School). The attempt to work at a more integrated approach can also be seen in the recent decision to try a "whole language" approach in Reading, which means teaching Reading and Language Arts in an integrated fashion. The school is conservative in its response to innovations, however, and is introducing the "whole language" approach on a trial basis in the second grade only.

A Research Approach. The curriculum has not changed much over the years. Two years ago computer studies were added, but basically the curriculum has remained traditional and academic. The school constantly seeks to keep up to date with the latest research, however, so as not to be seen as upholding outdated ideals.

> We're constantly looking at what we have, what's been developed in the field, what other schools are doing, what research is proving, and trying to ascertain whether we need to move in a different direction. That's one way we keep on top of things and keep what we're doing in a strong position. (Interview, teacher)

Research, with its rigorous, objective scientific basis[3] is seen to add legitimacy to the school's orientation. Moreover, a research

---

[3]St. Catherine's view of science contrasts with Waldorf School, where the science that is invoked is not the science of the modern world, with its faith in technology and instrumental rationality, but rather spiritual science that validates humans as capable of reaching the highest levels of "objective" truth.

approach is what the school is promoting to students, so it is important that this is also practiced by the school.

The use of research, and the conservatism of the school, can be seen in the school's retention practices. Children are sometimes retained, but this is a decision made after much deliberation by the homeroom teacher, the parents, and the Director of the Lower School. Again, research is used to support school policy.

> There's a lot of data that shows that, and this has been proven in longitudinal studies, that if you retained one child in third grade and don't retain another one they both function about approximately the same when you get to sixth and seventh grades. The sixth grader who has been retained is not better off. They're coming up with more data on that now. (Interview, teacher)

The one time when repetition does seem like a good idea, in the school's view, is when children test for entry to the school. Initial testing assists the school in insuring that students who are accepted will function well in the grade level in which they are placed. If there seems to be a problem academically, the school will repeat the child at that point of entry stage.

Textbook-Based Curriculum. The academic curriculum starts at the Pre-school and Kindergarten level, where the stated aim is to "cultivate a love of learning." Texts are used for kindergarteners: *Mathematics Their Way* by Addison and Wesley Publishing Company; *Resources for Creative Teaching in Early Childhood Education* by Harcourt, Brace, Jovanovich, Inc.; and *Sun Up, Happy Morning and Magic Afternoon* by Harcourt, Brace, Jovanovich, Inc. The texts may change and increase in number at each grade level, but they remain a core element of schooling for the duration of the child's schooling. Consistency in texts is maintained as one moves up the grades. Curriculum committees for each subject area (including faculty representation from each discipline in the Middle and Upper Schools) examine very closely the values that the texts are promoting before deciding to adopt them: "We look at the texts in selecting them and ask, What is the philosophy contained herein? What values are contained herein? Are there skills in there, too?" (Interview, teacher). Some years back teachers used different texts and there was no continuity in texts across grades. In moving to a situation where there is consistency through the grades the school looked, once again, to what other schools and research were saying about the idea: "We did look to what the research was saying. We did go to NCTE and other professional meetings to see what was going on in other schools" (Interview, teacher). While Mathematics texts are used on a daily basis in all classes, it is not mandatory that teachers use texts all the time. Teachers have autonomy in the methods that they employ, though they do not have autonomy in the content. Thus, some teachers may use the textbook more as a guide and cover the same material in other ways.

Successive Academic Challenges. In the first grade students are streamed for Reading groups 7 hours per week. The child's level is determined by performance on a standardized test and the judgement of the teachers. The standardized tests (produced by Educational Records Bureau, ERB, of which the school is a member) are given once a year in April or May. They are described, even in the younger grades, as having an effect on what goes on in the classroom:

> There's a certain amount of what they call "teach-to-the-test" kind of thing, that the standardized tests ɩ re coming up at a certain point, and so you spend however much time before that working on those kinds of things. (Interview, teacher)

Tests also set up the conditions for competition, leading teachers and students alike to seek ways of enhancing what will be displayed and reported about their performance.

Academic requirements are gradually made more stringent. When students reach the third-grade level, their work is "judged on its own merit, with less reward for effort and more emphasis on accomplishment. Although the judgments are made in a supportive way, this is the first time lower marks may appear on tests and homework papers" (Curriculum Guide). The pattern of increasing demands continues as one moves up grade levels. Teachers clearly have an agenda for each lesson and are focused in their efforts to ensure that the content is covered. The daily routines work well. There are few disruptions. Students are expected to accomplish the goals set for the lesson, to have their homework done, and to be ready to answer questions. They generally are prepared.

When students leave the Lower School, expectations increase, requiring a "resocialization, which is aided by the introduction of both the Honor Code and the demerit system" (Interview, teacher). This may be the official point of entry for the demerit system, but all Grade 6 children have already had at least 2 years in such a system. Demerits are used, along with more positive reinforcement, to strengthen the achievement thrust in Grade 6: "much of the academic emphasis is placed on strengthening any areas of weakness which may have accompanied the student from the Lower School" (Curriculum Guide). Study habits are also carefully scrutinized.

Grades 7 and 8 focus on the scientific method, "second level" or abstract thinking, and developing organized study habits. Algebra, required Latin, and Science are important components of the academic program. From Grade 9 competition intensifies. Teachers teach to the "top half of the class" (Interview, teacher). Also, in the Upper School a collegiate atmosphere is fostered, with students allowed more autonomy, but with an increased work load. Precollege mastery in all subjects is sought and many students take Advanced Placement courses; if they are successful, basic college requirements are waived. The curriculum is now exclusively oriented toward preparation for college at "levels of mastery expected of the nation's best colleges" (Interview, teacher). Thus, the school program is designed from preschool to Grade 12 to provide academic challenges which become progressively more difficult.

Homework.   Homework is considered essential to academic success. Only in Grade 1 is the homework requirement waived. In Grades 2 and 3 students are expected to spend 30 to 45 minutes per day on homework. By Grade 4 students spend up to an hour each day on homework. Grade 5 students spend on average an hour to an hour and a quarter on homework. During the middle school years students are expected to spend at least 45 minutes per class period on homework, which may amount to several hours work each night. Students who fail to meet these requirements are asked to attend supervised study hall after school. Parents are coached on how to cater to their children's homework needs. They are advised to keep a calendar in the child's study area so that due dates can be marked in and anticipated. They are also asked not to correct their child's homework: "Teachers need an accurate reflection of how well the children understand particular assignments" (Student handbook). If there is a problem with homework, parents are encouraged to contact the child's teacher. Communication between students, parents, teachers, and administrators is considered necessary for good schooling to occur. School and home tend to share the values of an achievement and success orientation.

Social Concern

The second aspect of St. Catherine's curriculum is its attempt to build a sense of social responsibility within the student body. I see this as representing two things. First, it is in keeping with the notion of a classical education throughout history. To be considered a member of the upper class, one had to have more than an accumulated body of knowledge. One needed "cultural capital" (Bourdieu & Passeron, 1977), that is, exposure to, and appreciation for, the fine arts, theatre, music, performance, literature, and so on. One also needed a proper sense of social concern in order to carry out the expected role in society as leader and benefactor of the people. This is no less true today than it was centuries ago. Second, the emphasis on social responsibility is an attempt to bring a more humanistic flavor to the depersonalized kind of thinking that is represented by an achievement oriented academic curriculum.

Social or spiritual needs of children are addressed in the curriculum through the ecumenical chapel program, the athletic program, extracurricular activities, the school's Honor Code and school rules, and in the Upper School through community service and a 1-year required religion course. It is in chapel, though, where the students receive the most direct guidance about ethics and morals. Chapel is a weekly ritual for the whole school. No specific religious doctrine is promoted, although there are aspects of the service that highlight its Christian focus (despite the number of Jewish students at the school) and also its Episcopal roots. The lessons at chapel are classic ones about social responsibility. Being kind to each other, honesty, having good manners, and giving to one another as members of a community are consistent themes.

Extracurricular activities are designed also to complement the academic emphasis in the school, reaching a culmination in the older grades.

> Traditions foster a sense of community and provide a historic continuity for the school. Upper school traditions include the Christmas Dance, Senior Easter Egg Hunt, Prom, Class Night, Moving Up Day, Big Sister/Brother and Little Sister/Brother Picnic, a senior-faculty Softball game, and a student–faculty field hockey game. Clubs give students with a common interest an opportunity to meet in groups in order to expand that interest. The Upper School offers the Latin Club, Cercle Francais, Spanish Club, Spanish Honor Society, St. Genesius drama club, Art Forum, and Ski Club. (School publication)

Clubs and traditions are thought to enhance school spirit. In the Lower School a math club was started last year by one of the Middle School teachers. Such interchanges among the school divisions are seen as important for maintaining whole school unity. A choir is also run by the music teacher, and an art club by the art teacher. Clubs are conducted on various afternoons after school, do not command a fee, and teachers' time is given voluntarily.

The achievement orientation of the school also carries over into the extracurricular realm, a point made by one of the teachers.

> Appreciation for achievement can be athletic, academic or extra-curricular. Because we're small we don't have a band or a great deal of extracurricular, but you can see the emphasis on achievement in the pop quiz team that is in the newspaper all the time. (Interview, teacher)

The pop quiz team competes in local, state, and national competitions, and has enjoyed a high level of success which has been flouted by local media, with headlines such as "Preps Undefeated in Past 15 Matches: Young Savants Hope Victory will lead to National TV Spot." Extracurricular activities are also promoted in the school as potentially useful activities in enhancing college possibilities: "In college applications they look for the kinds of activities that you've done in school" (Teacher's words). This would not happen in Waldorf School, where the notion of college entrance does not enter into school motives. Waldorf teachers say they want children to be able to go to college if that is their desire, but college is not promoted as an ideal that everyone is working towards. In contrast, college preparation is a key goal at St. Catherine's. Fundamental school cultural values are clearly embedded in the content of the curriculum, and elaborated through other means.

Evaluation

St. Catherine's students are formally evaluated four times a year, that is, every 9 weeks. Two of the reports are formally presented to parents at conferences; the other two are mailed home. All are written reports. Kindergarten and first grade use an assessment of developmental and educational skills that is nongraded, but does use an hierarchical scale.

> In the first grade they're not given letter grades. We have a checklist that we use. All kinds of things are on the checklist, verbal skills, auditory skills, comprehension skills, cognitive development. Then there are gradations, poor / good / fair, it just goes across and then space for comments. (Interview, teacher)

All in all, seven divisions are employed: socioemotional development, study skills development (divided into "work habits" and "listening skills"), fine motor development, cognitive development (reading skills, mathematics skills), music, art, and performing arts. Each of these is further divided into more specific skills, a total of 50 skills. The child's performance is then rated according to five performance criteria. Those criteria are: consistently, is making progress, sometimes, more time needed, not applicable now. By Grade 2 the hierarchy of grades A–F, with D a passing grade, is in place. The same system is used in the Middle and Upper schools, although there a grade point average (GPA) is computed in as well. Each year the school publishes the grade distribution for the Upper School, as well as

SAT scores[4] and Achievement Test scores. The school also lists the colleges and universities to which the graduating class has matriculated. The eastern Ivy League colleges are well represented: Harvard, Yale, Princeton, Dartmouth, University of Pennsylvania, and Columbia.

Students anticipate success because of their past academic performance, the planning that has gone into their program of studies, and also because of the advantages gained from family and school connections. Persell and Cookson (1989, p. 342) argue that "through the substance and reputations of their programs, the wealth of their students, and through personal bargaining, the prep schools help the admission of their students to selective colleges." Whether any or all of these claims are valid in respect to St. Catherine's is not an issue here, but it is noteworthy that the St. Catherine's school career has been carefully designed with university requirements in mind, even in the lower grades. College preparation begins with enrollment in preschool and intensifies as the years go by.

Testing is a regular and expected part of school routine. Performance or achievement is measured on tests. In assessing students through testing the school is endorsing the value of efficiency. The student who can efficiently master what is required on the test will perform better than the student who may have a broader base of knowledge but has not focused it to the requirements of the test and hence performs poorly. At St. Catherine's classroom instruction is built around units that vary in length from 2 to 4 weeks; at the end of each unit students are tested. Frequently they are given a practice test. If students score 100% on the practice test, then they are able to progress to the next unit. The procedure repeated in most classes is to teach a unit, test it, and evaluate. In fact, the whole curriculum is geared around testing. The reasons given for this emphasis on testing are twofold. First, tests are used as a legitimate teaching aid, a means of gauging a child's competence so that individualized

---

[4]It is salient to remember that the SATs (scholastic aptitude tests) were originally devised to predict a student's success in college, but as Atkin, Patrick, and Kennedy (1989, p. 74) point out, they are now used to "compare schools, districts and states; as a measure of accountability to the public; or to evaluate specific curriculum programs" (compare Goldman & McDermott, 1987, p. 283).

instruction can be given. Second, tests are a means of legitimizing the school. They are hard data that can be reported to parents to enhance the school's public credibility.

The use of grading as a motivational device and behavioral incentive or corrective was made clear during a homeroom discussion in fourth grade. Grade 4 children told their teacher in class that they misbehaved during a specialty class because the teacher failed to give grades for every piece of work done and failed to give demerits for misbehavior (Classroom observation). The significant factors leading to misbehavior, in students' own words, were the absence of grading and demerit points ("she doesn't always give grades," and "she doesn't know what a demerit is"). Evaluation thus has a carryover into classroom practices and disciplinary measures. Grades and demerits become rewards and punishments:

> Demerits are used for fourth and fifth grades for consistent misbehavior or disruptive behavior in class, for being rude, for being where you're not supposed to be. We don't give it for violating the dress code or coming to class without materials. (Interview, teacher)

The demerit rules are that students can accumulate two demerits per day without penalty, but once they get three they must do a "work duty," such as raking leaves or cleaning up "lost and found" property. While there is no direct connection between demerits and bad grades, students know that earning demerits antagonizes teachers, and that teachers give grades. Demerits are not excessively punitive, but they are construed as "bad" by the students, and hence serve their purpose well. Demerits are seen as a useful and unemotional way of giving sanctions.

Students who are seen to require stronger penalties than demerits provide are placed on the individual work contracts that allow teachers to closely monitor their behavior. A student on a contract must have each teacher sign the contract at the end of every lesson throughout the day. The contract specifies what is expected of the child in behavioral terms. An example of a fifth grade boy's contract is:

> Student A will 1) Will stay in his seat during class. 2) Will speak in class only when called on by the teacher. 3) Will not make faces

at other people in the class. Student A has agreed that he will work on these behaviors. (Teachers are to check yes, no, and write comments).

Contracts are tailored to the individual child, with an aim to correct his or her "bad work habits." Parents are kept informed about the child's progress with the contract. Parental contact is seen as critical in dealing with problems that may affect a student's academic or social development.

Parents are, by and large, concerned about grades. They have selected the school primarily for its academic focus, although there may also be motives of social exclusivity in some cases. Rohlen (1983, p. 317) found that the university entrance exam in Japan is the "dark engine driving high school culture," and I would argue that it is also the case in this U.S. elementary school, where university entrance provides an early and constant goal for students. Students are serious about their work because of grades and demerits and the fear that, if they are not successful, this may have repercussions in the short term (displeased parents and teachers) and in the long term (limited educational and career options). However, St. Catherine's students do not seem oppressed by the system. As researcher I was experiencing the children's school world, moving from class to class, observing them at work and play; I was never bored, for the children were always raising thoughtful questions and responding in interesting ways. If the school code is a rigorous one, then these students are in their right element. They are not overwhelmed by the school's achievement orientation, and I attribute this to the select student body, the quality of the faculty, and the school's structured attention to social and spiritual concerns.

CONCLUSIONS

School curricula have been shown to contain implicit values, different conceptions of the world, and a different theory of knowledge. In Waldorf School the three major rhythmical periods around which the curriculum is organized (0–7 years, 7–14 years, 14–21 years) are seen to correspond with physical, intellectual, social and emotional growth. Schooling is a process with teacher as guide "nourishing" the child with cultural content. The world is perceived as an organic, fluid, evolving, and ever-changing place with its own rhythm and pulse. In Waldorf School it isn't until students have left the grade school, around the age of 14 years, for example, the third stage of growth, that students are thought to begin to learn through formal, abstract thinking. Teaching as art, or music, and a pedagogy based on warmth, and in the early stages mothering, is what school is about.

St. Catherine's has a different conception of the world and how students learn. Critical thinking skills and the ability to think rationally are taught at St. Catherine's from an early age. Teachers do not wait until 14 years of age before children are challenged to think in an abstract and depersonalized way. Reflective and critical thinking is part of the school's intellectual orientation. The ability to work independently is noted and reported on to parents from the first grade. Sometimes group work is used as a means to an end, but not usually for its intrinsic value. At Waldorf School, in contrast, "working in a circle," the importance of cooperative relationships, is central. Thus, St. Catherine's is teaching norms of individual responsibility, creativity, and critical thinking in order to instil the concept of a rational world. It is not that Waldorf School is uninterested in science and the scientific mode of knowing, but that it holds a nonconventional view of science and maintains that children can best reach goals of formal, abstract thinking as adults through exposure to art forms in their childhood.

The difference in these two modes of thought, for example, logical rational thought, which is St. Catherine's model, and imaginative thought, at Waldorf School, is similar to the conventional distinction between art and science. Charles Darwin draws this distinction when he discusses his own overemphasis on scientific, logical decontextualized thought and his neglect of artistic knowledge. He wrote of his regret that his mind had become a:

> kind of machine for grinding general laws out of larger collections of facts . . . . If I had to live my life over again, I would have made a rule to read some poetry and listen to some music at least once

a week; for perhaps the parts of my brain now atrophied would thus have been kept active through use. The loss of these tastes is a loss of happiness, and may possibly be injurious to the intellect, and more probably to the moral character, by enfeebling the emotional part of our nature. (Darwin, quoted in Southworth, 1989, p. 3)

Waldorf School advocates are fond of quoting such recantations.

However, St. Catherine's sets out to focus, not just on academics, but to attend to both academic *and* social needs of children. The form of knowledge promoted in this school can be seen as primarily scientific and rational. Higher levels of learning are achieved, in this view, through the study of atoms of knowledge. Subject specialist teachers transmit their specialized body of knowledge. This is then counterbalanced by a concern for spiritual and social development. At Waldorf School, in contrast, knowledge is circular and (while seeking rationality ultimately) infused with intuitive and imaginative modes of thought, rather than the technical and abstract. The teacher stays with the child for 8 years, leading him or her on a "poetic" journey towards maturity and freedom. Through the study of myths, legends, and stories, students are seen to learn the rhythms of other peoples, to learn not only to know about them, but to learn to "know-with": "knowing-with entails empathy, receptivity, or a feeling of oneness with the object under investigation . . . . American Indians have long believed that one can unite oneself with other organic forms" (Uhrmacher, 1989, p. 7). Waldorf teachers thus adopt a whole class or rote learning style of instruction, for all the students in the class are age graded and believed to be capable of the desired level of empathy at a particular stage. At St. Catherine's a recitational teaching style, where the teacher asks a question, gains a response, and then evaluates it, is the norm (see Cazden, 1988; Mehan, 1979, on the recitation or IRE: initiation, response, evaluation). The IRE teaching style supports a view of knowledge as able to be broken down into parts and studied independently. The teacher is a businesslike professional teaching students about a world where scientific rationality prevails. Students are expected to be both instrumental and expressive, to create new knowledge while adhering to the traditions of the

Western intellectual heritage. A standardized curriculum with nationally distributed texts is part of this thrust.

The two schools could be seen as two different "tribes," each with its own myths that belong to that "tribe." The myths are stored up and passed down to the upcoming generation through the curriculum, the lore of the "tribe." One "tribe" believes in an holistic universe with humankind ideally united with that universe. It is seen as necessary to engage in "inner work" to attain spirituality: "Students discover that an intimate interplay exists between nature and self and that a mood of receptivity and quiescence opens them to an awareness of the earth's presence" (Mehlman, 1991, p. 311). The other "tribe" believes in a universe that exists according to laws that can be understood and to an extent controlled by humankind. In this view humans are a unique part of creation, but discontinuous with the rest of nature because of a higher intellect and spirituality. In the next chapter we will continue to explore how the curriculum is further elaborated and acted out through rituals and ceremonies in order to validate and sustain school cultures.

6

*THE POETRY OF RITUAL**

Isadora Duncan once said about dance, "If I could tell you what it meant, there would be no point in dancing it." The dancer has something to communicate and does so by becoming a strong example of that thing. People then perceive the message of the dance in their own way. They bring their own experiences to bear in interpreting it. Yet this is not just a private experience. The dancer is able to communicate a message that is more or less read by many different people in the audience in similar ways. Emotions can be simultaneously felt by many participants. The symbols in the performance become conventionalized and shared.

Schools use rituals in a similar way to communicate their cultures. Through rituals and ceremonial practice cultural values are held up for "collective inspection and validation" (Kapferer, 1981, p. 273). Rituals remind those in the school of what they value and how to look at things. Social contradictions are both masked and enacted, providing a sense of unity. But rituals are not static. They play a significant role in the *creation*

---

*An earlier and different version of this chapter is forthcoming as an article, "School rituals as educational contexts: Symbolizing the world, others and "self" in Waldorf and College Prep schools, in the *International Journal of Qualitative Studies in Education*.

of culture as well as its maintenance and change (Geertz, 1973; Turner, 1988). Rather than just reflecting a previously defined culture, they are an active part of culture, helping to generate values and norms and to bridge ideological gaps.

Rituals typically occur on two levels. On an overt level they perform functions. The Aboriginal youth whose chest is scarified and burned by his tribal elders is becoming a man in the eyes of his people. The ritual allows him symbolically (and with pain that is not merely symbolic) to assume a new and elevated status in the social group. Rituals thus display social relationships with a purpose of drawing boundaries and placing people in a relationship. On another level, rituals are a covert socialization process. Throughout the ritual social rules, obligations and responsibilities are being taught. The Aboriginal youth may be learning to identify no longer with his mother as he did when he was a child; instead he is to become one of the men.

In schools, no less than for an Aboriginal tribe, ritual occasions are often an elaborate display of a school's mission and goals, an attempt to bring about social unity, teach rules, or display social relationships. However, they do not always achieve their ends. Turner explains the differences in individuals' participation in ritual through the metaphor of an orchestra. He conceptualizes rituals as made up of a set of rules or culture (the musical score) and social processes (the orchestra). All the participants are "skilled musicians" and "well rehearsed in the details of the score," but they do not all play in sympathy with the conductor (Turner, 1968, pp. 135–136). Some people hesitate over certain passages, lapse in their rapport, or are sympathetic to each other in certain sections only. People present at the ritual may also place themselves emotionally outside the ritual. They may be unmoved by the ceremony, skeptical of its import and impatient with its performance. Others, however, may be transformed through ritual, "reborn" into the community. They internalize the event and become an intimate partner in the ritual, allowing it to have personal and social significance. In this case, what has been personally felt has been related to a social meaning.

We can also further differentiate between the social effect or meaning of rituals and their technical production.

" . . . drama as communion" emphasizes the experience created
by repetitive actions which have collective or public significance.
For instance, the feelings of inclusion and loyalty that one gets
when saluting the flag or participating in a graduation ceremony
with others are examples of the outcomes of the use of rituals. The
other approach views "drama as persuasion." It focuses on
expression rather than on experience, on the *way* something is
expressed rather than on the effects of that expression. It considers what some acted saying says, looking at the "reiterated
form, staged and acted by its own audience, which makes theory
fact." The ways in which the flag is to express pride and
solidarity are examples. (Bredo, 1990, p. 6)

It is the physical coming together of individuals that gives a
ritual the potential to do its work of building culture, such as
bringing about social unity, emotional bonding or the designa-
tion of statuses.

PROPERTIES OF RITUAL

A ritual has a "grammar," a set of formal properties that identify
it as such. The structure is like a musical score that repeats itself.
Each of the components of ritual thus has a special timing. One
could easily get it "wrong." Rituals also generally have a precise
order. At St. Catherine's chapel, for instance, the Benediction is
not said before the Invocation. Moreover, rituals are evocative in
their presentational style. Symbols are used in a dramatic and
expressive way. And the setting is a public or collective one,
whether indoors or outdoors, in a church or in a classroom
(Lesko, 1988, p. 25). The setting may also be indicative of
fundamental values. Chapel at St. Catherine's is held in the
auditorium, a large open space with carpeted, tiered seating on
three sides of the room and a stage at the front of the room. In
contrast, at Waldorf School rituals are frequently conducted out
of doors on a pretty hillside near the school.

Ritual Symbols

Certain elements are needed for rituals to work. The participants, the timing, its repetitive structure, the order of events,

and the "magic" of the performance may all be important components of the enactment. Certain objects are also accorded centrality. Flowers on an altar, a cross, or a white cloth are carefully placed so as to evoke a certain feeling among the participants. Certain colors are selected to convey symbolically an emotional, ideational, or social mood.

Schools, like other institutions, consciously or unconsciously select from among a wide array of possible symbols. Symbols in schools send a clear message of differing moral visions and different conceptions of the relationship between school and society. For example, the U.S. flag is nowhere to be found at Waldorf School and everywhere present at St. Catherine's. Waldorf School does not consider itself anti-American, but rather rejects the conventional meaning of being American. Flag waving denotes a nationalistic boundedness that is too limited in the Waldorf view. Instead, Waldorf School holds allegiance to a world community, not just a particular country. This is an important point because differing moral visions, evident in symbols, have a profound effect on the many daily realities of school life.

"High" and "Low" Rituals

Rituals are sometimes "high" ceremonies, in the sense of sacred or symbolic acts (as ritual is most commonly known in anthropology), and sometimes "low" or everyday rituals. Examples of high rituals include initiation, rain making, and peace and funeral rites. In schools, rituals that fall into this category would be beginning and end of school year rituals, chapel rites, sporting rites, special holidays, and religious rites. Such rituals have a special status. They are formal events to be conducted according to a deliberate and correct procedure. Some tolerance of flawed performance may be accepted in the ritual, but the emphasis is on a proper way to go about doing things with symbols.

Everyday or "low" rituals are instead simply ordinary practical and everyday events that have become sanctified. In schools these would include opening exercises, school assemblies, snack or lunch time, class tests, recitation rituals, and other rituals of instruction. There is some disagreement among educators and researchers over whether everyday rituals count as rituals or whether they are merely ritualistic. Kapferer (1981, p. 265) argues that they are not authentic rituals because they are not "set apart and distinctive from the routine order of everyday school life." In this view ritual is "an excursion from the mundane reality of everyday life" (Gerholm, 1988, p. 198). Other researchers, such as McLaren (1986), are careful to delineate rituals in such a way as to ensure that everything is not subsumed under this title, yet at the same time allowing for the routine and everyday; "According to Grimes (1982) a ritual is a form of symbolic action composed primarily of gestures (the enactment of evocative rhythms which constitute dynamic symbolic acts) and postures (a symbolic stilling of action)" (McLaren, 1986, p. 39). McLaren thus gives routine or habitual actions the status of "paler, less authentic, more "wraithlike" forms of ritualization" (p. 40).

Gehrke (1979), however, takes a broader view of rituals and argues that routines may be rituals. In this view to be a ritual an action must be symbolic of something beyond the experience itself: a "framework of meaning over and beyond the specific situational meaning" is constructed (Bernstein, Elgin, & Peters, 1966, p. 429). Gehrke explains using a ritual she remembers from her own elementary school days.

> Early each morning the teacher would pass gravely up and down the rows examining our hands and handkerchiefs. No guilt was greater than we felt when charged with dirty hands or "hankylessness." We were very cocky and self-assured when we could display relatively clean hands—first palms down, then palms up—on top of a neatly folded (never to be used) handkerchief. We were thoroughly convinced that cleanliness (or at least its appearance) was next to godliness. (1979, p. 104)

A sense of "rightness" and power was accorded to those who fulfilled the required behavior in the ritual. It was not just the rules of etiquette and procedure that the teacher was insistent upon (for example, the palms-up and palms-down routine), but also status distinctions. Teacher and students were engaging in a status ritual whereby the teacher determined the clean hands and hanky routine, and students were judged on their performance. Classroom routines and "interaction rituals" (Goffman, 1967) are thus potentially, but not always, rituals.

School rituals can also be analyzed in terms of their intentions and purposes. McLaren (1986, pp. 80-81), for instance, distinguishes between revitalization, intensification, and resistance rituals. *Revitalization rituals* are those aimed at revitalizing a school's mission or goals by inspiring participants to renew their commitment to its values. *Intensification rituals*, on the other hand, are intended to unify a group of teachers or students without necessarily reinforcing school values or goals. *Resistance rituals*, in turn, are rituals of conflict, where teachers or students consciously or unconsciously attempt to subvert or sabotage school rules, norms, or values. Inversion occurs, for unity is sought by the subgroup acting against the dominant one in a countercultural way. While resistance rituals were not clearly apparent in the two schools under study, subtle and individual acts of resistance to school cultural values were observed. As an example, a teacher at St. Catherine's abstained from saying the Lord's Prayer in chapel in a silent protest against the school's Christian bias. And at Waldorf School resistance was also seen in the uncooperative behavior of some of the boys in eurythmy lessons. Revitalization and intensification rituals were, however, a strong and consistent part of the daily life of both schools. For Waldorf School in particular, schooling was a dramatic performance of significant rituals.

RITES OF REVITALIZATION AND INTENSIFICATION

Rites for the Soul: Waldorf School

"Festivals are nodal points of the year which unite us with the Spirit of the Universe—Rudolf Steiner" (Handbook). The rationale behind the many festivals and celebrations in Waldorf School is that they:

> enable humanity to reach out to the spiritual world and the spiritual world to reach down to us from the cosmos . . . in the festival celebration, all is done with beauty and reverence, in an attempt to give the child a real soul experience through the

imagery of art, music, stories song and so forth. [They] need not be explained in an intellectual fashion. (Handbook)

Christian rituals celebrated at Waldorf School include those of Michaelmas (named for St. Michael, the "archangel of our time," November 29th), Christmas, and Easter.[2] Other rituals built into the school year include the Advent Spiral, Spring Festival, May Fair, Opening and Closing Ceremonies, Festival of Lights, and Thanksgiving. Students usually wear special costumes to these celebrations, and parents and friends attend. The community comes together. The rituals are concerned with enacting and sustaining important religious and cultural values, in addition to allowing children to demonstrate their achievements and growth, as can be seen in the following examples.

Thanksgiving Service. Classes have been preparing for Thanksgiving for weeks, carefully making their "offerings," a poem to be said, a song to be sung or a tune played on recorders. The fourth–fifth graders have brought food offerings of pumpkin pies, muffins, bran cakes, popcorn, pumpkin bread, and apple juice. "Are these chocolate?" I ask, pointing to the muffins on the table. "Oh, no! Carob," is the quick reply. Main lesson finished early this morning, and the classes have moved outside into the fields surrounding the classroom cabins. This is where the ceremony is to take place, in a grassy hollow on the side of the hill. A picnic table covered with a bright yellow cloth has been set up to display nature's gifts. "Oh yes, yellow is just perfect for Thanksgiving," says Autumn. In the center are eight beautifully decorated and handmade yellow and orange candles in a menorah. But the children cannot get the candles alight because of the cold wind. "Oh well, don't worry," says the teacher. "It'll just have to be symbolic." The table is laden with Indian corn, pumpkins, squash, a cotton plant, a leaf wreath, and a bowl of grapes, oranges, and nuts.

The wind and cold chill to the bone, making us thankful for the fire that has been lit. It is a large fire. Flames crackle fiercely. Soon ash is swept up by the wind, dropping tiny, grey flecks

---

[2]*Christengemeinschaft (Christian community)* is the term used for anthroposophy's worshipping community in Waldorf communities across the world.

onto the participants. Teachers have carried buckets of water to the site as a safeguard against the fire getting out of control. All the classes are assembled in a semicircle around the fire. Teacher moves to center stage. "We are all gathered here today to give thanks for what we have and to share with one another. You've all been bringing in food for others less fortunate than yourselves and that is in the spirit of Thanksgiving—to give thanks, to share with others what we have."

Each class, in turn, then presents its offering, a musical, poetic, or dramatic performance, followed by enthusiastic applause. First graders, with their teacher, recite two poems about a miller grinding corn, and bagging it, and using the flour to make bread. Second graders sing songs and play their recorders. The older children recite Lewis Carroll's "The Walrus and the Carpenter." They also play canons on their recorders and sing songs in solo then in unison. The children's musical talent is highly developed and they seem to appreciate the chance to perform. To conclude the ceremony third graders play a grace on their recorders. Each class, in turn, moves to the Thanksgiving table to partake of the Thanksgiving meal. The youngest children go first.

To understand this ritual it is useful first of all to place it in the context of Thanksgiving as an American tradition, and secondly to consider how the Waldorf School ritual differs from the conventional meaning. Thanksgiving is, after all, a rite with quintessentially American historic roots. For it to be celebrated in a Waldorf school demonstrates the situated nature of this form of international schooling. In English Waldorf schools, the students play cricket; in the U.S., Thanksgiving is celebrated. The U.S. tradition of Thanksgiving dates back to 1621, when the Pilgrims first celebrated Thanksgiving. (It was later officially proclaimed an all-American celebration by Abraham Lincoln in 1863.) Moreover, thanksgiving has traditionally been viewed as a time of worship and celebration within a family context. Family reunions occur at this time. People rekindle and reconnect their familial ties. However, Thanksgiving has also come to signify big toy parades, particularly in the large cities. Santa Claus, in a tinsel-covered sleigh, leads a procession of extravagant toys, which is the start of the "Big Sell" for Christmas; American capitalism at its best. California also flaunts the heroes of Hollywood and television in a big brassy parade that is now a tradition. The commercial meaning of Thanksgiving is what Waldorf School is rejecting in its ceremony. Instead of media and glitz, the school draws upon the family concept of Thanksgiving. The school is saying "we are a community like a family" and we, too, need to come together to worship and feast and share with others. The teacher's simple yet eloquent statement of what the ritual is about, "to give thanks and share with others," is then demonstrated through the class offerings of music and poems. The ideal demonstrated is one of caring. The fire symbolizes the warmth and energy provided by the school community. Students are praised for bringing food for those "less fortunate." And the closing grace places the giving of thanks within a framework of religiosity. Thanks are given to God for providing food, which is then celebrated by the breaking of bread together. The cycle of preparing the food, opening "prayer" by the teacher, the offerings (the climax), the closing prayer (grace) and eating the food also echoes the rhythm of life and the seasons that is celebrated throughout the Waldorf School. The youngest children go first to the table, in keeping with the care ethic and the biblical injunction, "the first shall be last and the last first."

The Advent Spiral. Advent begins on the Sunday nearest the feast of St. Andrew (November 30), includes the four Sundays prior to Christmas and continues through Christmas Eve. To mark this event, Grades 1 to 5 take part in an "Advent Spiral" held in one of the classrooms. A spiral of greens and tree stumps leading to a candle in the center has been made. The spiral is like an Advent wreath with its greens and circular symbolism, said to be an adaptation of the pagan fire wheel. The room has been darkened and the children are assembled. Each child has an apple with a candle in it, and they walk the spiral, lighting their candles from the main candle and then putting their little candles around on window sills and ledges. The teachers tell stories. This is one story:

> Once upon a time there was a little angel who looked out of a window in heaven. On seeing the dark earth, it became sad and asked if it could take a light there. The older angels thought about

it for a long time. They asked the Father God for His advice.
"Well," said Father God, "get together as many little angels as
you can, give each a red apple with a candle in it, let them walk
down the spiral of the stars, and light their candles from the light
which never goes out at the center of the spiral, then they will be
ready to make the journey to earth." And this is exactly what the
angels did. Many years passed . . . . When the angels were
grown-up on earth, and their wings had long since been neatly
tucked away in the bottom drawer between layers of tissue paper,
they came together again, saying, "let us make an Advent Garden
for our children." So they built during Advent, when the days are
darkest, a spiral garden of rocks, plants and flowers. In the center
of the spiral they put a mound of twinkling stone crystals. On top
of the mound they placed a candle. Then the curtains were drawn
and the room became dark and quiet. The candle was lit, and the
stone crystals twinkled like stars on a dark night. Then came the
children and as they entered the room a red apple with a candle
in it was placed in their hands. The children made a circle around
the garden, and the first child walked down the spiral path and lit
its candle from the center light. On its return journey it placed the
burning candle somewhere along the spiral path. Soon the garden
was filled with twinkling candle lights, and the grown-ups were
singing just as they did when they first came to earth. (Story
attributed to the Christian Community, North Hollywood)

Another teacher tells the children that the candles that have lit
up the room are their own special talents, and that, when they
are all together, they have a dazzling effect. She also tells them
how wonderful it is to be able to accept and celebrate each
other's differences. We are all unique, "different, and special"
is the message, and together we make a strong and fine community.

In the Advent ritual the value of community is again promoted, with attention to the importance of allowing individuality and community considerations to fit together. It is a
dramatic rite. Teachers argue that, even though many of the
children will not understand the meaning of the rite, its beauty
and mystery will be part of the child's experience and hence
available for later reflection. Symbols have been carefully selected. Human fallibility is represented by the red apple and is
reminiscent of Adam and Eve in the Garden of Eden. Red is the
color of passion. The candle, in turn, is symbolic of God and the

spirit triumphing over the flesh. The evergreens symbolize life. The darkened room helped set the stage for a spiritually up- lifting experience. The darkness not only showed up the can- dles, but also enhanced the drama and prepared the participants. An attitude of spiritual receptivity was sought to set the tone for the climax of the children lighting their candles. And the spiral shape is a variation on the circle or eternity theme, suggestive of the cosmos and an ever expanding universe, found so often in Waldorf School. Such concerns of spirituality and community, and the place of humankind in the cosmos are fundamental to the school.

The Festival of Lights. It is 7.30 p.m. on a wintry night. Snow and ice cover the streets. A winter gale blows. Inside a large Episcopal church hall, some 400 people wait for a cere- mony, the Festival of Lights, to begin. Teacher comes forward and welcomes everyone. Third graders walk up the stairs and onto the stage to light the menora on the right hand side of the stage. All the children stand and sing as a choir accompanied by the piano. The Advent Wreath on the left of the stage is lit by one of the teachers. Silence is observed, for this is the spiritually significant moment of the evening. People bow their heads in prayer or reflective thought. Then, people look up, waiting expectantly for parents also came to see their children. Each class's offerings of music and poetry are bracketed by hymns sung by all the participants. The hymns are distinctly Christian: "Hark the Herald Angels Sing," "Oh Little Town of Bethle- hem," "Silent Night," "Joy to the World," and "Angels We Have Heard on High." All the hymns proclaim the birth of Christ, making the ritual appear to be Christian (but it is called the Festival of Lights, which is a Jewish tradition, and the lighting of the menora is a central part of the ritual). The final performance is a choral item presented by the faculty. They sing harmoniously, bringing the evening to its joyful resolution. With strains of Silent Night wafting in the air we are all wished a "Happy Holiday." Children rush outside, displaying all the excitement of opening night.

The Festival of Lights is a celebratory community gathering. The children enjoy performing and their parents are keen participants. On one level the ceremony is religious. Jewish,

Christian, and other faiths are given a public opportunity to come together in worship that is not aimed at conversion. The community feels its common values centered around spirituality. The ritual also signifies a break in the school year and brings closure to the first half of the school year. Since the school is very strong in the arts, particularly in voice and recorder, the ceremony also gives students and teachers alike an opportunity to share those talents in a way that affirms them. Repeating the Advent Spiral theme, the Festival of Lights also symbolizes and reinforces the idea of the gifts of each individual together making for a strong and meaningful community.

Eurythmy Lesson.   Second graders sit in a circle on the floor with their shoes off. The teacher, a young German woman, wears "eurythmy slippers," snug socks made of soft white fabric. She is wearing a black cotton skirt with shiny sequins and embroidered flowers on the hem, and a white cotton, folk-style blouse. Standing very erect, she smiles at the children. Furniture has been moved to the perimeter of the classroom to make space for free movement. The children stand and face their teacher. They follow her body movements and repeat the verses as she recites with arms outstretched and circling, "Sun, Moon, and Stars, Shining white, Shining far, Shining in my heart." For each phrase there is a particular movement to be made. Verses and movements are repeated.

The children have done eurythmy before, so they are able to say the verses and perform the movements without difficulty. Each movement has a clear pattern. "Go round and round the village (repeated), Go in and out the windows (repeated), As we have done before, Now stand and face your partner (repeated), And bow before you go." When the teacher says *willage* instead of *village* and *oh-ven* instead for *oven*, there are some taunts from the cheekier boys. "Follow her to London, As fast as you can go, Now shake her hand and leave her, And bow before you go." Teacher leads the group in a circling movement (to London); some of the boys whack the door jamb as they wind past in the circle. "That's not nice. We'll do it again. Only be quiet," says the teacher. This time some of the boys make rabbit ears on the person in front. They snatch at the dried flowers hanging from the rafter and hit the walls, only not so loudly this time.

The teacher ignores them. "He's stepping on my toes." "Well, he's kicking me." "He's pulling my hair" are some of the children's cries. "All faces looking at me" commands the teacher. She hums the next tune and shows the movements, in and out in lines, then into a semicircle. For each of these forms the teacher has a detailed sketch on a notepad showing the directions of the movements. When they finish the verse about the "peach girl" who has "come home too," they are told to sit and watch the teacher.

Next is an interesting exercise in writing the alphabet with our bodies. The teacher shows how to make an s on the floor. She walks an s, then asks for volunteers. Students take it in turns to do this until everyone has had a turn. Teacher says, "Very good," after each child. "Now I will show you the alphabet. What is your name?" "June." "All right. This is J for June." Teacher does a little jump, which surprises me. I have never seen anyone "do" a J. For an A her arms are uplifted, she moves back a couple of quick steps. The K is hard, a chopping motion on the floor. For every letter of the aphabet the teacher has a special dance or movement. The children are fascinated. Some of them quietly stand up and try doing their own letter, all the while carefully watching the teacher.

"Adam he had seven sons" is the final movement. The children wind around in a circle following the teacher, arms moving in wide gestures. Attention is given to the group making a "perfect circle." At the completion of the activity the teacher stands quite still. Children and teacher join in the verse that began the lesson: "Sun, Moon, and Stars, Shining White, Shining Far, Shining in my Heart." "Auf Wiedersehn, class," says teacher. "Auf Wiedersehn, Frau Loetze," the children reply.

Eurythmy is said to be the "poetry of movement." Steiner argued it was the language of the soul: "one should not think that any eurythmy movement is ever arbitrary. At a given moment, a particular movement has to be brought forth as a musical or poetic expression, just as in singing a specific tone is produced or in speaking a specific sound occurs" (Steiner, 1980, p. 92). The shapes of eurythmy are spiral and flowing, consistent with the shapes of form drawing and so many other Waldorf School activities. And the circular rhythm is representative of

the "life forces" that one finds throughout the Waldorf School
structure. Craftspeople are said to use these rhythms in their
work. The name *eurythmy* is a combination of the Greek *eu*: well
and *rhythmos*: rhythm (Pouderoyen, 1980, p. 3). Harmonious
movement, the capacity to move freely and rhythmically, is at
the heart of eurythmy. Thus, it is not merely physical form or
technical precision that is sought, for one can find this in ballet,[3]
but rather a spiritual expressiveness. Eurythmists are thought to
"speak" with their bodies.

Young children, 7 or 8 years old, boys and girls, are required
to do eurythmy in all Waldorf schools. However, we see a gender
difference in the children's response to eurythmy. Eurythmy
resembles the so-called "feminine" art forms in our culture. Its
origins are said to be in the ancient temple dances of the East:[4]
"It is a renewal, but in a totally modern form, of the ancient art
of temple dance . . . the development of the art of eurythmy is
based on the sensible—super—sensible insight into the human
body's capacity for expressive movement" (Kisseleff, 1980, p.
28). Hindu dances are soft and "feminine" and flowing, in
comparison with, say, Spanish dancing which utilizes hard,
staccato movements. As Simons (1980, p. 31) puts it: "the
Hindu dance lifts us off the ground, while the Spanish stamps us
right into and under it." Thus, in the eurythmy class it is
perhaps not surprising that it is the boys who are distracted.
They have also been socialized into mainsteam American culture with its separation of "masculine" and "feminine" identi-
ties. And however much Waldorf School might like to set up
different values, asking the boys to spiritually express them-

---

[3]Eurythmists see ballet as too technical and uninspiring to be worthy of the
child's attention: "young children should not be made too conscious in their
movements. The precision of movement by which some dancing schools make
little girls into accomplished ballerinas with all the tricks of the trade is to be
heartily deplored. It has even been observed to produce a dullness of mind at
a later age" (Harwood, 1980, p. 140).

[4]Eastern philosophies and religions were of interest to Steiner. Steiner had,
it seems, a close knowledge of both the East and the West. His many references,
in *Occult Science* and other works, to the Vedas, Zarathustra, and many other
Eastern sources of inspiration, indicate this intimacy. But it was his closeness
with Goethe and his own place in Western culture that provided the main
influence on his philosophy.

selves through poetic movement is stretching the limits of their compliance. The school says everyone must do eurythmy, for it is a *required* subject, so the boys find their own ways of having fun. Boys at Waldorf School may not have football coaching to foster masculine culture, but they do collect baseball cards and have their own baseball heroes. When they are confronted with a school activity that emphasizes gracefulness and is like dance, their reaction is largely one of disinterest.

Waldorf School is not unaware of these problems. One of the parents complained that her three boys did nothing else but play wars and guns and shooting games. "It seems to be genetically wired that way," she concluded. Another parent said her boy was incredibly competitive and "macho," and that this was the reason Waldorf School was so right for him. He needed to have, in her view, "that other side of his personality rounded out." She gave a talk to this effect at one of the meetings designed to attract new students to the school. One of the parents at that meeting had commented that the curriculum seemed distinctly feminine in form; she had boys and wondered how they would fit in. The school's argument, that all children would benefit from aesthetic awareness, imaginative thinking and sensitivity training, would seem to be a reaction against the dominance of bureaucratic and impersonal institutional models in today's rapidly changing world. People who are "whole," able to do whatever they set their minds to, rather than being narrowly trained for a specific technical skill, are said to be better educated, in this view, for they have the ability to adapt to changing circumstances. Critics reply that the Waldorf School view is essentially isolationist and idealistic.

Yet the children are being exposed to ideas and a physical form (even if they never achieve the spiritual dimension) that has the potential to transform ways of thinking and being. The anthroposophy movement, with which the school aligned, is dedicated to peace and a better humanity. It is through exposure to these ideas at an early age through activities like eurythmy that the school hopes to give children the opportunity to hold values other than those of the excessive competitiveness, materialism, and violence that are seen to pervade American culture at large.

Nature Ritual. "Take delight in nature" (Steiner, 1937, p. 112). One of the central motifs in Waldorf School is that of nature. In all classrooms one finds only natural materials, wool, wood, cotton, beeswax, and clay, for instance; plastics and synthetics are absent. There are no computers, indeed, no modern technology, not even many books, and no books in the kindergartens. On the other hand, nature is everywhere. It surrounds the classroom; all one can see in all directions is the forest. Inside the classrooms, nature is celebrated. A recurring symbol is that of mother and "mother nature." For instance, the kindergarten classrooms display a large framed painting of the madonna and child on the wall. In another corner of the classrooms is a Nature Garden. The Nature Garden consists of offerings of fruit, flowers, berries, acorns and branches placed on an altarlike table covered with a white linen cloth. A candle is lit in the Nature Garden at the beginning of the school day, and verses celebrating life and nature are said, such as the following poem said at the beginning of main lesson in Grades 1 to 3:

> The sun, with loving light, Makes bright for me the day. The soul with spirit power, Gives strength unto my limbs. In sunlight shining clear, I reverence, O God, The strength of human kind, Which Thou as gift of love, Hast planted in my soul, That I may love to work, And ever seek to learn, From Thee stream strength and light; To Thee rise love and thanks.

At the end of main lesson the candle is extinguished, bringing closure to the lesson and a sense of rhythm and harmony to the school day. The older grades say a different verse that also celebrates nature:

> I do behold the world, The sun, the stars, the stone, The plants that live and grow, The beasts that feel and live, And man to spirit gives, A dwelling in his soul. I do behold the soul, That living dwells in me, God's spirit lives and moves, In light of sun and soul, In heights of world without, In depths of soul within. Spirit of God, to thee, I seeking, turn myself, That strength and grace and skill, For learning and for work, In me may live and grow.

Within the nature ritual a dominant symbol is that of the circle.

The classroom itself in the early grades is altered from a hard rectangular shape to become more circular and "womblike." Soft muslin drapes in the corners of the room transform it into a circle. Further, the colors of the classroom and the colors that the children use in their paintings are not strong, angry, or passionate colors, but soft pastels of pink, green, blue, and yellow. And during creative play, for the young children it is "homey activities" and artistic "work" that occupies them, which is suggestive once again of mothering and domesticity. At "Circle Time," the children follow the teacher into a circle, where they listen to a story and engage in singing, verse activities, and rhythmic chants. For these chants the teacher leads the class in saying or singing a verse (or times tables in grade school) and at the same time performing bodily movements, often to the rhythm of a drum. At the grade school, too, the circle theme and the use of rhythm are continued. During main lesson, in eurythmy, in games and during specialty classes, such as handwork, a circle formation is used. When circles are formed, attention is also paid to making the circle "perfect" in shape.

Repetition and rhythm in all aspects of school life, argued Steiner, were essentials of education (Steiner, 1937, p. 86). Within the cycle of nature, the child, as part of the cosmos, is seen to respond well to patterns. The rhythms are not considered empty or meaningless routines, but spiritually moving and significant events that provide a worthy foundation for each child's moral, spiritual, and intellectual development.

It is noteworthy that Waldorf School does not include the Pledge of Allegiance or the singing of "America the Beautiful" in its daily ritual (as St. Catherine's does). Neglect of rituals such as these, and the substitution of rituals to nature, demonstrate the school's alienation from mainstream American culture. Instead of patriotism or statist loyalties, the beauty and importance of nature is taught. The school attempts to counteract the depersonalization, fragmentation, and alienation of humans from nature in an economy and consumer-driven culture, and hopes to affirm the spiritual in nature.

Steiner once said that his schools were like country schools in their methods (1937, p. 91). He admired the recognition in country schools that children were not mere "resources" to be programmed or managed, but complex creatures with emotions, with a will of their own and a latent intellect capable of wonderful things. Country schools were located in nature. They responded to the seasons and rejoiced in what they could teach. Teachers in these schools knew each child intimately. Often the students were related. The school was located in, and very much a central part of, the community. Steiner was not against the modern world with its movement away from intimate community as such, but he was against humans becoming isolated from nature. Steiner believed humans were all of of nature combined, a synthesis of other forms (1937, p. 99). At Waldorf School humans are held to be part of the cosmos and that therefore they ought not put themselves out of touch with the cosmos. The school does not, however, posit a return to primitive ways. Steiner believed in knowledge and civilization and the quest for perfection. But he felt humans must try to grow spiritually and live in tune with their environment.

Steiner used the example of Goethe's educational experiences as a child to show more clearly what education should and should not be. Goethe disliked learning the piano in the way he was taught as a child. The piano was regarded as an instrument separate from him. Goethe began to take an interest in the piano only when he made the connection between his different fingers and the sounds they were producing. Steiner relates how Goethe protested the uninspiring, unconnected with nature way he was being taught at the age of 7: "He built his own altar to nature, taking for the purpose his father's music desk, laying minerals upon it, and plants from his father's rock garden, and on top putting a little fumigating candle; then he caught up the beams of the morning sun in a burning glass and offered a sacrifice to the great God of nature—a rebellion against what people wanted him to learn" (Steiner, 1937, p. 102). Steiner's view of this was that Goethe had been treated like an automaton, and that this is no way to teach, evidenced in his outrage. Instead, Waldorf School teachers are to attend to the whole child in a family approach to schooling. Families, ideally, love and care for children within a structure of authority. Parents do what is best for the child. Waldorf School views the school community as like a family in its caring function and commitment to each child.

"Earth Who Gave Us This Food" Ritual. Food rituals are common to all peoples. Some foods are made taboo, others are highly prized and desired, and still others form the staple of the diet. Set rules and etiquette also surround the selection, preparation, and consumption of food. Schools also engage in symbolic actions regarding food that reflect and support a culture. In the two schools under study quite different aproaches to food are seen. At Waldorf School the emphasis is on all-natural health food. St. Catherine's also emphasizes good nutrition, although to a lesser extent, and with a more traditional approach to nutrition.

In Waldorf School kindergarten, for a fee of $2.00 per day the school provides a vegetarian lunch, which is almost mandatory:

> if for medical/religious reasons you do not wish the school to provide lunch for your child, please supply a medical exemption signed by a doctor or a religious exemption written by you. (*Handbook*)

Because lunch is a central part of the school day, a time for sharing and giving thanks as a community, the idea of students excluding themselves is avoided.

> Grace is always said by the kindergartners at snack and meal times: Earth who gave us this food, Sun who made it ripe and good. Dear Earth, Dear Sun, By you we live. Our loving thanks to you, We give.

Foods served at snack time are all natural: juices, such as apple and orange, natural teas, whole grain breads, seeds, and fresh raw fruits and vegetables. These snacks are prepared by the teacher and students, an activity that is believed to help establish bonds. During the shared mealtimes a sense of communion is fostered. Another element of the food ritual is that it is a time for the display of manners. Etiquette is to be obeyed, mostly instilled through the example of the teacher. A proper way to approach mealtimes is modeled, which includes the saying of grace and unobtrusive, unhurried eating.

For those students in the kindergarten who bring food from

home, rules are also stipulated about the type of container in which to transport food to school:

> In order to cut down on the influence of the modern media in our children's lives, we do not allow lunch boxes to be brought to school. The clanking of metal boxes can greatly add to the noise of an already excited lunchroom. Please send lunch in a basket or backpack. (*Handbook*)

Baskets made from natural materials, or soft backpacks, are acceptable, hard metal is not. Moreover, in the grade school all students must bring lunches and beverages from home. No food or refreshments are sold in the grade school on a daily basis. At certain times of the year, 1 day a week homemade muffins and apple juice are sold by students to raise money for school trips. At other times there is no provision for food to be sold in the school.

> As in the kindergartens, grade school students also recite graces before meals. (Sung) All praise to thee, My god, this day, For all the blessings of the light, Keep me, Oh keep me, King of Kings, Beneath thine own almighty wings. (Said) Blessings on the meal. Amen.

Grace might also be a simple statement by a child about what he/she was grateful for. For instance, one girl gave thanks for her baby sister born on the weekend in a home birthing experience. Dewdrop had told the class about the new baby and the home birthing process during main lesson, and the grace became a collective expression and celebration of the event. In another class grace became a verse that the teacher liked for its emphasis on the importance of kindness and fraternity:

> A faithful friend is a strong defence, And he that hath found such hath found a treasure, Change not thy friend for any good thing, A faithful friend is the medicine of life; And they that fear the Lord shall find him. Yea, whoso feareth the Lord shall direct his friendship aright; For as he is, so also shall be his friend.

In addition, the verse is used to signal a change in class activity, part of the rhythm to the school day.

Snack and meal-time rituals are also an occasion for teaching about proper social relations. For instance, the teacher who uses the verse "A Faithful Friend is a Strong Defense" also admits that the saying of verses to mark a change of "lessons" has a disciplinary function.

When the students are saying the verse, they are not talking: When they hear that verse "A Faithful Friend is a Strong Defense," then that means put everything away and get ready for snack. I love it. When they're putting their things away the confusion and madness is toned down because they're saying that. And so the verses that they say during the day cue them to the next move that they make. So that's a wonderful thing. Plus it goes along with my effort to get the children to care for one another. If I said to the children every day, "All right children, I want you to be nice to each other," that would go in one ear and out the other. (Interview, teacher)

The verse comes from Ecclesiasticus, a book written between the Old and New Testament. The teacher says she selected it because the verse represents some kind of middle ground between the Christian and Jewish faiths, since the book is recognized in some way by both faiths.

Consistent with the rituals described earlier, lunch and snack time rituals display and reinforce social values. The school asserts the importance of spirituality, saying grace, giving thanks for food and being kind to one another. It also highlights the school's concern about the media dominating and distorting children's perceptions of the world. The problem addressed in the "no metal lunch box" rule is that television shows children on *Sesame Street* and other children's programs bringing their lunch to school in metal lunch boxes emblazoned with *Sesame Street* and other television characters. Children the world over watching *Sesame Street* then want to imitate such TV personalities. Waldorf School teachers believe this is detrimental to a child's proper development. They argue that, if a child is to become a free, independent individual, he or she ought to be kept away from the negative influences of the media, particularly television. The rule is one small part of this overall effort.

In addition, the role of nutrition for health and well being is taught and reinforced through rules and example.

The food that we eat affects our total being: our energy, concentration, interest and vitality. At [Waldorf School] we encourage the eating of natural, whole foods. We ask that parents consider carefully the effects of "junk food" and foods with chemical additives, preservatives, sweeteners, *etc.* Such food can have a marked, detrimental effect on the child's organism and undermines the work of the school. (*Handbook*)

Parents and teachers across the nation and elsewhere have also protested the pervasive effect of nutritionally hollow food in our society. Waldorf School is perhaps just more vigilant in its naming of the junk food way of life as negating the effects of good schooling. The emphasis on "natural whole foods" is also symbolic of a commitment to a whole and natural world.

The 'Secret Pal' Ritual. It is the last week of school before Christmas. The classroom is decorated with a Christmas tree, an Advent Calendar, and various festive ornaments, such as pine cones and holly. Underneath the tree are presents, beautifully wrapped. The children are very excited, for today is the day they will find out who their 'secret pal' has been, an event marked by the giving of gifts. Early in Advent the children had, with the teacher's direction, selected their 'secret pal.' Each student then "did something," a kindly act, for his or her secret pal "whenever they felt like it." Then, just prior to going on vacation they are gathered together to open the gifts and try to guess the identity of their "secret pal." The children were instructed to handmake a gift, so as to teach more completely the concept of doing for others, but not every child has done this. Homemade gifts range from heart shaped cakes to jewelry made from colored clay. Store purchases include stuffed animals and games. Everyone seems delighted. Children chatter with excitement as they unwrap the gifts, in turn, so that everyone can see the gifts and join in the fun of guessing. Most of the children already know who their "pal" is. Some of the gifts, such as the heart cake baked by one of the students, are immediately shared.

In the "secret pal" ritual the teacher's motive was one of social cohesion, "trying to get them to be more of a group" (Interview, teacher). The value of good social relations is at the center of her philosophy of good teaching.

I want to give them the opportunity to become well-rounded social beings, not academic automotons. What we have here is a little society where co-operation is what is needed. It is more important for them to mature and grow in the ability to care for human beings and work as a unit, the more highly developed values, than for them to pass test scores. Sometimes it worries me, "oh, it's not academic," and then I think, Well, if you took any one child out of here and you put them in a structured school, they could do anything. Anything you ask them to do, they can do. And because I'm not drilling them so that they're miserable, that doesn't mean they're not capable. If placed in the public school, they would fit in within a month because of what they have inside. They're a group with a lot of spirit and soul and consciousness. (Interview, teacher)

The value of community has been a traditional thread in educational circles, but Waldorf School teachers make it the mainstay of their schooling and define community in terms of a concern for spirituality. Here in the secret pal ceremony, as in the other rituals described earlier, the ideals of giving, sharing, and holding communal values are celebrated.

We now turn to a consideration of rituals in another elementary school, St. Catherine's, seeking to understand the organization, interests, and purposes of particular rituals and what this tells us about school culture.

Rites for Academics and Character: St. Catherine's

Lesson Ritual. A sign on the fourth grade classroom door declares, "You're somebody special. Nothing can stop this class. Welcome." Inside the classroom three or four small groups of children sit talking to each other. The girls talk quietly while two of the boys play "sword fights" with rulers. Other boys are engaged in "war games": "I shot you." "You can't come over on the other side you dipstick. It's a deadly war zone." "This is dumber than Star Trek, you guys." "Who cares." "You're dead, I shot you in the you know what." "Paul, I shot you dead." "Everybody dies." It is recess. I sit on the bench near the window watching the lively activities. A bell rings, and children swarm back into the classroom. The talking quiets as they enter the room. Teacher is not yet back, but the children take a test from the folder on the back shelf and sit down. All social contact ceases at once. What matters now is doing the test. Heads are down and bodies oriented toward their tests. Ten minutes pass. Eventually the teacher returns. Nothing changes.

When the teacher comes to stand by me, I ask her a question, and she replies, "I really need to set an example, and if we're talking I'm not doing that. I want them to know tests are serious business, because that's what it will be like for them later on." I remember now how seriously they took the last test, and the rule that, if they talk during the test, they lose points. As the students continue their work, teacher writes on the chalkboard. "If you finish early, check for errors then bring it to me and read *quietly.*" The test is an English test requiring children to circle proper and common nouns, write compound sentences, pluralize words, write definitions and abbreviations, and understand possessive case. As an example: "To make a singular noun that ends in s possessive, add _____ ." Every child finishes the test within the 40-minute lesson period. They hand in their papers and begin reading silently. Presently the bell rings. Teacher announces, "Don't forget your homework. We'll discuss the results next class. Jimmy may I see you during the break, please? You may go to Science now." Talking begins once more as students move noisily out of the classroom to their lockers in the hallway to get the materials they will need for their next lesson with a different teacher.

The contrast between "play" and "work" in this testing ritual is profound. Students are able to make that distinction without teacher supervision. When it was time for the test, they responded as the teacher would have wished had she been there. The teacher had clearly established the testing routine through a careful delineation of rules and consistency. Thus, when I contravened the rules, she did not bend those rules. The teacher wants to impress upon the children the value of work, and individual responsibility for students to be their "own policeman" (Interview, teacher). In addition, the value of planning and structuring is endorsed. The teacher gives the students clues for good test taking—"check for errors." Then students are to begin the next activity, reading *quietly,* so as not to disturb others for the remainder of the period. They are schooled in the rhythm of the testing event: start test / finish test / check for errors / hand in test / read quietly / end of lesson. Time is to be carefully considered and apportioned to gain maximum success.

Students' adherence to the testing norms is highlighted by their quite different behavior before and after the lesson. The children switch immediately from the play mode to a work mode, on the signal of a bell ringing, even without a proper lesson opening to orient students. They are motivated to begin without the teacher. The close of the lesson is again demarcated, as in many schools, by a bell ringing, a "mirror image of its opening" (Mehan, 1979, p. 46). After the teacher closed the lesson, students immediately began talking and physically moved from their seats. The behavioral rules implicit in the lesson no longer applied. In the testing ritual the school further endorses key school values of the work ethic, individualism, achievement, and responsibility.

A Mealtime Ritual.   The 12:30 p.m. bell has rung, and fourth- and fifth-grade students are out in the playground, running and jumping or talking to friends. At 12:45 another bell rings. Students return to their classrooms, collect their lunches from their lockers, and line up at the door. They are still in a playful mood, laughing and full of energy. The teacher arrives. "Quiet, please." They settle and are led to the cafeteria where they wait in the corridor while the younger children who have just finished their lunch return to class. Once inside the lunch room, the children go to their assigned places. Gender and grade distinctions are significant in seating allocations. Fifth-grade boys sit together, third-grade girls, and so on. The children start eating. They talk among themselves. Some of the children are served a hot meal from the cafeteria. They have ordered it early in the morning in their classrooms. Teachers are seated at a round table in the center of the room. The students' tables, in contrast, are trestlelike. Mr. Jackson, the teacher on duty, gets up from the table, walks to the side of the room, and rings a small hand held bell. There is silence. Heads are bowed. All say together: "For these and all God's gifts to us, May God's Holy name be praised. Amen." The eating of lunch resumes. Every now and again Mr. Jackson stands and asks students to settle

down. The last time he does this, he says, "It's your responsibility to settle down now, ready for class." Presently, a bell
rings. Some of the students leave the lunch room, wending their
way back to class. Others work in teams to clean up the lunch
room, wiping down the tables and sweeping the floor. "That's
the clean up bell," one of the boys says to me. A few minutes
later another bell rings. "I've got to go," my 10-year-old informant says as he rushes off. "That's the bell to be back in class."

What is immediately apparent about the St. Catherine's lunch
ritual is how well ordered it is. Plans have been made and
executed concerning the time of entrance and exit, the tolerated
level of noise, when to eat and when to say grace, the clean up,
and so on. The grace is a confirmation of the school's concern for
the children's religious upbringing. Also, the facilities show the
school to be well equipped and established. The lunchroom is
not luxurious, but compared to Waldorf School, where students
must eat in their classroom or outside, it is well set up. Here at
St. Catherine's, for those students who desire it, hot lunches are
available every day of the week. And Mr. Jackson's exhortation
to students to take responsibility for their actions and prepare
themselves for class is in keeping with the value the school
places on individualism and achievement. The idea for students
to have recess first and lunch to follow was a conscious decision
to enhance the afternoon work environment in class. Previously,
students had eaten their lunch, then had recess, before going
back into class. But students were too excited from the play:
"they were so unsettled, we found it was impossible. This way
we get much more work done" (Interview, teacher). Implicit in
the lunch time ritual are norms of religious observance, individualism, and achievement—ethics that are also reflective of other
areas of school life.

Chapel Ritual. Whereas for Waldorf School festivals are the
"glue" holding its cultural values in focus, for St. Catherine's it
is chapel.[5] Once a week the Lower School, kindergarteners to

---

[5]Sporting and athletic events have a similar effect to chapel in bringing the
school together, although they rarely involve the whole school centered
around a particular ritual. Sporting rites are more likely to be centered around
teams who go off to compete with a rival group in order to bring back glory and

THE POETRY OF RITUALS

grade 5, come together for 30 minutes of prayer, hymns, and a moral message. The Middle and Upper Schools also hold chapel. Chapel is the unifying event in the school's weekly routine. It is an event that is revitalizing and aimed at injecting a "renewal of commitment into the motivations and values of the ritual participants" (McLaren, 1986, p. 80). Chapel also has the function of recharging the "emotional batteries" of teachers and students, or *intensification*, for example, drawing out the personal side of the ritual or what it means to the participants.

A poetic or music "score" was played each time chapel was held. The form stayed the same, only its content varied, depending on the rhythm of the school calendar. Always a minister led the service. The homily was always given. Hymns or songs were always sung. The Lord's Prayer was always said. The candles were always ceremoniously lit by a kindergartener, and extinguished by that child at the end of chapel. The opening and closing prayers were always the same. The birthday blessing was always given. The altar was always formally arranged with a white linen cloth, flowers, candles in gold candlesticks, and a gold cross. The focus in the room was always towards the leader positioned at the front or near the side of the altar. The setting was thus formal and hierarchical, as opposed to the circular formations common for rituals at Waldorf School.

Variation in chapel comes from the religious and secular calendar. When it was Martin Luther King's birthday, the sermon addressed the issue of racial discrimination. When it was Valentine's Day, the theme was love. The seasons are also

---

honor to the school in much the same way that warriors might bring back glory to their people. And sporting rites occur primarily at the Middle and Upper School levels. The one sporting event when the whole school comes together is the annual "Field Day," held near the end of the school year. At this event, egg and spoon races, sack races, and other novelty events are the central focus of the day, with students competing with faculty in some events. The day is attended by parents and is generally a "fun" day, which is an inversion of the seriousness with which the entire school year has been conducted. Whereas "crushing your opponents" (Interview, students) is a bona fide attitude at the school with regard to interschool sporting competitions, and indeed academics, one finds the reverse at Field Day. Here, rather than the traditional competitive track and field, the school takes a step backwards to "laugh at itself" and momentarily deny the strong competitiveness that is a motivating force in the school.

symbolically represented by the floral arrangements on the altar. At Christmas an Advent wreath graced the altar; in Spring fresh pink roses; in Winter a cornucopia of dried flowers. Songs for Martin Luther King (with clapping and rhythmic chants), and the African-American spiritual "Swing Low, Sweet Chariot," contrasted with hymns sung in Latin. The music played on the piano to signify the school's entry and exit from chapel also ranged from the high tones of "Pacelbel's Canon" to the children's refrain "The Magic Penny."

To look more closely at what the ideas of chapel were, the cultural values put forward, we now turn to some chapel experiences.[6]

The Beginning of Advent.   An electric bell sounds in all the rooms in the school indicating that it is chapel time. Inside a large auditorium a 5-year-old boy is lighting the candles on an altar with the assistance of a "chapel mother." A small group of adults are already in the room. Reverend Cameron, the headmaster, talks to Mr Moore, the Director of the Lower School. A "chapel mother" is watching the small boy. Mrs Post, the music teacher, sits at the piano, selecting her music. She begins playing a hymn. I smile hello and take up a position near the door. Out in the corridor there is bustle and movement, talk and laughter, as the whole school makes its way to chapel. Children in pairs, boys with boys, girls with girls, file quietly into the auditorium. In each of the pairs there is one older child, a senior in the school (10 or 11 years old), and one younger (5 or 6 years old.) Students do not talk to each other, but rather sit in their usual "place." They know where they are to sit. Children with "chapel buddies" (the pairs) sit on the carpeted floor, kindergarten in a column on the far left, first grade next to them, and so on. Some whispering begins now as the assembled group waits for the service to commence. "I hate it when it's noisy," says Mrs. Wright. "Chapel is supposed to be quiet." Everyone in the room is positioned to face the center front space, where an altar is covered with a white linen cloth. On the altar are a pair of gold candlesticks holding long white candles that are alight,

---

[6]These accounts of chapel are my reconstructions of the events *post hoc.*

a large cross in the center, and an Advent wreath. The wreath, as is traditional, is made of evergreens with four candles.

The headmaster, Dr. Cameron, stands in front of the altar. There is silence. "Good morning," he says. "Good morning," the students reply. "Let us pray." Heads are bowed and eyes closed. "Our father who art in heaven, Hallowed be thy name . . . " is chanted in monotone. When the Lord's Prayer is over, Mr. Moore invites the school, "Please be seated." Mrs. Post steps to center-stage position. "Now we will sing Dona Nobis Pacem. What does that mean?" Children raise hands. She selects a child to answer. "It means give me peace. Let there be peace." "Yes, that's correct. Good." Without accompaniment the children then sing: "Do-oh-na, No-oh-bis, Pa-ah-cem, Pah-cem, Do-oh-oh-na-ah, No-oh-bis, Pa-ah-ah-ah-cem." Some of the children look at the words in their red folders that contain the hymns, prayer and order of service. The homily begins:

Dr. C: It's getting near Christmas and one of the things you often hear about this time is how terribly commercial Christmas has become. Well, it's people who make it that way. You decide what you're going to do. A few years ago my wife and I went to France to a beautiful monastery called Mont Saint-Michel. Some of you may have been there already. It's so beautiful. I hope all of you have a chance to go there one day. This monastery is on an island up on a hill, and on the way up there are many shops selling drinks and ice cream and little plastic trinkets. My wife thought this was terrible that commerialism was there, but as long as there have been pilgrims going to Mont Saint-Michel there have always been shops there. So it's the same here at Christmas. It's people who make Christmas commercial or not. It depends what's in your heart. And at Christmas time we need to be thinking about what happened to Joseph and Mary and the baby. God allowed his most precious thing, his son, to be born in less than optimal, not nice, circumstances. He didn't have a feather bed, but rather was born in a barn. God didn't build a new motel so they could spend the night, but allowed them to be turned away from the inns that were already full. God's only son, the King, was born in a barn. God allowed this to happen, and he also allowed Jesus to die in horrible circumstances. Why would he do that? Do you think your parents who love you so very much, would allow something nasty to happen to you? No. And yet parents at some point, even though

they love you so very much have to let you free to live your own
life. Now at Christmas I want you to take something, the thing you
love the most, it might be a toy or some clothing or a skill that you
have that you are not teaching your younger brother or sister, and
give it to someone you really love, and see what you learn from
that. Often people just give away things they don't want, and
that's generous, but it's not the same as giving away something
really precious to someone you love. Also, this year we have Toys
for Tots again so I want you to bring in toys or games or stuffed
animals for someone less fortunate than yourselves.
(There is a pause.)
O.K., Now, I'm wondering, who has a birthday this week?
(Five children stand.)
Oh. George and David, Sally and Sue and Pamela. Great. Let's say
a prayer for them. Bow your heads and hold your hands together.
All: Dear Lord, Bless these children that they may grow and learn
and live in peace. In Jesus' name. Amen.
Dr. C: So don't forget Toys for Tots this week. You will notice that
we have the Advent wreath to mark the beginning of Advent and
we will have a whole school chapel in the auditorium to mark the
end. Everyone will do something at that service, reading scripture
or singing. And at Christmas time be thinking about what God is
teaching us.
Mrs. P: (Stands and leads the school in another hymn, also in
Latin.)
All: (Heads are bowed for the closing prayer.)
(The piano is played softly while students exit. They return to
class for Reading. The small boy who lit the candles extinguishes
them with a gold candle snuffer. It is 9:00 a.m. and school has
been in session for 40 minutes.)

This service at the beginning of Advent, like other religious
events, such as Easter, serves to remind students of their
religious commitment. Advent means "the coming" and is
meant to prepare people in spirit for the Second Coming of
Christ. Advent is also, in the immediate present, a preparation
for Christmas. Dr Cameron, the headmaster, does not want
students (or teachers) to forget the religious meaning of Christmas: "be thinking about what God is teaching us." The Advent
Wreath, evergreens shaped in a circle, suggest the "cycle of the
thousands of years from Adam to the birth of Christ" (Interview,
teacher). The circle of the Advent Wreath symbolizes also the

continuous nature of God's love, the candles signifying that "God's word is Truth that lights up the world" (Interview, teacher). Dr. Cameron also wants children to share, to be spiritual in the way that God demonstrated we should be. He stresses that God allowed his son to be born in a manger, demonstrating purity and nonmaterialism. By giving to others something really precious, not just that which is superfluous to us, Dr. Cameron suggests, one can grow in goodness. Another version of Christian charity is the Toys for Tots program, whereby Christmas toys are donated to less fortunate children. The story of how Mont Saint-Michel became materialistic once people were there is intended to teach the need for constant work to make our lives more spiritual. Dr Cameron hopes that participants at chapel will see that they can, with God's help, make Christmas an event that is more than just materialism, presents and tinsel. The "chapel buddy" scheme, where each fifth grade child "adopts" a buddy in Kindergarten and escorts his or her kindergartener to chapel each week, has become a popular tradition in the school, with parents claiming that children "just love chapel and still talk about the person who was their chapel buddy when they were in Kindergarten." The practice demonstrates the school's commitment to fostering caring social relationships, charity, and social responsibility.

A Moral Message: "Laugh at Yourself."   Songs sung today are "traditional black American" spirituals, although Pacelbel's Canon is played on the piano to usher the children into chapel.

Mr M: Girls and boys, we still don't have absolute quietness.
(Pause and there is silence.)
Chapel needs to be a really quiet time. (Pause.) Next week is Martin Luther King's birthday. You'll be hearing more about that in class, I expect, and we will talk about him at chapel next week. (Pause) Who has heard the expression "He can laugh at himself?" (Various students raise hands.) Yes, you've all heard people say Johnny is really good at school or good at sport, and do you know what? He can really laugh at himself. Or, Sally is really smart and really pretty, and she can laugh at herself. Well I've been thinking a lot about laughing at myself, and I've been practicing. I have a mirror for this purpose. (He produces a large round mirror approximately 12 inches in diameter. Students

laugh. He shows them how he laughs at himself. Students laugh again.) Is there anyone here who thinks they know how to laugh at themselves? (Some hands go up. Mr Moore selects a girl to demonstrate. She pokes her tongue at herself in the mirror and pulls silly faces. Everyone laughs. Then he chooses two boys to do this. They say "Ha ha ha ha ha," which encourages more laughter. The whole class then has a turn at laughing at itself.) I have an anecdote that's about laughing at myself. What is an anecdote? People in my reading group should know.

SS: (Students volunteer "It's a story with a moral," "It's a personal experience.")

Mr M: Yes, it's a story about yourself, I will give you an example. About 6 months ago—remember this was before all these countries became free and before the Berlin wall came down—I was sitting watching TV. Now, I don't watch TV very often, but I was sitting there with my daughter and we were watching Alvin and the Chipmunks. (Students laugh.) Now, Alvin and the Chipmunks, as you all know, is a rock band. And they have been around at last since my childhood. They might have been around as long as the Rolling Stones. Now they've branched out into lunch boxes and cartoons. (Some laughter.) We were watching this cartoon and Alvin and the Chipmunks were in Germany. There was a little girl on the West German side of the wall crying because her brother was trapped on the East side. So Alvin and the Chipmunks said, "We'll help." They put on their disguises and went over to East Germany. But they were caught by the authorities so they took off their capes and glasses and other disguises and they started playing their music. And the wall came tumbling down. Now I was thinking, "Is this a good TV program?" You all know we think a lot about whether TV is good. Your parents and teachers don't like you watching too much TV, and they don't think some programs are any good. Well, they're right. I agree with them. So I was thinking about this program. I thought, it's good in one way because it shows a real life situation in Germany. But I thought it was bad because it was completely unrealistic. This would never happen. Now of course I read in the newspapers and I see on TV that it has come down. So I was wrong, and I need to laugh at myself. Laughing in the mirror is only one way, a silly way, to laugh at ourselves. But we shouldn't take ourselves too seriously. Dictators take themselves very seriously. What is a dictator?

(Students reply, "A communist", "Someone who comes to power by force.") Well, yes, he could be a communist. A dictator is someone who is not elected, but just takes over the country. Dictators put on these big suits with medals all over here [Mr Moore is not wearing a suit, but rather slacks, tie, and sweater.] They have given themselves the medals, and they never laugh at themselves. But all the dictators in the world are being over-thrown, which shows it cannot last for long. They need to not take themselves so seriously and laugh at themselves more. That's my idea for today.

The main focus here is character development. At St. Cathe-rine's, where achievement is so important, the Director of the Lower School perceives the need to cultivate humor. "Laughing at oneself" is a foil to overinvolvement with self that may arise out of an achievement emphasis. Mr Moore does not merely preach "do this," but attempts to show how wrong he had been in one instance (the Berlin wall did come tumbling down). The message is, we shouldn't take ourselves too seriously, because that is no way to live a full and enriched life, and that it is oppressive to always think you are right. To highlight this point, he uses the example of a dictator. Interestingly, the student's response that a dictator is a communist is a response that might be expected in a nation where communism is frequently por-trayed as the enemy.

Martin Luther King's Birthday. Today the minister is a woman minister from the Episcopal Church.

Rev. T: Good morning. I'm very happy to be here because I had two girls who went to this school. When I come into this room I feel happy because I used to come here and see them in plays and other things. This week is somebody's birthday. Do you know whose? (Some hands go up.) I can see you've been studying this. Yes.
S: Martin Luther King.
Rev. T: Martin Luther King was born at a time when black Americans had to eat in a separate restaurant and go to a separate movie theatre and ride on a separate part of the bus. Martin Luther King thought this wasn't right. But he didn't try to change things by forceful means. He used peaceful means to change the whole of America so that everyone would be treated equally. He gave his life for this cause. And we remember him also because he showed

us that if something is wrong you can change it through peaceful means.

(Reverend Taylor then selects children to act out a play that she narrates.)

Mrs. Rosa Parks, who is black, comes home very tired from work, and she sits down at the back of the bus. Now a white man got on and he said to Mrs. Parks, "You've got to give me your seat." And she said, "I'm too tired and I'm not moving." So then he got the policeman. (She selects a girl to play the part). Oh we have a policewoman today, not a policeman. And so she took Rosa Parks off to jail. Now Rosa Parks was Martin Luther King's friend, and he and their other friends got her out of jail and decided this wasn't very fair. So they said, "We won't travel on buses any more until you speak to us respectfully, and until you allow us to sit anywhere we want, and you employ some black bus drivers." For a full year they refused to travel on buses. They walked to work.

S: Why didn't they drive?

Rev T: They didn't have cars. And eventually they won the right to travel on the buses sitting anywhere they pleased, and with black bus drivers. Most importantly, we remember Martin Luther King because he changed America through peaceful means.

[African-American songs were then sung: "We shall overcome" and "Lift Up Every Voice and Sing" (African-American national anthem), followed by a chant performed by the kindergarteners: "Mar-tin Luther King, Mar-tin Lu-ther King, Peace. Love. Brotherhood." The chant was accompanied by clapping and finger clicking and the stamping of feet.]

The Civil Rights message given during the week of Martin Luther King's birthday combined a religious intent with a social ethical purpose. Significantly, Reverend Kathryn Taylor is an ordained minister in the Episcopal church, thus symbolizing the church's movement towards correcting gender and other inequalities. Her story about Mrs. Rosa Parks was aimed at showing the injustice of American society in pre-civil-rights days, and the work that Martin Luther King did in an attempt to remedy social injustices. Black and white children acted out the parts, with a girl playing the role of police officer. Reverend Taylor stressed that social change should come about through peaceful means, a point further reiterated by the kindergarteners' chant "Peace. Love. Brotherhood." The message was one of peace, and an attitude of social responsibility and care.

Valentine's Day. Mr. Miles, a Methodist minister and an African-American, smiles at the chapel congregation. He gives out to teachers and students many craft items that he has made himself, a tote bag "made from the legs of my son's jeans"; a teddy bear; two wooden chopping boards and some apple jelly he has made himself. He says "These are my talents. They're gifts that I have; the ability to do these things." Then he reads a lesson from the New Testament, the lesson about the person who had five talents and multiplied them five times, the person who had two talents and multiplied them two times, and the person who had one talent who just buried his in a "dark hole." "The lesson is, whatever your talents are, use them and share them with the world, don't bury them in a dark hole."

Also at this service Mr Moore tells the students that the school has adopted a whale called White Moon. He shows photographs of the whale and tells the children he lives off the coast of Maine during the summer. Happy Valentine's Day greetings are also exchanged. Most of the women teachers are wearing red dresses with other Valentine-type decorations, such as silver heart earrings. Students are also dressed up in formal red dresses or shirts, many of them with valentine motifs.

Christian giving, charity, and love are again emphasized in the Valentine's Day chapel. The minister is a black American, and in a symbolic inversion of American society he gives out gifts to students and teachers in the school. Black Americans have not been able, by and large, to reap the gifts of American society, but here is a black man giving away his gifts to a school with a student body that is predominantly white and materially gifted. The symbols of personal cost—"these were made from the legs of my son's jeans," and investment—"these are my talents," are used to teach a lesson of charity and generosity, as well as the virtue of hard work. The biblical example of the person who buried his talent while others multiplied them is intended to encourage students to develop their own individual talents and to use them for the social good. The adoption of White Moon, the whale, is yet another symbolic act of the attitude of personal and social responsibility. Through all these means students are being offered membership to the "community" of St. Catherine's and a set of traditional values intended to support, not only the school, but its place in the wider society and nation.

Noah, the Individual. Reverend Holloway, a Presbyterian minister, conducts the service. He is a large man with a kindly, grandfatherly manner.

Rev. H: Let's imagine you go home after school. You get changed and go outside to play and you see a man out in his yard building something. Well you know this man and so you go and ask him what he's doing and he says he's building a boat. You think that's O.K., but how is he going to get it to the ocean, because by now it's about the size of half a football field? And he says, "Don't worry. It will rain." But the weather forecaster doesn't predict rain for ages, and so you think he's crazy. He keeps building the boat, and pretty soon it's finished. Does anyone know who this man was?
(Many children call out "Noah")
Yes, Noah. Then the moving vans pulled up and unloaded bales of hay and lots of feed into the bottom of the boat, and people still thought he was crazy. But it did start to rain. And Noah didn't say this, but he thought, Now who's crazy? He loaded up two of every kind of animal you could imagine. Kangaroos. Everything. Because what had happened was that the world had become such a wicked place that God needed to start over. He made provision though, for Noah and his family and two of all the animals to be saved. Now people thought Noah was crazy, but he was really doing something very important. It's the same thing when you have your own individual talents and skills which you are trying to develop, and others think you are crazy or pick on you for not being like them. What if Mozart hadn't kept writing music? The others all said to him, "Why aren't you like us?" What if Diana Ross hadn't done all that singing with the church choir? The others said to her, "Come and play with us." What if Abraham Lincoln hadn't done all that reading? The others said, "Why not just play soccer and not read?" What if Jesus hadn't been a dreamer and doing all that praying? They were each following their individual talents and developing them. And that's what you should do.

Once again a biblical example, this time the story of Noah building the ark, is used to demonstrate the importance of following God and developing one's own individual "self," gifts and abilities. The minister argues that Noah did not blindly following others, and he brings in modern day people, Abraham

Lincoln, Mozart, and Diana Ross, to add weight to the argument. The service ended with the singing of "America the Beautiful," signifying patriotism, and the school song, signifying school spirit.

CHAPEL THEMES

Chapel has been shown to be about nurturing the spiritual growth of students. It reinforces the religious life of the school and is an integral part of the school. A number of structural properties of the ritual contribute towards its effectiveness as a culturally validating event.

It is significant that everyone in the school goes to chapel from kindergarten to Grade 12. The mandatory nature of chapel attendance applies even for the Jewish students, who have had to "come to terms with it" (Interview, Director of the Lower School). Chapel thus has an important status. It is held in prime school time, first period in the morning on the middle day of the school week. That chapel has been in existence since 1910 in the original Episcopal school also adds a feeling of tradition and constancy to the ritual. Spatially, too, students are located in a key area, a public place, which is the school auditorium. Attention is then focused on the central space in the room, the position of the altar. The minister leading chapel, as the purveyor of God's word, stands in front of the altar. To give the sermon from another position would not have the same effect.

The quietness of chapel, its removal from the hustle and bustle of the everyday secular world, is also important. Students know that chapel time is "quiet time," a time for reflection and prayer. While the auditorium is also used for other purposes, such as dramatic performances and school assemblies, the rules that make chapel unique have been established and accepted. How one behaves during drama lessons in the auditorium is not the same as for chapel. Despite the reflective emphasis of chapel services, they demand students' attention, and are well organized and divided into distinct segments. Chapel time is what McLaren (1986, p. 197) and Hall (1973, 1984) refer to as *monochromatic time*. In monochromatic time the emphasis is on schedules, segmentation, and promptness. To be late for chapel

would be a violation of implicit chapel rules. Monochromatic
time is also that of traditional classroom lessons and contrasts
with *polychromatic time*, which is how one is in a state of play
or "street-corner state" where events are loosely structured. In
the "street-corner state" there is much interpersonal involvement and a whole range of things happening at once. The
children in the corridors coming to chapel, if not too closely
supervised by the teacher, are in polychromatic time. Once
inside the auditorium, however, students transfer to a new
thinking register where focusing on the service is all important.

The chapel service also has a symmetry. The beginning and
ending are a mirror image of each other, giving centrality to the
homily or sermon, which is the climax. All else is to underscore
the significance of the moral message. Sometimes what is said in
the sermon is supported by readings from the bible. At other
times the connection is symbolic. The pattern or rhythm of the
liturgy is only ever slightly varied, its standard form being:

1. Candle is lit by the altar boy/girl (if necessary, the
   minister calls for the candle lighter to come forward).
2. Music; school enters
3. Welcome, secular announcements
4. Religious ceremony begins: Invocation (opening prayer)
   Leader: Lord, open our lips.
   Response: And our mouth shall proclaim your praise.
   Leader: The earth is the Lord's, for he made it.
   Response: Come let us worship him.
   Leader: Let us pray.
5. The Lord's Prayer
6. Hymn or song (All)
7. THE HOMILY
6. Birthday blessing
   Leader: Would anyone who has a birthday this week
   please stand for a birthday prayer. Let us pray.
   "Look with favor, we pray, on your children as they
   begin another year. Grant that they grow in wisdom and
   grace and strengthen their trust in your goodness all the
   days of their lives. Through Jesus Christ our Lord.
   Amen."
5. Hymn or song (All)

4. Religious ceremony ends: Benediction of minister's choice, or
   "The grace of our Lord Jesus Christ, the love of God, and the fellowship of the Holy Ghost, be with us all evermore. Amen."
3. Closing remarks, secular announcements
2. Music; school exits
1. Candle is extinguished by the altar boy/girl after being motioned toward the altar by the minister.

The sermon is the high point and framed by the other parts of the service. Its central role is emphasized. The repetitive structure allows for poetic moments. The theme of the sermon may be echoed in the hymns and prayer that are its precedents or antecedents. It is intended that participants are personally involved and moved by the sermon.

The explicit content of the sermons focuses on the themes of Christian giving, charity, and love, as well as on personal development, having a sense of humor, caring for others, using one's skills and talents for the betterment of humanity, and in the "glory of God." The services have some secular messages, for example, Valentine's Day, and are attuned to the values of the prosperous middle class, but also attempt to maintain traditional religious character. Moreover, the values of Christianity are of a traditional flavor, not the born-again Christian kind. No overt proselytizing takes place. Rather, a commitment to traditional Christian values underpins chapel and the school.

CONCLUSIONS

The rituals of a particular school, its *ritual literacy*, give it its power and *poetic wisdom* (Kapferer, 1981; McLaren, 1986, p. 235). Such poetry and its underpinning values can differ dramatically. Even the "same" ritual, for example, Advent, signifies something quite different at Waldorf School and at St. Catherine's. The mechanical performance of the ritual as well as its meaning differ. At Waldorf School the use of tree stumps, candles, and apples is symbolic of a search for God in nature and humankind's location within nature. At St. Catherine's, in contrast, Advent is more conventionally celebrated in the manner of the Episcopal church, where God is "above" nature: "the earth is the Lord's for he made it." Advent, as preparation for Christmas, is marked by the lighting of the Advent wreath and a special liturgy. Waldorf School's ritual is an *organic ritual;* St. Catherine's ritual is a traditional Christian and *rational ritual.* By *rational* is meant the acceptance of tradition and conventional norms and ways of doing things. The Episcopal Church and a prep school tradition have been alive for centuries, constantly adapting to modern changes, but basically supporting and reinforcing a social order that is rational and instrumental in orientation, one where purposeful action and freedom to choose guides decision making. Bredo points out that schools typically adopt a rationalistic culture.

> Recently, John Meyer called for use of religious and ritualistic explanatory imagery in the sociology of education. "(Instead of) the assumption that the technical knowledge and socialization of the educational system has any real substance, one sees the system as analogous to a religious celebration of rationalistic mode values . . . a ritual of rationality" (Meyer, 1986). Adopting this imagery Meyer and Rowan saw schools as building their structures in ways that fit the *prevailing rationalistic culture of our society, and, indeed, the world.* School structures with their instrumental forms . . . then become rituals for the display of instrumental-rational values, conforming to rationalistic myths. (Bredo, 1990, p. 7)

Clearly, however, not all school structures have instrumental forms and not all embody instrumental–rational values. The case of Waldorf School is an example of a school where an organic metaphor, not a rational one, prevails. The values being promoted by St. Catherine's are like those found in business and the professions. The rituals of Waldorf School, on the other hand, are those of an extended family which holds alternative ideas to mainsteam society with its economic base of business interests. The purpose of business and the professions is to organize and manipulate the world for both personal and collective gain. Businesses typically thrive on the principles of efficiency and organization as well as caring for those within the bounds of the institution and its clientele, and hopefully distributing wealth in the form of charity to others outside the institution. The emphasis of the Waldorf school community, in contrast, as demonstrated through ritual, is to educate students towards a particular worldview, one that holds "spirituality" and harmony with the world to be paramount.

Rituals thus support culture by making the school's meaning or interpretation of events seem natural. Rituals are used for control, as a medium for reflection, to establish harmony and order, or to instruct.

Rituals for Control. Rituals are carriers of *cultural codes.* People's ways of thinking and acting, their cognition and their gestures, are guided by cultural norms. Rituals socialize students into the prevailing school order (Kapferer, 1981; McLaren, 1986, p. 3). The school's hegemonic or mystificatory role is thus raised as an important issue. We are led to question the school's motives, and are cautioned against naively accepting rituals as a positive phenomenon. While promoting harmony rituals might also be exploiting and manipulating people into accepting dominant norms, even ill-conceived norms. Giroux, for instance, sees school culture as an expression of the dominant mainstream culture through such means as revitalization and intensification rituals. He views mainstream culture as characterized by injustice and manipulation: "School culture is really a battleground on which meanings are defined, knowledge is legitimated, and futures are sometimes created and destroyed. It is a place of ideological and cultural struggle favored primarily to benefit the wealthy, males and whites" (Giroux, 1984, p. 133).

The two cases examined here have quite different purposes, but we might also critique the morality of their "missionary" activities carried out through ritual. Waldorf School and St. Catherine's are engaged in generating particular cultural belief systems with different perceptions of the world, different relationships to others, and different views of the individual or self. Other schools generate their own responses to these problems. What is the "right" answer? Of course, it depends on one's purposes, and St. Catherine's and Waldorf School have defined themselves differently. It is helpful, however, to remember that the potential is always there for schools to step over the limits of presenting a worldview and begin indoctrinating. As Lisman (1990, p. 2) points out, the educated person is one who has been "socialized to be a good person and support those institutions of society that enable us to obtain goodness, but at the same time, look with a critical eye at the institutions in which he or she is engaged." This is a timely lesson for all educators.

Rituals for Reflection.   Chapel at St. Catherine's and the many daily rituals at Waldorf School provide reflective time, an opportunity for time out from the business of classroom instruction. The characteristic bustle of school life leaves little time for reflection by students on what they have learned or on their own feelings. Teachers, too, busy themselves preparing for the constant demands being made on them, and rarely take time out to think critically or reflectively. Administrators tend to have more discretionary time, but they are engaged in administrative tasks, to coordinate and direct others' efforts for the organization, and do not always take time to consider the school holistically. As Barr and Dreeben point out, schools are often like:

> switching yards where children within a given age range and from a designated geographical area are assigned to teachers who bring them into contact with approved learning materials, specified as being appropriate to age or ability, during certain allotted periods of time. (1983, p. 6)

Fixed time schedules and constraints, and teachers working in individual classrooms, teaching their specialized subjects, means that teachers are isolated from adult–adult contact for most of the school week. Many of the school rituals described here provide an opportunity for the whole school to come together for time out, a time for reflection and community. The cases given provide practical examples of rituals with distinct educational intentions and meanings for consideration by those looking to vitalize school spirit and enliven schools through ritual and ceremonial practice.

Rituals for Order.   Rituals may also be a way of achieving order and purposive engagement of students in an otherwise "crowded" situation (Jackson, 1968). Rituals have a stabilizing effect on the classroom, as we saw in the Waldorf School, where verses and prayers said between lessons served to effect a smooth transition and to establish order in the classroom. When students were saying the verses between lesson "the confusion and madness is toned down because they're saying that" (Interview, teacher). It is salutary, however, to exercise some caution with regard to rituals for order. Carried to extremes, we could envisage students becoming mindless automotons going through the motions of school life but never really being engaged. Constant routines might not only have a calming effect on the classroom, they might also dull the bright and lively interchanges and the impromptu social dynamics that make school unpredictable and fun.

Rituals of Instruction. Rituals are also used to socialize students into the way things are done in a school. Schools take people who are "less than fully socialized" (Lortie, 1975, p. 138) and teach them the norms, ideas, and values of the school and its community. A school's symbolic resources are used to nurture the child in a particular direction intellectually and spiritually. In both Waldorf School and St. Catherine's education means much more than merely instructing students in technical skills and a set body of knowledge. Their ideas on education differ, but they share an appreciation for education as much more than the mere transmission of knowledge. St. Catherine's cultural horizons include a great deal of attention to the competitive realm, as well as to advocating social responsibility and integrity. St. Catherine's teaches students how to achieve in a competitive and status conscious society. Work is rigorous, yet students here are privileged. They are, in Cookson and Persell's (1985) terms, "preparing for power," for taking on leadership roles. Waldorf School focuses instead on aesthetic forms, such as music, art, and eurythmy. The school sets out to teach students how to live an aesthetically enriching life in harmony with nature.

School rituals thus play a significant part in the social construction of reality. The school is able "tacitly to mediate the conceptual development of students" (McLaren, 1988, p. 121). Further, when viewed in concert with other cultural elements—

the history, myths, philosophy, curriculum, use of time, space, and social relationships—the potential of the school to create and sustain realities is powerful indeed. Like the air we breathe, school culture is everywhere present and not always evident until we begin to think about alternative ways of doing school. Waldorf School and St. Catherine's provide us with remarkable figure–ground comparisons. In the next and final chapter of analysis, we will further examine the schools' approaches to the use of time, space, and social relationships, highlighting their social and cultural meanings.

7

TIME, SPACE, AND SOCIAL RELATIONSHIPS

Time and space are often thought to be objective, knowable realities. People "spend" time, "make" time, "have" time, "carve out" time, and "waste" time. Space is also conceived as a thing to be used by people. But time and space have subjective and aesthetic dimensions. One school may "chop time and space into similar units" and "egg-crate corridors and class-rooms" (Page, 1991, p. 51). Another school may create a culture less punctuated by bells and timetables and with less clear spatial boundaries. Schools' use of time and space signifies particular social relationships and cultural values. The concepts authority, work, and teacher's role at St. Catherine's, for instance, mean something quite different from authority, work, and teacher's role at Waldorf School.

KAIROS TIME AND CHRONOS TIME

Anthropologists have made a distinction between *kairos*, or *organic time*, and a second conception, *chronos*, or *mechanical time*. The distinction stems back to the ancient Greeks. The organic conception of time is the time of "human history, seasons and weather" (Erickson, 1982a, p. 160). In contrast, mechanical or technical time, refers to the literal duration of time and is mechanically measurable (Erickson, 1982a, p. 160; Hall, 1973). The schools in this study create aspects of both kinds of time in their school cultures, but one or the other view predominates.

In Waldorf School the conception of time is cyclic. Main lesson is held for the first 2 hours every day, with the content of main lesson alternating every few weeks. No electric or mechanical bells punctuate the school day. Instead, the movement is slow, with an aim to integrate oneself with the environment. This kind of time is the time of nature and the "cosmos." It is an organic conception: "Early peoples used the cycle of recurring natural phenomena familiar to them in everyday life as a guide to the passing of time. The most obvious and precise of these phenomena were the alternation of night and day, the phases of the moon, the position of the stars and the changing of the seasons" (Massad, 1979, p. 4).

The school's view of child development is that of a slow cyclic rhythm of development or evolution:

> the concentration of consciousness which we call growing up is a living process, and like all living processes it takes place in rhythms. . . . Today we investigate so many details of childhood that we often do not see the forest for the trees. The pattern of life is lost in its details. (Harwood, 1977, p. 17)

Rhythmic 7-year periods in the life of the child govern the school's approach to teaching and learning. For instance, it is the child's body (with the loss of baby teeth) that indicates when it is time to learn to read.

St. Catherine's mainly embodies chronos time. In this school the prevailing ethos is one where time moves quickly, from past to present to future. People work constantly to "keep up with time," and to use it to change and master the environment. The day is divided into eight 40-minute periods marked by the ringing of electric bells, as in most schools today. The bells ring 17 times each day, when it is time to get ready for class, time for movement from class to class, and for recess and lunch. This view of time, as a linear progression, is one of the characteristics of the modern Western world. It is associated with the values of promptness and efficiency and doing things "on time" and according to an imposed structure. Waldorf School is asserting, in opposition, that its values and purposes are different and have to do with the location of humans within their natural environment.

The concept of time and its control in Waldorf School is one which gives way to human interaction. Time is important, even at Waldorf School, for Waldorf School is located in a larger American culture with a concern for progress and a brighter future. But time as a ruling principle is subordinated to human concerns. For example, the school's policy on decision making by faculty demonstrates a commitment to people over efficiency. Complete unity is considered desirable before a group acts. Parliamentary procedure, where everyone has the right to speak but is ultimately silenced through the one person, one vote principle, is not practiced. In faculty and board meetings if any individual does not agree with something that has been put forward, he or she has the power to completely hold up that decision. Power is conferred on the individual. However, the impracticality of the desire for perfect unity in all decisions has become clear, and in practice compromises are made. Because it is inconvenient for committees and individuals to put time and energy into a proposal only to have it rejected outright by a minority of one, there is a fair degree of social pressure on those who might disagree with any particular proposal to ''have a pretty good reason for disagreeing'' (Interview, teacher).

More than in any other school I have seen, however, teachers at Waldorf School have the right to a voice irrespective of the time cost involved. Teachers are in control.[1] They are informed, because they are joint administrators as well as teachers, and more often than not, parents, too. Thus, the load for teachers is not light. When a school does not make time efficiency a priority, ironically the demands on teachers increase. After a full day's teaching teachers are expected to attend lengthy meetings: for the whole school faculty 1 day a week, core faculty meetings on another day, committee meetings, board meetings and the anthroposophical study group meetings. At these meetings the

---

[1]When the first Waldorf school, the Freie Waldorfschule, opened in Stuttgart in September 1919, it was from its inception a faculty-run school with Rudolf Steiner as advisor.

efficiency/achievement drive so prevalent in modern societies ("life in the fast lane") is subjugated to a more considered and reflexive use of time, one which places a high value on human concerns as can be seen in the following example.

Waldorf School Faculty Meeting.   It is 3:45 p.m. The children get out of school at 2:45 p.m., but by the time they hike down the hill to the pick-up point and are collected by their parents, it is usually around 3:15 p.m. Teachers have since come back up to the cabins, and are now in the "office," a small room adjacent to a classroom. It is a cosy room decorated with children's paintings and craft items. Kindergarten and nursery teachers have driven out from town, a distance of five miles on a winding country road, to be here. Fifteen women teachers, one male teacher, and myself are present. People stand around the table fixing tea and chatting. The room is quite crowded. We each find a chair and place it in a circle formation. Everyone stands. We hold hands, saying the verse that we always say at anthroposophy meetings:

In the free human being
The Universe gathers itself together
Then in the free resolve of your heart
Take yourself in hand
And you will find the world
The spirit of the world
Will come to be
Through you.

For the next hour we sing. The music teacher, who is also a parent, leads the group in singing, in preparation for the forthcoming Festival of Lights, when the teachers will present a choral item. At other times teachers sing for the sheer joy of it, without a conscious purpose. One of the songs is a local folk song, another is about the bitter winter, "In the Harsh Cold of the Morning." The singing is exceptional, including singing in three parts. Miss King, the music teacher, uses her recorder to give the pitch. At first Mr Lopata, the only male teacher in the group, was speaking on the telephone in the corner of the room, while the women sat in the circle singing. But he now joins in also. "Oh good, terrific. We're finally getting it together," says Miss King. Every now and again a child runs into the room seeking mother's solace, then leaves happily to play outside again. At the conclusion of the singing a supper of apple cake, cinnamon slice, crackers, and cheese is shared. The remainder of the meeting is devoted to business items, including a discussion of the budget, a Board Faculty retreat,[2] the possibility of a third kindergarten for next year, and a forthcoming open house. The meeting concludes around 6:30 p.m.

Two concerns in the school, democracy, on the one hand (everybody having a voice), and getting things done (the time element), create some tension. The faculty sing together in an attempt to establish group bonding, but a time limit is placed on this. There is an agenda. In addition, when the structure of the school is one of teacher power and equality amongst faculty it is sometimes difficult to make decisions. One teacher explains:

> the problem with a democratic faculty is that sometimes in these faculty meetings something needs to be said to someone and there is no-one with the authority to do that. You have to work together and not set yourself up above others and so it's difficult. If everybody's voice is equal and valid then everyone has an opinion and these meetings run on for hours. So we had to set limits on what is reasonable. (Interview, teacher)

Though the ideal has been constrained, neither the faculty meetings nor any other aspect of school life is ruled by time concerns.

The meeting is like a family ritual, with a pattern of greetings, verse/prayer, song, supper, business, closing, and farewells. Teachers do not place their children in child minding while they attend faculty meetings. Instead, children play outside, the older

---

[2]The Board of Directors is comprised of teachers, parents, and community members. On the board are 11 women and 1 man. The Board's role is officially that of "sounding board" for certain faculty decisions, but the faculty tends to view Board meetings as a chance to inform board members of decisions and events rather than to seek approval. The Board selects new members to serve a 2-year term from those who express an interest in serving the school. At the same time, however, parents and teachers work co-operatively. What unites them is their commitment to Steiner's methods of educating.

ones supervising the younger children. Children are permitted to interrupt the meeting because this is a family oriented school where everyone contributes to a common welfare. The business agenda is important, but the social event is the focal point of the meetings. If the emotional cohesiveness and strength of the group is in order, according to the school's line of argument, all else will fall into place.

St. Catherine's Faculty Meeting. We meet in one of the kindergarten rooms after school. Teachers take turns hosting a faculty meeting in their classroom, giving the faculty a chance to see others' work. The host teacher, Victoria Wilson, provides the introductory session by giving us a "talking tour" of her classroom. It is a large room packed with what looks like wonderful things for kindergarteners to do. At one end of the room is a pigeon, Gatsby, in a cage. He was found wounded on the road by one of the teachers, and the kindergarteners, with the help of a veterinarian, nursed him back to health. A Stamping Center, Lego Center, Art Center, masses of bookshelves, a table with dinosaur fossils on it, Storybook Village, and Blocks Center provide color and interest in the room. A large American flag hangs above the chalkboard, with an alphabet mural and a huge computer printout of numbers on the same wall. The children have been learning their numbers, and one of the activities has been to count how many days are left in the school year. The printout shows that we are 100 days into the school year. The story book area is carpeted, while the rest of the classroom is tiled with linoleum. A bathroom adjoins the classroom. We sit at two large tables which would normally provide seating for twenty kindergarteners.

Most of the faculty are women (23), and there are 4 men, including the male director. When Victoria has finished her "talking tour," faculty ask questions. Mr Moore, the Director of the Lower School, then gives a report on a recent conference he has attended in New York. He sets up a makeshift podium from cardboard boxes that are in the room, placing them one on top of the other. He talks about the fifth annual conference of the "Elementary School Center." The theme of the conference was "Children in a World at Risk: Joining Forces for Advocacy," which drew on work of the U.N. Convention on the Rights of the

Child. The plea at the conference was a heart-wrenching one, and Mr. Moore is firm in his support for the ideal. He displays a book he has purchased which sets out the kinds of things that the group is fighting for, such as protection of children by enforcement of minimal age employment conditions, protection against exploitation in employment, protection of children from parental abuse, and improving children's standard of living.[3] The faculty comment: "Of course it's wrong; the U.S. has the money, it's just a matter of priorities. No child should suffer. But the money is going to things like Star Wars and other defence initiatives." "What are the implications? How would this be implemented?" asked another teacher. "Well, it happens right here in South County, you know, you don't have to go to New York to see this." "It sounds a bit socialistic to me. I don't like the idea of more regulatory legislation. Big Brother is already very present in our lives." "What about the issue of cultural sensitivity?" said Mr. Jackson, "The Amish, for instance, rely on child labor. It's part of their way of life. I don't hear that in the argument." "You'd be better to spread the word to the parents. They're the ones with the money to do something about it," argued Mrs. Page. The conference report ends on a note of interest and questioning.

"Midterms are due February 26th, so mark that on your calendars," said Mr Moore. Discussion then centers around what teachers would like the parents' auxiliary to purchase. Suggestions include a computer, movie screen, furniture, VCR, curtains, or cafeteria tables. Another item on the agenda is the problem of the movement of children from one play area to another. (There are three play areas in the school.) One of the teachers leaves for another appointment; another is talking on a cordless telephone she has produced from her handbag. Mrs. Cohen sits grading students' test papers.

The upcoming parents' night is announced. An agenda for the evening is given by Mr Moore and commented on by the teachers. Mr Moore says that he will talk to parents about study habits, different ways children learn, parents' role in homework,

---

[3]The book displayed: Castelle, Kay. (1989). *In the child's best interest: A primer on the U.N. Convention on the rights of the child*. New York: Foster Parents Plan International, Inc.

and attitudes to homework. The fifth grade teachers say they hope to use the occasion to inform parents about some of the forthcoming spring events for fifth graders. Details of the evening are discussed. Finally, preliminary ideas for the next faculty meeting are announced by Mr. Moore, and he closes the meeting at 4:50 p.m.

In this meeting we see a concern for time and its control blended with a concern for democracy. However, the school leans more towards the control and efficiency end of the spectrum. At St. Catherine's faculty meetings, in contrast to those at Waldorf School, there is one leader, the Director of the school, and while every participant is free to voice an opinion, the agenda is more closely followed. Mr Moore directs the group's attention to the task at hand and defers what he deems as irrelevant items to a future date. Time is not "wasted." The faculty is busy. Someone makes a telephone call during the meeting. Someone else leaves to go to another appointment. Another teacher grades test papers while the meeting is in progress. And yet the Director, with his kindly yet efficient manner, strives to allow space for fruitful discussion amid all the time pressures.

We also see that the concerns of the school center around keeping parents in touch and helping them to help their children to do better at school. The proposed pep talk to parents on how to help with homework is one of the ways the school does this. A concern with achievement is not peculiar to St. Catherine's:

> Jean Piaget complained that Americans nearly always asked him the same question about his work: How can children be accelerated through your stages of cognitive development? (Fitzgerald & Brackbill, 1976). Piaget called this, sarcastically, "the American question." (Tobin, Wu, & Davidson, 1989, p. 173)

Nevertheless, as we have seen, the idea of achievement differs between the two American schools studied. Achievement at Waldorf School is more like a journey towards self-expression and holistic personal growth. Achievement at St. Catherine's is one of structured acceleration towards the goal of a high-quality education and entry to the best colleges and universities.

Also noteworthy about the faculty meeting is the difference

between the two presentations that are given. All the teachers are seated around the students' low tables and on kindergarteners' chairs. Mr Moore stands at his "podium" to give his address and to lead the discussion, whereas Miss Wilson simply stands and moves as she talks, pointing out features in the room. Controlling the timing of the meeting is also the privilege of Mr Moore, giving him power over the teachers, whereas at Waldorf School all the faculty are equal and the decision to close the meeting is a group decision.

School Time, Work, and Play. The schools have different expectations about the number of hours that students are required to be at "work." St. Catherine's and Waldorf School years begin on September 5 and 6, respectively, and end on June 1. However, between these beginning and ending points the schools have devised different calendars. St. Catherine's takes a 2-week break at Christmas and a week's vacation in March for spring break. Overall, St. Catherine's is in session for 180 days, the same as public schools. Waldorf School begins September 6, has a 2-day holiday for Thanksgiving, 2-weeks at Christmas, a day for Martin Luther King Day (January 15), 2-days for Presidents' Day (February 19 and 20), and 1 for Memorial Day (May 28th). In addition, the school has a 9-day Spring Break, which includes Easter (April 13–22). Waldorf School is thus in session for 167 days, 13 days fewer than St. Catherine's.

The length of the school day also varies. At Waldorf grade school each school day starts at 9:00 a.m. and ends at 2:45 p.m. At St. Catherine's students are in school from 8:20 a.m. until 3:00 p.m., 55 minutes extra each day. The difference in time spent in school amounts to an additional 153 hours per year that St. Catherine's students spend in school (for example, 23 St. Catherine's length days, or 27 Waldorf School length days). Then there are the 13 more days St. Catherine's students already spend in school, equalling a total of 36 extra (St. Catherine's length) days in school. If we consider the time that Waldorf School students spend walking the trail to school as P.E., because it serves a fitness function quite well (and is necessary, since P.E. is underrepresented in the curriculum) and consider also the time St. Catherine's students spend moving from class to class, some of this time difference falls away. However, we also need to take into account that St. Catherine's school time is spent on an achievement-oriented academic curriculum, and Waldorf School time is spent on a holistic curriculum (spiritually and aesthetically enriching and not driven by test scores). The overall picture of life in the two schools and their use of time is thus profoundly different.

At St. Catherine's, with subject specialization, tasks are broken into discrete units and to be completed in specific time periods. Reading, for instance, is taught during Reading from a specialized teacher. *Reading* comes to be seen as a task done at specific times. Because children physically leave their classrooms at least three times a day to go to other buildings or rooms, clear transitions between lessons occur. At Waldorf School children only leave the classroom for play time outside. The children, then, are more dependent on and connected with the teacher and the class. And the Waldorf School day is integrated, with the lines between subjects blurred.

However, both schools separate *work* and *play, schooltime* and *free time.* McLaren (1986) calls this distinction a ritual separation of free time or "street-corner state" and school time or "student state." Even at Waldorf School, which has a strong overlap of school and home, the distinction is clearly made between work and play. The following interchange occurred in a German class in the third grade:

> **T:** The German children typically go to school, and I'm going to ask you if this is a good deal or not, typically go to school until 12 o'clock, noon.
> **B:** That's not fair.
> **T:** They go to school at 8 o'clock in the morning then go home at noon to eat a big lunch, the major meal of the day. But they make up the extra time through a lot of homework in the afternoon. And they also go to school on Saturday.
> **B:** Well, it is fair. I wouldn't want to go to school on Saturday.

Waldorf School and St. Catherine's would seem to reinforce the idea of freedom and play versus work and school. Rohlen expresses the American ideal in comparison with the Japanese:

> As youth, Americans have some opportunity to live out a bit of the Tom Sawyer dream, even as they work at a Summer job, but urban

Japanese grow up harnessed both to study and to a single organization. No dream of ultimate innocence and freedom is given
credence by the [Japanese] school calendar. (Rohlen, 1983, p. 161)

The Tom Sawyer ideal may not be a strong part of school life
for achievement-oriented St. Catherine's, but students nevertheless hold dearly to the idea of summer holidays (as opposed to
the Japanese unification of work and play in a singe goal focus.)
However, both schools use time for their own ends, and a Tom
Sawyer level of adventurousness is for play time, not school
time. At Waldorf School, where "nothing is arbitrary" (Interview, teacher), the child who would imitate Tom Sawyer might
find his freedom somewhat constrained. And at St. Catherine's
time is highly task oriented, and school time carries over into
home time, with demanding levels of homework and the pressure of testing and evaluations. While testing and grading does
not drive Waldorf School's use of time, nevertheless, school
time is also carefully structured so as to highlight and promote
school objectives.

"HARD" SPACE AND "SOFT" SPACE

Spatial relations established in schools also implicitly teach
students about their place in the material and physical world.
Waldorf School grade school students are located in quaint
cabins in the woods. St. Catherine's is also on the edge of town,
but its setting is quite different. Rather than a country road, a
tree lined avenue leads up to the school, which is in an area also
populated by exclusive country clubs and old Southern mansions. Waldorf School's setting is suggestive of country life, and
as one critic put it "backwardness" (Interview, ex-parent), while
St. Catherine's setting is suggestive of wealth and prestige.

Waldorf School buildings are on two sites separated by a
distance of five miles. The kindergartens and nursery school are
in rented rooms in an Episcopal church hall in the township
itself and adjacent to the university. The grade school is in
rented buildings in the woods five miles out of town. The road
is treacherous for the last two miles, particularly in icy or wet
weather, as it is quite narrow. The practice is for parents to

car-pool their children to the pick-up point at the bottom of the hill, then teachers hike with the children to the cabins (a distance of about half a mile). A similar procedure occurs at the end of the school day. Teachers say they love the area, but there are difficulties involved and the image for the school is a little too rustic for some: "we need a classier act" (Interview, teacher). Also, the distance of the grade school from the township and its location in a position of isolation (one cannot see any evidence of human existence in the surrounding landscape, only mountains) increases the mystique of the school. No buses or any other form of public transport comes anywhere near the school. Spatially the school is set apart from Southville itself. It is readily accessible only to a community of insiders.

The immediate experience students have on arrival at the grade school is one of unbounded space. Heavily wooded hills are all around, a spectacular sight during fall with the turning of the leaves, and equally as magnificent when the branches of the trees are laden with snow. The lake sparkles in the sunlight and turns into a solid frozen block in the dead of winter. Horses and foals graze in nearby paddocks. Yet children cannot roam free to explore the wilderness, for during "school time," the school must exercise caution in the amount of space it allows students. They are carefully shepherded, under the watchful eye of two or three teachers, during the walk up the hill. Before that, while at the pick-up point, students must wait in a designated area. "Do not go over there," says the teacher. "Wait here." Once students arrive at the "school village" there are no fences to designate boundaries. Nevertheless, students know clearly where the out-of-bounds areas lie. Students play on the grassy knoll in the central area before school, and at lunchtime. During inclement weather a large shelter without walls, the "pavilion," provides protection from the rain.

St. Catherine's students are also located in spaciousness, and in this case most of what the eye can see is owned by the school. The Lower School has a separate campus to the Middle and Upper School, and together they comprise some 63 acres of highly valued property. Rolling playing fields, the headmaster's residence, and a pretty, wooded area surround the school. During P.E. lessons students are able to go bicycling or jogging and never leave St. Catherine's property.

Architecturally, the schools also provide a point of contrast between what is called *hard* and *soft* architecture. Rohlen (1983) describes *hard* and *soft* architecture as reflecting cultural differences. He uses the example of the use of space in school architecture in Japan and the U.S.:

> Our school architects would in fact like to create buildings with dimensions that encourage a sense of freedom and pastoral beauty. Robert Sommer (1974), one of the most articulate and persuasive, condemns our typical schools as "hard" and "tight," qualities that dehumanize. What he might say of Japanese schools, which are tighter and harder, remains to be seen, but clearly the Japanese see Spartan training as "humanizing," and Japanese classrooms as places where much group socializing does occur. Sommer's assumption that human qualities grow best in soft, open spaces is, if not uniquely American, nevertheless only one of many views on the subject. (1983, p. 152)

"Anthroposophically correct" buildings have distinct architectural features that suggest the softness to which Sommer refers. Waldorf schools in the U.S. that have been built in this style are a close replica of the buildings in Germany (where the anthroposophical movement was founded). Such architecture lacks symmetry and hard right angles. The buildings are circular, although not a regular circle, rather "organic" and somewhat asymmetrical, similar to Steiner's Goetheanum in style. Accordingly, no garish or artificial tones are used. Instead, earthy colors, browns, rust tones, greens and beiges, subtly shade the external walls of the buildings to blend in with a natural landscape.

Since Waldorf School is in rented buildings it sets out to simulate an anthroposophically correct style by rounding the hard corners of the rooms with muslin curtains and painting the rooms in soft, warm colors. The kindergarten rooms have had their corners made "soft," and soft things are inside the classroom: a fleece in a basket, cotton dolls, nature gardens, and so on. As the children mature and their teeth and bones harden, the classrooms are designed to become more "hard." Rounded corners and many natural things in the classroom are considered no longer necessary. The classroom becomes a more spartan environment. The progression in the school's use of space from soft to harder in the older grades is reflective of the school's developmental view of learning.

Waldorf School classrooms are in separate wooden buildings (two grades per cabin), each with its own bathroom and porch. Separate grade buildings have had the effect of promoting insularity of classrooms, even though the school's ideal is to have a more connected building. Separateness is not something that is part of Waldorf philosophy. The ideal would be to have a school built in a circular design with interconnecting hallways and enclosures, rather than separation of parts. At Waldorf School, however, finances are in short supply and rented buildings place limitations on the realization of their philosophy.

Despite the separation of the classrooms, though, feelings of association and community are strong. The layout of the buildings is semicircular, with the lower grades on the low ground and the higher grades on the high ground. Whether by design or fiat (the school did not build the cabins, but their rustic charm did appeal), the arrangement is reminiscent of the spatial arrangment of so-called "primitive villages" with the customary circle formation and elevation connoting higher status.

All classes at the grade school are also exposed to both the softness and the hardness of nature. With the change of seasons students directly experience Nature, for the electric heaters in classrooms are unable to provide enough heat unless the rooms are kept closed, which then creates the problem of a lack of proper ventilation. In the hotter months open windows and doors are the only defense against the heat. Another problem of living in bucolic splendor on a mountain is that of plumbing. Pipes freeze and burst, leaving teachers to fetch and carry buckets of water for bathroom and drinking needs. Students are thus intentionally or unintentionally close to Nature, learning about its harshness, as well as the beauty, and they are learning what the simple life is like. No classrooms are air conditioned. There is no lavish principal's office or gym facilities, such as one finds at St. Catherine's. Instead, everyone has to work together in a somewhat spartan situation.

In contrast, St. Catherine's school architecture is well designed and schoollike, although not ostentatious. Here, once again, we see a blend of "hard" and "soft." The buildings are solid, brick constructions, elegant in design, large, and interconnected. Wide hallways and bright windows looking out onto playing fields and wooded parklands add to the feeling of spaciousness and exclusivity. The Lower School is made up of a preschool and kindergarten wing, principal's office, library, teacher's room, specialty rooms, such as computer, art, and drama rooms, dance studio, auditorium, cafeteria, gymnasium, and classrooms. The modern brick buildings are well equipped with the most up-to-date science, athletic, and other equipment. Implicitly, the high-quality facilities teach students that they are among the privileged. Even if they remain in an insular environment and somehow fail to recognize that not all schools are so well equipped, the norm of ample provision has been established. Students are in spacious surroundings and provided with quality resources. Students have a science laboratory with microscopes and other equipment, a large, up-to-date library, and a modern computer room. Lunch is not eaten in the classroom, as it is at Waldorf School, but in the lunch room. Art is in the art room, dance in the Dance studio, and so on. The physical environment reflects the school's belief in specialization and provides optimum conditions for teaching and learning in that mode.

It would be simplistic to say Waldorf School uses soft architecture (open spaces, circles) and St. Catherine's hard architecture (bricks, angular rooms with hard corners), although there is some difference in this regard. Both schools incorporate elements of hard and soft, but Waldorf School is more towards the soft end of the spectrum and St. Catherine's is more oriented towards hard architectural design. The schools' use of time (kairos/chronos) and space (hard/soft) then carries over into other domains of school life, including the social relationships that are so critical—between parent and teacher, administrators and teachers, and most importantly, between teachers and students.

PERSONAL AND PROFESSIONAL SOCIAL RELATIONSHIPS

Social relationships are signified in the way time and space are constructed in schools. For instance, from their first day in grade

school children in Waldorf School have made a commitment for
the next 8 years of their lives. They are wedded to a particular
teacher. The teacher moves up each grade with the children
until they reach high school, then the cycle is repeated, the
teacher returning to first grade to accept a new group of
students. (The practice is in its third year of operation at Waldorf
School.) The idea of having the same teacher for an extended
period of time is a departure from normal school practices.
Parsons (1959) points out that one of the lessons students usually
learn at school through changing teachers every year is the norm
of universalism. The teacher is just one of many who could fulfil
that role. He argues that children in elementary school change
teachers every year to grow:

> accustomed to the fact that teachers are, unlike mothers, "inter-
> changeable" in a certain sense. The school year is long enough to
> form an important relationship to a particular teacher, but not
> long enough for a highly particularistic attachment to crystallize.
> More than in the parent-child relationship, in school the child
> must internalize his relation to the teacher's role rather than her
> particular personality; this is a major step in the internalization of
> universalistic patterns.

However, Waldorf School professes to teach freedom, not the
dependence that is generally seen to come from particularism.
Here we see the concepts of universalism or particularism
breaking down. Waldorf School believes that the best way to
teach universal principles is through the particular. A teacher
who is personal and more like a parent is held to be best
equipped to guide the student through the various stages of
development. The school teaches students that they belong to
categories (third graders, sixth graders, and so on,) and this is
part of universalistic training. Yet the "family" structure of the
school, such as teachers staying with classes for 8 years, close
relations with families, and so on, could also be seen as teaching
in-group or particularistic norms. That the community is somewhat bounded, an anthroposophists' enclave, is further evidence of particularism. (On universalism vs. particularism, see
Dreeben, 1968.)

At St. Catherine's the idea of interchangeable teachers is a central tenet. While some of the teachers have been at the school for a long period of time, there is no sense of teachers acting in a role other than that of professional. Teachers are people who are there to inspire students in their quest for truth, knowledge, and achievement, an aim expressed in the school song:

> Though years may find us far apart, each gone our separate way, The memory of these special days will ever with us stay. The mem'ries of the people who inspired us in our quest. For truth and knowledge will, through time, inspire us to our best. New challenges 'neath giant spreading trees, each day unfold. A chance to grow, a chance to learn each lesson new and old. The games we win, the games we lose, the times we give our all. The laughter and the tears we share through winter, spring and fall. Refrain: So raise our voices to Saint Catherine's; Through life her memory will light our way.

Children rotate from class to class, having as many as five different teachers in the course of one school day. Besides teachers, other people in the school have clearly defined roles. The Director of the Lower School has his role, as do the secretaries, groundsmen, lunch servers, and so on. That we are living in an age of specialization is made clear to students.

Waldorf School teachers, however, do everything with very little support. The only support staff are two mothers who work in the office in an administrative capacity (one of them also teaches classes if a teacher is absent and a substitute teacher unavailable). The boundaries between roles are loose rather than tight (see Weick 1982). Teachers are expected to pay themselves, do clerical work, balance the budget, make policy decisions, walk students to and from the pick-up area, maintain strong links with parents, legitimize the school, give extra help to students who need it, mark children's copy books, organize class trips, engage in their own self-development through anthroposophy, and teach the same group of students for 8 years.

The rationale behind the extraordinary dedication of teachers is that only through close, personal, and consistent contact with a strong mentor or guide will the child's soul develop properly. The child is seen to grow spiritually along with the teacher. In

Grade 1 the teacher is more like a mother, but by Grade 7 he or she has taken on the role of wise older friend and advisor. Another aspect of this structure is the development of community, which is seen as a vital part of the school's role. Continuity in teacher–student relations, and close contact with families, is seen as necessary in an age of fragmented social relations and superficial meetings.

The teacher's authority is strengthened by the external structure of the school where teachers are also administrators. With no higher authority than the teacher, his or her word is law. This form of organization is not usually taken into account in studies that claim to show how schools work. For example, Meyer and Rowan (1978) argue that schools are loosely coupled organizations, with few links between the various levels of the organization. In other words, administrators undertake the task of legitimizing the institution while teachers are mainly concerned with their immediate task in hand, that is, to get through the day with their students. Waldorf School teachers, however, are concerned with both teaching and governance responsibilities.

At Waldorf School teachers' authority is also strengthened by the internal organization of the classroom. Much of the school day involves teacher-led discussions, singing, poetry, and recitation.[4] Even at the kindergarten level the teacher's role is central. A pattern of strong authority relations can also be found at St. Catherine's, but here the school hierarchy bolsters and supports a hierarchical view of authority.

Authority Patterns. In Waldorf School students are called "children." In contrast, at St. Catherine's teachers generally refer to students by their first name and sometimes call them "sir" and "ma'am." The difference in terms of address is not accidental. At St. Catherine's the child is regarded as mature and sophisticated. Many are not, of course, but that is the aim. At Waldorf School the child is considered a child. He or she must pass through designated periods of growth before reaching

---

[4]Teacher control of time and space is not unusual in the U.S. in general. Some researchers claim that teachers in American classrooms monopolize 85% of class space and 100% of class time (Sommer, 1974; quoted in McDermott, 1974, p. 110).

maturity. Therefore, students are treated with a high degree of nurturing and protection. Waldorf School teachers believe a positive authority figure can do much more to instill integrity and right behavior in a child than any amount of punishment. Children are thought to need to learn to control their "lower impulses," and this is done through adults caring for their souls. "Authority" is taken to mean an older person possessing strength and wisdom which is used to guide younger people. Authority is not imposed or "authoritarian," but seen to arise from a situation where students love and respect their teachers. Authority is seen as a precursor to freedom.

How then is authority established and discipline maintained in Waldorf School? With no hierarchy in the school, no principal or deputy to administer punishment or formulate policy, responsibility falls on the teachers. They respond to this challenge in a number of ways. First, just as Steiner advocated that teachers consider each pupil "allowing a picture of him to stand before the mind" as preparation for lessons (Carlgren, 1972, p. 19) so, too, do teachers at the school believe in and practice this daily ritual:

> I spend a few minutes each day visualizing each child to allow a spiritual communication with each child and establish harmony in preparation for the next day. Sometimes that's all it takes to understand the child and be aware of his needs. (Interview, teacher)

Knowledge of each child is seen as essential for good teaching. And since the school is teacher centered, despite its progressive goals, authority is something that is nurtured by example and reinforced through school rituals and other practices.

Another approach to discipline is the *child study*, which is part of the weekly faculty meetings. At a child study the teacher will present a profile of the child to the whole school faculty, providing samples of the child's work and a history of the problem. The team works on finding possible strategies to deal with the problem, part of the school's commitment to equality and sharing within the community. Still another protection against disciplinary problems arising is the screening that takes place prior to the acceptance of the child (Interview, teacher).

And suspension and expulsion of a child from school are always possibilities. This applies to both schools, a feature that sets them apart from public schools. According to one of the teachers at Waldorf School, "we have never had to expell a child, although we've come close. If the problems are too difficult to be dealt with in this setting, we would not hesitate to recommend to parents that they go elsewhere, hopefully to a place tailored to the child's needs" (Interview, teacher).

St. Catherine's may recommend also alternative placement for students who do not seem to fit in, although this is rare, and every effort is made to ensure that children's needs are met. One of the key stategies to deal with discipline problems at St. Catherine's is to put the offending child on a monitoring and reward system called a *contract*:

> If a child needs a contract to help him behave, to help achieve what he can achieve in school, then oftentimes a child will be given a contract. Anthony has done a complete about on behavior. He was doing beautifully for 2 weeks, and so we decided to reward him because he was doing so well, so we put him on a contract to give him that reward, so that eventually he will do beautifully without it.[5]

At St. Catherine's the authority of the school director, and ultimately the headmaster, if necessary, is used to support teachers in their endeavors. The school also relies on testing to identify problems, unlike Waldorf School, where the teacher's knowledge of the "whole child" is used to gauge progress.

Teacher Talk. At Waldorf School, while spiritual development is a goal of the school, this does not mean scientific thinking is not valued. On the contrary, Steiner held that it was through observation and development of sensitivity that one

---

[5]It is boys at both schools who have more difficulty fitting in with the school's order. There may be gender differences in children's reactions to the constraints of school time and space. Boys are socialized, by and large, into a sense of independence and freedom, and girls into more compliant and obedient roles, which may make girls more at ease in the orderly and regulated environments we call school. Schools themselves may also be contributing to these differences.

could become more rational and logical in one's thinking. Through stories the child is thought to come to appreciate how things work and think more deeply about the complexity of people and events. Instead of educating through "technical rationality," Waldorf educators believe they are better preparing the child to live in a world where science needs to be informed by human concerns. The process starts in the grade school where students study nature, past civilizations and ancient peoples. The following excerpt comes from a fourth–fifth-grade main lesson:

T: Why do you think you might have a festival around December and January if you were a very ancient person? We're not getting ready to go to the mall. Very ancient. What do you think about this time of year?
B: It's cold enough.
T: It's cold.
B2: And Jesus was born.
T: We don't even know about Jesus yet. We're very ancient. He hasn't even been here yet. Think about it. The days.
G: Snow, cold, and dark.
T: Yes, we have a lot more what than usual?
B: Darkness.
T: Darkness. Now if you were a very ancient person and you had a lot of darkness what might you be praying for?
G: Light. You would pray for the sun to come out.
T: Light. All right. You're going to be praying for the light to come on, and you have the festival of?
SS: Lights.
T: The Festival of Lights. Now what about spring? What are people going to be celebrating in spring?
B: Planting things.
T: What are they going to be praying for then?
G2: That they'll grow.
T: That they'll grow well and that you have grain and that you have favorable conditions to grow your crops. And so our festivals come out of these very ancient traditions. [She goes on to explain how thanksgiving came about.]

The teacher attempts to place the festivals in their historical context and to encourage the children to imagine what conditions were like then ("We're not getting ready to go to the mall''). The school accepts religion as legitimate and able to be held in conjunction with a scientific attitude. The approach in Waldorf School is one of using stories and imagination as a means to growth. The child in the period 7–14 years is seen as beginning to develop the capacity for objectivity and understanding of universals, which will come later.

St. Catherine's teachers emphasize a conventional scientific understanding of one's environment. Religion, however, exists in parallel with a scientific approach to the world, the former serving spritual or humanitarian needs, the latter to improve the quality of life. Reverence is held for both science and God. Science is seen as providing objective truth to enhance human control of the environment. Religion is an important link to the past as well as an avenue for social and emotional expressiveness.

An example illustrates this point. One of the fifth grades was reading an American Indian myth explaining the cause of thunder and lightning. The teacher provided background information on the author and elicited from the children four different functions of myths. The students said myths were stories told orally, that they explain natural events, and that they explain events in terms of power from spirits or gods. The question and answer sequence that followed allowed no room for the suggestion that God made the lightning, which one may well find in a fundamentalist Christian school:

> T: Now what would we say lightning comes from?
> B: The heat in the, the friction of the cold and the hot hit each other and that makes sparks/
> T: /Yes. Electrical charges that crash in the clouds. Right. So we've got this wonderful scientific explanation that takes away from our fear, because we understand what's happening out there. Did the American Indians have that?
> SS: No.
> T: They didn't have that advanced technology that we have, so they would have to imagine that the lightning was some spirit who was larger than they were, wouldn't they?

A view of the compatibility of science and religion is in keeping with Episcopal epistemology where God is seen to work through natural laws. The church has no problem with the teaching of science, including evolution and biology, unlike, say, Christian fundamentalists, who take the Bible literally and see evolution as at odds with the Creation story in Genesis.

The idea of Progress is also taught. Humankind is placed on a unilinear continuum starting with "primitives" at one end of the scale and progressing to modern postindustrial societies at the other.

> **T:** Imagine primitive man before we had nice strong concrete buildings to protect us and before we had a steady food supply and before we had to just go to the grocery store to get whatever we needed. Would thunder and lightning have a different significance in our lives?
> **SS:** Yes.
> **G:** Like you wouldn't be protected as you are now. You'd be in a small, little tipi which is animal skins.
> **T:** Right. Animal skins between you and the outside world instead of glass and bricks and stone and insulation to keep you warm. O.K., now, the closest that I can think of to help you understand how thunder and lightning felt to the American Indians is if we search back in our memories to when we were 2 or 3 and we remember our first big thunderstorm. Remember being scared?
> **B:** Yeah.
> **G:** My sister was scared when she was 11 or 12.
> **T:** Well some of them are still scary now even with our nice, safe buildings. But we can imagine how Indians felt living out in the wild much more than we do if we search back in our memories to when we were young.

In the teacher's view "primitive" native Americans made up myths about thunder and lightning because they did not have the "wonderful" scientific knowledge that we have to explain these phenomenon. Her use of the "primitive people equals small child" example is revealing. The teacher also speaks of modern technology in positive terms: we have "nice, safe buildings to protect us," "a steady food supply," "a world with telephones and electric light bulbs and computers and supersonic jets," "the advanced technology that we have." Native Americans are portrayed in a way that renders them vulnerable to the elements and irrationally inventing spirits to explain what they were unable to comprehend. The example has been included to underscore the ways cultural values shape teaching, even in supposedly fact-oriented lessons.

CONCLUSIONS

Time, space, and other school relations orient students towards quite different ways of perceiving and acting in the world. Attitudes towards time in the two schools can be seen as supportive of mainstream urban American society, or at odds with it. Chronos, mechanically measurable and literal time, is concerned with promptness and efficiency in the modern world. This is important at St. Catherine's. On the other hand, Waldorf School sees the emphasis on chronos time as having led to a loss in the quality of life and in the products of our endeavors. Waldorf School upholds "natural" rhythms or kairos, which is more like "time" found in traditional rural farming communities. The school sees its approach, however, not as a return to old ways, but as a precursor to a new age of unity and enlightenment. The schools' cultural values implicit in their orientations toward time, space and social relations differ between an organic form, in the "tribal village" of Waldorf School, and the "professional academy" of St. Catherine's.

Moreover, the rituals of Waldorf School, the practice of teacher as guide, and a different approach to science set the school apart from St. Catherine's. Waldorf School culture would seem to be a reaction against the progressive domination of much of modern life by science and technology. Waldorf School is spatially and temporally unique in its attention to natural rhythms and rituals. The mode of teaching and learning is one built around personalized relationships and storytelling. In contrast, St. Catherine's firmly embraces an achievement oriented and intellectually based form of schooling that is the essence of our modern and fast-paced technological world. Here the teacher is concerned with imparting specialized knowledge or skills in a rational and scientific manner. Some attention is given to creativity and the arts through specialist teaching, but for the main part a scientific approach governs school life. The scientific view can be seen in the value St. Catherine's places on testing, its curriculum, the use of space in the school and also the lessons that are taught, subtly through the use of space and time, and more overtly through teacher talk. St. Catherine's is an academic-elite school devoted to the education of able students for university, and careers in business and the professions. Waldorf School is devoted instead to the socialization of the young in conjunction with school families. While anthroposophy is not propagated in Waldorf School in an overt fashion, we can see that its principles guide much of what goes on in the school day.

In the next and final chapter we review the cultural values of Waldorf School and St. Catherine's and consider the implications for both school and society. School cultures can be profoundly different in their day-to-day realities, but this is more than a matter of preferences or style. Fundamental orientations towards the world, others, and the individual or "self" are created and sustained daily in schools everywhere.

8

CONCLUSIONS

Schools have been shown to construct cultural meanings embodying epistemological and ethical viewpoints that have implications for the way that students perceive the world, others and themselves. We will first review the particular meanings created in each example, and then consider the importance of these findings for education in general. St. Catherine's is a clear example of an academic elite model of education. Prep school traditions underpin the school's approach, with an aim to prepare students' intellects and to develop character through religion and service. Waldorf School, on the other hand, demonstrates holistic education. The school focuses on human values and feelings and is concerned with developing each child's innate potential. Children are seen as unique individuals to be nurtured in a natural environment "worthy of the child" (Interview, teacher). Waldorf School downplays cognitive development, believing that if the child's soul is nourished, all else follows.

UNIVERSES OF MEANING IN SCHOOLS

Perceptions of the World, Nature, the Cosmos

Developing the "feeling self" is the touchstone of grade school education in Waldorf School. Attention to feelings is deemed so important, not only for the child's stage of development, but also because of the times in which we live. The loss of human interaction with nature in the modern world and its replacement with automatic, unthinking motion (such as turning on the light, xeroxing, and so on) has led, in this view, to a lack of experiences where people are fully engaged with the world "body and soul." Just as an artist is someone who has felt deeply the pangs of love, loss, or sorrow, and is able to express those feelings, in the Waldorf School view children ought also to be brought to a closeness with nature and with the "feeling life." Through aesthetic experiences the child is thought to learn to be fully engaged and express feeling.

People are seen as "part of nature," and the environment is to be protected and valued, not mistreated and exploited as it is in contemporary society. It is believed possible to develop a different way of perceiving things. Waldorf School encourages students to look at plants, the sun, moon, stars, and "beasts that feel and live" as parts of an organism, a cosmos in which they are located. Mary Catherine Bateson (1990) makes a similar point when she suggests that, if we consider a tree as a woman, then one's relationship to that tree is likely to be substantially different than if we consider the tree as a lump of cold matter, which is expendable. The Waldorf School manner of perceiving the world is not one of control over one's environment, changing it and mastering it through a better technology and science, but one of developing individuals who learn from and are responsive to their environment.

Connected with Waldorf School's emphasis on human's location in nature is a reaction against the modern world's one-sided approach to schooling. The dominant model of education in contemporary society is seen to focus solely on a scientific, utilitarian or materialistic mode of thinking. The Waldorf alternative philosophy of humans as an integral form of nature is similar to that of many traditional oral-aural societies, and contrasts with the view commonly adopted in highly technologized societies where nature is conceived as serving humans. The use of technology and laboratory equipment in so many modern schools misses the mark, argue Waldorf School teachers, because it is all too often used exclusively without attention to spiritual aspects of teaching and learning. In the Waldorf perspective the educated person is seen to have both personal direction and control, as well as submitting to "God's plan." Students are nurtured to grow in body, soul and spirit, compared to mainstream public schools which are seen as concerned only with the intellect. The science that Waldorf School promotes is one which claims to attend to "spiritual" aspects of existence, thus asserting to be a "higher science" (Interviews, teachers) than that which merely attends to physical phenomena and their effects.

In contrast, St. Catherine's view of the world as a rational world is supported by science. The school's use of testing to gauge student progress is evidence of this view, as is the centrality of science and technology in the school. Religion is also important at St. Catherine's, but it is as if religion is in a separate social sphere, helping one to live a better life, and scientific truth prevails in terms of the productive sphere. Nature is seen as somewhat separate from humankind and to be used for our purposes. There is reverence for nature; God is seen in the wind rustling through the trees or the magnificent whale, but God is more than this. These assumptions about the world and nature are only subtly different, but they are important differences.

Relations to Others

St. Catherine's is focused on both academic and social concerns, imparting a degree of social exclusiveness on its students. St. Catherine's confers privilege on those it serves. The goal is to gain entry for students to the best universities, and in this sense the school is oriented towards a competitive relationship with others. The school proudly lists college placements of recent graduates: Harvard, Stanford, Princeton, Vassar, Yale. An interesting parallel can be made with the situation for the individual child. The school faces the challenge of competition with other schools by striving to create a position for itself within a system of schools as "the IBM of schools." Similarly, an individual child faces the challenge of competition in the academic arena from an early age, with the ultimate goal of college placement. Of course, public school students also gain admission to the best universities. But the social status that derives from having attended a prestigious school is considered just as important as academic achievement in terms of preparation for professional pathways. Students have expectations of successful careers, and having attended the "right" type of school is an advantage. Parents send their children to St. Catherine's because they want their own legacy of social advantage to be enjoyed also by their children. The minority of parents who are not so advantaged (single mothers and the like) are hoping for improved circumstances for their offspring and are prepared to make personal sacrifices to achieve this goal.

Another key to schooling at St. Catherine's is the relationship between families and the school. St. Catherine's parents share in having purchased what is considered by many to be the premier schooling in the community. They share an elitism and an identity that is suggestive, though sometimes inaccurately, of affluence. Some tension exists in the school, nevertheless, between the prep-school values of a tradition bound hierarchical world and modern day equity concerns. The school is seeking to embrace a broader school population representative of U.S. society. An effort is underway to admit students from diverse ethnic (and to a lesser extent social class) backgrounds. In recent years the minority population in the school has increased to 8%. However, the consequences of taking a step towards diversity "too far too quickly" are not known. With a tradition of academic success and prestige, the school is somewhat reluctant to take steps that might dramatically alter the infrastructure of the school and possibly diminish its stature as a college-preparatory school. The value of "self-help" which underpins the idea of breaking down social class barriers is part of the American vision, and self-help is taught in the school. But many of the students in the school have a background which has the potential to lead them to expect privilege: "there are students here who think they are entitled to everything" (Interview, teacher); "we try to teach equality but rank and status are also important especially with money" (Interview, teacher). And the school is ambivalent about this, for it sets itself up as at the top of a hierarchy of schools and encourages "excellence," which is then translated into competition, while claiming an ideal of equality.

Waldorf School sets itself somewhat apart from mainstream

society; it seeks an alternative social and cultural form. The body of knowledge and worldview is particular and shared by those who have been initiated into the Waldorf community. While fees are not high enough to establish socioeconomic exclusivity, the pedagogy and practices are distinctive and have the effect of selecting a group of people who are committed to these goals. A number of people have actually moved to the area in order to have access to a Waldorf school. A positive outcome is that the school is a collective enterprise, but at the same time we ought not pretend that Waldorf School or St. Catherine's promotes equity principles in a broad sense which is a public school agenda.

In both schools there is a strong sense of community. Cohesiveness is facilitated by the fact that the schools serve a select group of students. Parents and teachers voluntarily elect to support and participate in a particular school. There are no zoning regulations or public requirements encouraging support of the school. Rather, people decide freely to support a school. In many cases this may not be a conscious or well-informed decision. Parents, for example, may learn about a school through friendships formed in a sporting or social arena and decide on the basis of that friendship to send their own children to that school. Finances may be another limiting factor in decision making. Parents may not want public schooling for their children for any number of reasons, but their choice of an alternative may be limited by the number of schools within the family's educational budget.

However, community means something quite different in each context. At Waldorf School, community means an alternative social group to mainstream society, like a new age commune. A network of obligations and social ties are established with others in the community. Equality within the community is critical. There is no place for hierarchy, rank, or status distinctions. The individual is expected to be able to retain individuality and keep the group's welfare in mind. At St. Catherine's community is less tightly bounded and constructed, although the concern here is for cordial social relations within a community of people who share a belief in a humane, achievement oriented society.

Each school can be seen as an institution with a highly developed culture and parents as committed to that culture to some degree. Much is expected of the parent body. It is not assumed that schooling is an affair separated from family concerns, as may happen in the public sector. Instead, the school's life's blood, financial as well as emotional, comes from the parent body. The school must work with parents to establish and maintain the school's culture. This is not to argue for homogeneity or an overly integrated system, but rather to posit an analysis that recognizes that a school community has its own cultural milieu, despite the contested nature of social relations and their inherent diversity.

Perceptions of the Individual or "Self"

Waldorf School's emphasis on the value of cooperation and "working within a circle" (Interview, teacher) permeates school life. Working within a circle means being bonded to a social group, taking into account the effects of one's actions on others in that group. The metaphor of a "family" or "commune" is a useful one, for here children are allowed individuality and autonomy within the parameters of a sharing social group.

It is also useful to see Waldorf School's emphasis on stages of development as similar to the growing child's independence within a community structure. In the first stage of life (0–7 years) the child's body is seen as central to existence. The child learns through imitation, with the kindergarten and nursery school teacher's expert guidance and role modeling serving to develop the will of the child and interest in learning with others. During these years much interaction occurs between students and teachers, with free play, preferably with natural materials, predominating. Because the child is considered to be capable only of physical, not intellectual tasks, and to learn through imitation, emphasis is given to creating an environment "worthy of the child's attention." The school attempts to recreate a situation in the past when children lived on farms in small cohesive communities and children could be engaged in many activities imitating their parents and relatives' real life endeavors. In Waldorf School kindergartens and nursery, the idea of country family life prevails; children play house, build, put away, sweep, clean, wash, cook, and bake. They plant seeds and seedlings and where possible play with animals and become acquainted with the seasons. Toys are natural toys, made from wool and cotton fibers, not plastics and synthetics. Colors and harmony and rhythm are central aspects of the school day. It is the rituals of circle time, story time, nap time and lunch time that are seen to be so important for the child's development. Colors are part of this, and are used consciously for educational ends. Colors are selected for their calming or their stimulating properties; a careful use of color in relation to stage is considered helpful.

The next stage, the feeling or sensation stage of grade school (7–14 years) is seen as a period of creative–emotional growth. The child is thought to experience the world primarily through the senses, not the body, and the teacher's task is to ensure that the academic curriculum is translated into an artistic form. Imaginative stories, myths, parables, and pictures are selected to convey the so-called objective processes, facts, and laws of life. It is argued that the child is not being indulged in a world of fantasy for its own sake, but as a means of acquiring a truly "scientific" frame of mind in later life. In storing up beautiful poetry and other cultural riches, teachers believe the children are being prepared well for their later independent use.

The final, thinking stage (14–21 years) is considered to be the time when the student begins to intellectualize experience. Teachers take what has been experienced and felt in the grade-school years through concrete knowledge, stories, and narratives, and transform it into "laws" that govern these phenomena. At the age of 21, according to Steiner, the student develops the ego, the unique capacity to engage in self-education and self-direction as an autonomous human being. Freedom is not seen, however, as coming through an anarchic "do as one pleases" attitude. Instead, freedom is thought to come through proper living and a disciplined approach to living. The community sees itself as part of the cosmos, a unified, harmonious whole—a "new age" conception of society.

Waldorf School's perception of the "self" also places credence in the individual's stages of development as somehow connected with larger society. The present stage in earth history is called the fifth epoch, which began around 1400 A.D. and is expected to be followed by the sixth and seventh epoch. The individual human's growth and development is held to parallel social ontogeny. Grade schoolers study the Greeks before the Romans as a conscious part of an overall plan to teach children an ideal of cultural growth and evolution. It is not the ideology of progress that we see in the technical–rational world of computers and supersonic jets, but it is nevertheless an ideal that assumes stages of development.

For the teachers in Waldorf School such maxims on evolution are taken seriously. Individual teachers may not be comfortable with all of Steiner's reasoning, for example, no reading until the second dentition, but they are willing to overlook minor difficulties for the sake of the overall plan. After all, they argue, "nothing is ever arbitrary in a Waldorf School. There is a reason for everything." Thus, the kindergarten teachers see themselves as mother figures offering help and suggestion to youngsters engaging in play activities. Children begin the school day with the ritual of an hour and a half of free play. No toys in the sense of what modern society defines as toys are provided. No trains or Barbie dolls or Fischer-Price toys can be found in this kindergarten. The child is given free reign in a structured environment stocked with quite different toys. Cords of firewood, baskets of small building blocks cut from a tree limb, and hidey holes made from drapes of colored muslin provide opportunities for the children to invent their own fantasies and express their developing imaginations. As adults express their experience of the world through thought, so are children seen to express their experiences through play. Grade school continues with the idea of teacher as authority, but learning is seen as taking place through the body—and the media of music, story, and eurythmics. Whereas "in public schools the acquisition of knowledge mainly occurs through sight and sound," in Waldorf School sight and sound as well as "imagination, touch, movement and feeling" figure largely in the learning environment (Interview, teacher).

Consistent with the belief in the natural world as conducive to the development of the imaginative, thinking capacity of the child, television is regarded as potentially harmful. Watching television is seen to involve no inner activity on the part of the viewer. Instead the screen "shoots images" at the viewer, which are taken in unconsciously (Interview, teacher). Waldorf School's quest is for children to become active in their own imagination and creativity. Everything in the school day is designed to enhance creativity, and allowing children to sit passively in front of the television is regarded as counterproductive.

The education of parents is thus seen as important. Waldorf School makes a conscious effort to inform parents of the school's approach to matters of child raising. Parents, of course, do not always comply as well as the school would like. Commercial toys do occasionally turn up at the school; they are discreetly confiscated by the teacher and returned to the child at the end of the school day with clear instructions about keeping "home toys" at home. All these aspects of schooling are part of a conscious plan to nurture children towards creativity and the ultimate goal, "freedom."

But what does Waldorf School mean by freedom? The development of the "free human being," the aim of Waldorf School education, is seen as allowing for a meaningful communion with fellow human beings and a better human society located in the larger "cosmos." The free human being is sought in each child; the free human being is seen as being in control of his or her own destiny and yet at the same time able to show care and compassion toward others, as can be seen in the verse said at faculty meetings and anthroposophy study group meetings: "In the free human being, The Universe gathers itself together, Then in the free resolve of your heart, Take yourself in hand, And you will find the world, The spirit of the world will come to be, Through you." Ironically, "freedom" is thought to develop best in the highly structured and controlled environment of Waldorf School.

In contrast to the communal self of Waldorf School, the conception of the "self" and individual development that is adopted at St. Catherine's has roots in the philosophies of Plato and Aristotle and is more competitively based. The teacher's role is one of imparting a distinct body of knowledge drawing on a specialized area of expertise to receptive individuals. The emphasis is on knowledge to be acquired. Students are perceived as bright, and those who are experiencing learning difficulties are directed elsewhere or assisted through tutoring programs. The curriculum is traditional, competitive, and academic. Education is a preparation for daily life, and more importantly a preparation for the future goal of college admission. Furthermore, not a great deal of attention is paid to individuals or individual differences. Teachers at St. Catherine's teach to the class which is assumed to be more or less homogeneous. Group work is the exception, but even group work is more often used as a means of completing a task, such as science experiments, than a tool for tailoring work to the child's level of learning. The teacher is also an authority figure, not in an overbearing sense (most, if not all of the teachers are liked by students), but they nevertheless possess a formal relationship to students, one which endows them with power as mentor or teacher as it has been traditionally defined through the ages. Students are expected to remain relatively passive and quiet while they are working. Those students who prove unable to do this are placed on a contractual reward system designed to teach conformity to the norms of being a student in this school.

St. Catherine's academic emphasis is evident in the collection code curriculum (discrete subjects) and strongly framed knowledge (teachers control what is taught), which is also the case at Waldorf School. However, the knowledge that is selected for study in Waldorf School is not discrete units but interdisciplinary, and intended to be more child centered, with its focus on stories and music and movement. Alternatively, the knowledge and skills selected by St. Catherine's is traditional school knowledge, the teacher's conception of what students ought to know irrespective of students. At St. Catherine's, tradition and the goal of social recognition and status are involved. While the school is forward looking, it does this through traditional knowledge. Thus, Latin is taught. New knowledge is included in that the school attempts to keep abreast of scientific and other knowledge that is constantly being created, but nontraditional content, such as courses in personal development or self-esteem that might be found in other schools in this country, is not. Confidence and self-esteem are thought to come through the experience of learning and the intrinsic reward of gaining mastery in skills or content. Development is seen as a matter of growth through intellectual challenges.

Academic schooling for what is sometimes described as the ruling class (cf. Connell, Ashenden, Kessler, & Dowsett, 1982) has always been along these lines. In the English public schools

one would not expect to study courses in "self-esteem" or
"practical" subjects, or be allowed a vast range of choice in what
to study. Neither at St. Catherine's is there a place for vocational
subjects nor a smorgasbord of subject offerings. Specialist
teachers in traditional academic areas transmit their disciplines
to primarily goal-oriented students who rotate from one specialist to another according to a tight schedule, in the manner of
secondary students. The world is one where everyone is considered gifted. So while academic distinctions between those at St.
Catherine's and those who are not are emphasized, academic
distinctions among those who belong to St. Catherine's are
downplayed. Standardized tests are used for formative evaluation of teaching practices and to instill in students the importance of test performance, not to confer academic merit on some
and to discredit others.

St. Catherine's school also strives to prepare students for
leadership and to develop the individual through competitive
athletics. Academics and sports are deemed good producers of
leadership qualities, such as responsibility, high performance,
and team work. Developing an all-round education, rather than
just an academic one, is considered important. A status value is
also attached to sports. Students in the elementary school are not
only getting fit; they are gaining membership to a centuries old
prepschool tradition. Moreover, in emphasizing interschool
athletic and academic competition, the school is competing with
other schools to establish and retain its high status position
within a broader base of schools. The school considers itself a
quality school and works at retaining that status.

St. Catherine's aims to teach students to be responsible individuals: "to become the best human beings possible and to
prepare them to contribute usefully to society" (Interview,
teacher). The religious or moral dimension of St. Catherine's
education attempts to strike a balance in the development of the
individual between materialism and spiritualism. Achievement
in U.S. society is often measured in terms of economic success,
and while St. Catherine's does not support a view to economic
success devoid of social concern, the drive for efficiency and
success is strong. These students for the most part come from
families where the parents themselves are demonstrating strong
economic competence, and the school itself is grounded in a

sphere of economic strength. Students are thus being exposed by both family and school to a model of success that is based at least in part on economic success, and then balanced by spiritual or religious devotion. Obligatory weekly chapel where a variety of ministers conduct services proclaims the value of religion as a part of high culture, and also the value of social concern. It is considered important for St. Catherine's students to develop a sense of civic, moral, and social responsibility, which is also a prep school tradition. Nevertheless, the school has not adopted a doctrinaire approach to religion. The school wants to inculcate moral stature or growth of character in students so that they may be prepared for high level positions and responsibilities, part of an ideology of success; no one religion is seen as necessary to do this.

Religious or moral values are also taught at Waldorf School, in contrast to a perceived void in public schools' teaching of morality and the degeneration of moral values in contemporary American society. Contemporary society is seen as corrupt in its focus on materialism and acquisitiveness: "Ahriman," that which is materialistic within us, is thought to be destroying the moral fiber of people in Western societies (see Steiner, 1972). Waldorf School claims that it is "responding to an educational dream of parents that includes more than the academics" (Interview, teacher). That "dream" emphasizes non-materialism. Waldorf School seeks to promote and inspire "spirituality," "moral integrity," "self-esteem" and "harmony." While the school does not have a curriculum based on any one religious doctrine, it is vigilant in its attention to spiritual needs. Each individual child is seen to harbor the potential for the development of higher levels of spirituality (see Steiner, 1972, pp. 255-346, on "initiation" to the spirit world). There is no one all-powerful divine God, according to this view, who will protect them from adversity.

Instead, it is the individual who needs to be nurtured to "grow" spiritually. While many of the students are attending church and Sunday schools that promote the view of one Christian God (and others are Jews, Sufis, and so on) Waldorf School offers a "personal journey toward God" (Interview, teacher). In place of any one religious doctrine the school posits a comparative religious approach. During "main lesson" stu-

dents study the evolution or development of ancient civilizations in the plural, and they discuss the ideas behind the various
myths associated with these peoples. A variety of perspectives
are thus covered, with no one right answer to the question "Who
is God?" The mix of children in the school militates against a
unified religion (although the school's world view could be seen
as a "religion" in itself). It is not that students do not believe in
one or another religion according to their home background.
They do. But in the school context they are gaining an appreciation for a diversity of religious styles. Christian rituals such as
Easter and Christmas are important in the school year and
celebrated with enthusiasm, but at those self-same rituals, for
instance, the Jewish faith is also celebrated.

   Thus, on all three levels: perceptions of the world, nature, the
cosmos; relations to others; and perceptions of the individual or
"self," the schools create different meanings. In their *views of
the world*, the schools offer a contrast between humans as united
with the cosmos at Waldorf School, and humans as rational
beings who are able to control Nature at St. Catherine's. In the
first case God is in Nature. In the second, God shows himself
through Nature amongst other things; but God is more than, and
"above," Nature. The *form of relations to others* differs in that
Waldorf School stresses equality and personal connectedness,
whereas St. Catherine's embodies a notion of social relations
built around status distinctions and hierarchy, with professional
relations between students and teachers, and parents and teachers. In Waldorf School the teacher is more a close friend of the
family; in St. Catherine's the teacher is a professional. *Perceptions of "self"* and the evolving individual also differ. Waldorf
School views the individual as a member of a group who passes
through fixed stages of development and requiring authoritative
direction from older and wiser spiritual "guides." St. Catherine's view of the "self" is that the individual's development is
able to be nurtured, accelerated and perfected through a variety
of well-chosen tests and challenges.

IMPLICATIONS FOR POLICY MAKERS

The study reveals two different school cultures where community is important and where education means much more than

merely instructing students in technical skills and a set body of knowledge. Though the ideas on education are quite different, both schools share an appreciation for education that is not simply the transmission of knowledge. Whereas St. Catherine's cultural horizons include a great deal of attention to character development and the athletic realm, Waldorf School's focus is on aesthetic forms, such as music, art and eurythmy. However, both are concerned with a unified public context and co-operative relations amongst the parent, student and faculty bodies. The potential divisiveness of student, teacher and parent concerns are given unity through ritual and other cultural practices. St. Catherine's and Waldorf School cultures provide clear examples of the embodiment of different ideals that schools can hold, and show quite different forms of action.

What does this mean for policy makers? Those involved in restructuring schools may want to consider the following issues, paying attention to discrepancies between stated goals and lived practices in schools. (a) *Curriculum:* Does specialization of disciplines and tasks facilitate learning? In this study we have seen specialization at St. Catherine's and integration of subject matter at Waldorf School successfully serve quite different intents and purposes. We also need to consider whether the curriculum should be based on "school knowledge" or on student experiences. (b) *Pedagogy:* Should rote learning, grades, GPAs, and "covering material" be rewarded? St. Catherine's has been shown to emphasize challenging, clearly defined and measurable learning outcomes. Waldorf School instead down-plays outcomes and evaluation and seeks holistic growth in students. However, rote learning and the use of rhythm and ritual are common teaching tools in Waldorf School, so even in a "progressive/holistic" model there is much that can resemble traditional learning models. What we see in both Waldorf School and St. Catherine's, however, are *caring* teachers who define their roles as much more than teaching skills and knowledge. (c) *Purposes and Goals:* Ought credentialling and graduation be a central goal for students, or is it possible to promote a love of learning for its own sake? Is schooling truly exciting and involving for students? Are they motivated and challenged to learn? Are students taking responsibility for their education? Does a "community of learners" exist? Are parents, students, faculty and staff fully involved in the school? In the schools studied here students are keenly interested in school and learning, though St. Catherine's places more emphasis on future goals. Both schools demonstrate strong communal bonds. (d) *Governance*: How can a school be structured to provide for optimal growth of students in all areas—social, emotional, physical, and intellectual? What is the best size for a school? How ought the school be run? St. Catherine's relies on a formal organizational design based on hierarchy, while Waldorf School utilizes a structure of equality, where teachers and parents take on administrative roles. Nevertheless, both schools demonstrate a strong commitment on the part of teachers and students to the schools. With participants in school cultures emotionally invested in it, any struggles over governance are less likely to interfere with the core technology of teaching and learning. (e) *Cultural Values*: Should character development and ethical concerns be an integral part of school life? What are the cultural values towards the world, others and "self" that a school promotes? As this study shows, a complex web of significance is "spun" by all those involved in a school.

"Can we create good school cultures?" Can we just change culture to suit our own purposes? McLaren's (1986) study of a "tough" Catholic junior high school in Toronto led him to propose that schools' impoverished environments could be improved by deliberate attention to the creation of rites. While I saw the rites in the schools studied as central to school culture, I do not think one can invent rites or any other part of school culture and artificially impose them to "make" culture. Rites come out of a larger picture which includes the history of the school, the school population, the parent body, the school's traditions, its philosophical and mythical foundations, and so on. What is important for policy makers and for those who would change schools is an understanding that cultures evolve, and a recognition of the interplay of cultural dynamics and the power of symbolism. School symbols are an important and understudied part of the teaching and learning process and environment. Symbols help create universes of meaning. They "establish powerful, pervasive and long-lasting moods and motivations in people by clothing their conceptions of a general order of existence with such an aura of factuality that the moods and motivations seem uniquely realistic" (Geertz, 1966, p. 4). Educators seeking positive learning experiences for students need to attend to symbolic meanings and qualitative differences in schools.

A related outcome of my work is thus its attention to the normative aspects of schooling. Commonly accepted views of schools as concerned mainly with knowledge transmission and teachers as the purveyors of value-free knowledge are misguided. Teachers are often portrayed in research as insulated in the classroom, in isolation from school cultural values. They are thought to be primarily concerned with controlling in-class behavior and teaching the academics, not molding student's character. Lortie (1975) and Schofield (1989), for instance, have understated the ways in which that which is outside the classroom influences classroom practices. Admittedly, in public schools socializing activities are seen as "at best a means of achieving overt and essentially nonproblematic instructional ends, at worst an illicit interference in individual and private familial concerns" (Kapferer, 1981, p. 260). Nevertheless, even in public schools the industrial and bureaucratic model on which public schools are founded surely intrudes; public school cultures are simply not as easily recognizable as they are in private schools. Pragmatic and instrumental norms are what we have come to think schools (in the generic sense) are about. It is only when we begin to confront other ways of seeing the world, as in St. Catherine's and Waldorf School, that such assumptions become evident. Socialization can take many forms, and what students learn through participation in school cultures, whether industrial, academic-elite, holistic, or any other form, is of vital importance to the developing worldviews of students.

Within public and private schools a vast array of school cultures are created. Dell Hymes's (1980) question, "What kinds of schools are there?" has not been adequately addressed by educational researchers. In the study of school cultures we are, as he argued, "about one hundred years behind knowledge of American Indian kinship." This book is a useful contribution towards finding out about the many possible varieties of schooling and their educational and social messages. By focusing on St. Catherine's, a college-preparatory school, and a Waldorf school, we have seen how the distinctiveness of schools

is culturally embedded. Peshkin's (1986) study of a Baptist
fundamentalist school, McLaren's (1986) analysis of a Catholic
high school in Canada, and Nancy Lesko's (1988) Catholic high
school in the U.S. are other efforts in this direction. The many
varieties of public, parochial, Montessori, learning-disabled,
and other alternative school cultures also need to be examined in
close detail.

Concrete lessons can be learned from the study of school
cultures. For those who are concerned with how to make schools
a better and more efficient place, St. Catherine's shows us how
we can do this within a framework of social concern. Though
some may balk at the elite nature of the school (with its critics
pointing to "social pretentiousness"), it is nevertheless a fine
example of a school where morale is high, where students are
excelling in school and where moral and religious concerns have
not been forgotten. Students at St. Catherine's are learning
traditional subjects, but in a way that allows them to keep up
with the modern world. The school is aiming, not only to
transfer a set body of knowledge, although this is important, but
to cultivate people who will think about the broader implications of knowledge. Richard Rorty (1990) stressed the need for
students to be "located in time and space," in other words for
them to know the when and where of events such as the French
Revolution and Hiroshima. Students at St. Catherine's are developing such knowledge as well as being oriented towards
knowledge as something more than "cultural capital" (Bourdieu
& Passeron, 1977). The school is preparing students for leadership in society by attending to academics, not in isolation, but
with reference to social concerns.

Waldorf School teaches different, but also important, lessons.
This school draws attention to the danger of fragmentation in the
modern world, concerned as it is with task orientation for a
bigger and better future. In an age where academics and accelerated learning is a primary goal (kindergarteners and preschoo-
lers can "fail" in some schools), and when the average number
of years spent in school is ever increasing, it is refreshing to find
a school that believes in the ability of children to learn through
the stories, myth, and magic that were once the basis of childhood. While many other schools seem to be overly concerned
with a rapid output irrespective of the cost on the child, Waldorf

School seems determined to preserve the childhood years. Also, the emphasis on multisensory learning is important. Even if we do not accept some of Steiner's more unusual explanations (for example, categorizing children as cholerics or melancholics is medieval, to my frame of thinking) there is much in the pedagogy that speaks to my experience as an educator. In our quest for "more," we may be overlooking other foundational dimensions of a truly educational experience. Waldorf School suggests an alternative strategy. Instead of focusing only on narrow goals and ignoring the context, Waldorf School teaches us that we need to consider things in a more integrated and holistic manner. Waldorf School also teaches community. With an emphasis on continuity, students learn to develop and sustain relationships and forge long-term social commitments. These attributes are also key values that are overlooked in many educational institutions. The message from Waldorf School is of the value of integration, harmony, wholeness and ritual in education. St. Catherine's has a solid, conservative approach to education and mainstream American culture, with a forward-looking view of scientific and technological progress. Waldorf School is taking a radical departure from traditional educational practices in an attempt to create new cultural impulses. In reframing and restructuring our schools, the issue of the particular "universes of meaning" we want to create is a critical consideration. What kinds of school cultures do we want for our children?

APPENDIX

Research Assumptions

Research is a value-laden enterprise. The researcher frames questions, selects, and edits the field experience. The choice of focus is a statement of value, as is the theoretical framework used to make sense of field material, and the setting is imbued with values. The ethnographer must be aware of these issues and attempt to clarify background assumptions. Recognizing that there is subjectivity in research does not mean the exercise becomes one of "anything goes," but rather that this awareness can lead to the production of more credible research findings.

Anthropologists disagree about the type of knowledge produced through anthropological fieldwork, with various factions claiming it to be literary, scientific, or somewhere in between. The anthropologist needs the methodological rigor of a scientist to guard against using inadequate evidence, and to recognize his or her own perspective, among other concerns. The researcher also needs to be an artist while engaged in fieldwork, and in doing analysis and interpretive work. The task of the ethnographer is similar to that of the artist, for both set out to defamiliarize that which we have failed to perceive. The problem with becoming too familiar with something is that we fail to notice when it changes; we fail to notice its complexity. As Clifford

Geertz noted, "it would hardly be the fish who discovered water." Shklovsky (1965), the great Russian Formalist critic, said the purpose of art is to "recover the sensation of life; it exists to make one feel things, to make the stone stony . . . to impart the sensation of things as they are perceived and not as they are known." Instead of responding in a dull and habitual way, art sharpens our senses and causes us to pay greater attention to something, to see it anew. To arouse critical consciousness, the ethnographer needs to be skilled at weaving an artistic allegory, using unusual metaphors, and questioning what is generally considered unproblematic, normal, or "natural." So, the question of whether the knowledge produced is art or science may be wrong. There is art in all science and science in all art.

Anthropologists recognize the importance of particular settings and tend to be modest in their claims. Some focus exclusively on the group they are studying without extending their analysis outwards. Others engage in situational analyses that start from the concrete and then move out to show general processes. Whichever approach is used, contextual analysis is critical. Every rite or symbol studied in schools, for example, cannot be taken to mean something out of context. It is embedded in a framework. Just as words in a sentence are arranged according to a syntax, and their meaning is limited and shaped by that arrangement, so too is this the case in social life. The meaning must be taken from the context. A single utterance only makes sense when placed with other utterances that mark it as belonging to different frames (for example, "everyday life" or "in school"). McDermott illustrates this in a "What time is it?" story. He shows that the same question, "What time is it?" asked in different settings provokes quite different responses ranging from "Hey, man, this is my watch" in a New York subway, to "Going to bed already, dear?" in a strained marriage, and "ten o'clock" followed by the reply "good work, Joe" in school (Varenne & McDermott, 1986, p. 206). Bateson (1955) similarly discusses the analytical implications of "this is play," showing the complexity and levels of meaning. Messages are rarely simple or unambiguous. They can be taken on many different levels, and the validity of any one level does not discount other possible meanings.

Cause and effect are also seen as difficult to identify. There is a recognition of mutually interlocking systems. Any part in a system might be seen as either cause or effect. In a couple's dance routine, for example, anthropologists might question the idea that only one of the pair is leading the other. Perhaps both dancers are subtly signalling each other and indicating direction and movement.

Mary Catherine Bateson's account of her involvement with dolphins during a visit to her father illustrates further these points. Gregory Bateson had spent several years in the mid-sixties studying dolphin communication in the Virgin Islands and later in Hawaii. He invited his daughter to go into the pool with Peter, a young male dolphin, instructing her that the dolphin would treat her in a protective manner, as he would a dolphin cub. She recounts how the dolphin charged at her, whirling her around in the eddy created by his movement. Then he courted her "like a cat that rubs against one's ankles, soft and luxuriant, dolphin skin shimmering at human touch" (Bateson, 1984, p. 171). She felt reduced to helpless infancy, strangely seduced by this powerful creature. No longer could she record her experience with scientific detachment:

> "How on earth," I asked Gregory, "can anyone remain objective working with dolphins? How do you keep from being sucked in?" "The same way I do with Iatmul or Balinese or schizophrenics," he said. "You can't work with human beings without allowing for your own involvement. But biologists don't know that—they're used to working with fish or birds, all creatures that don't try to seduce them—they are not able to observe themselves in the relationship, so they produce nonsense." (Bateson, 1984, pp. 171–172)

The point is that the researcher is in the research. One cannot draw a frame around the phenomenon being studied and separate it from context. The anthropologist in the field is as much involved in producing the findings as the informants. It is the questions that are asked, the verbal and nonverbal interchanges between the researcher and the "natives," that sets a tone or metamessage for the communication that takes place. Thus, no clear line can be drawn between subjectivity and objectivity. The researcher must attend to his or her own self-consciousness and construction of "reality" in the findings. Such reflexivity rests on the assumption that there is no pure unsullied objective social reality to be recorded untarnished by human thought and emotions (see Marcus & Cushman, 1982; Marcus & Fischer, 1986, pp. 54–55; Watson, 1987). As Bateson says, "trying to be objective, you may think you are separating off an experience by setting it in a frame, but actually the frame changes the meaning of what is within it" (Bateson, 1984, p. 172).

The Study

The school year 1988–89 was spent engaged in fieldwork in nine private schools in a community. The funded study was concerned with understanding patterns of value, curriculum, and pedagogy in a variety of schools (see Bredo & Henry, 1989). The following year, 1989–90, I began the study reported here, focusing on just two of the nine schools, Waldorf School and St. Catherine's. To gain formal entry into the schools selected, I sent a written submission to each school, outlining what I proposed to do, and followed this up with telephone calls to answer questions and clarify points of ambiguity. I was already well known to the people in the schools through the previous year's study. Some weeks went by while they deliberated over the decision, requesting permission from faculty and school boards. Then access was granted. The way I was "in" varied considerably, and this reflected quite profound differences in the schools.

St. Catherine's preferred that I come on a regular basis each week to a particular class. All the teachers were informed and had a schedule of my yearly program of visits. I was to spend every Thursday at the school, although in practice I ended up alternating the days on occasion, so I was able to observe routines on other days. In addition, I frequently went to chapel on Wednesdays. Chapel was an all school affair which seemed to embody many of the social principles of the school. This gathering also gave me a chance to see all of the faculty together. Interviews were held with teachers after school, in evenings, lunch times, and during free periods in school.

At the other school, Waldorf School, I was "in" much more

tentatively at first, although this became a firm embrace. The school had some reservations about the potential costs of research to them. I was coached on what was expected of me if I wanted to maintain their full co-operation: "to understand our school, it needs to be studied as a full gesture, not as an isolated entity." There were no schedules for my visits to this school. It was agreed that I would set aside Mondays and that I would negotiate with teachers from week to week about who would be observed next. Once again, days were alternated to suit schedules, although most frequently I was there Mondays throughout the school year.

I observed lessons, plays, school festivals, and celebrations during my time in the schools. Other meetings observed included parent–teacher meetings, faculty meetings, meetings for prospective parents, and those of the anthroposophical society, which met on Monday evenings at a member's house out in the country. I carpooled with other members to travel to anthroposophy meetings. Attending the meetings was important, because a number of the founding parents of Waldorf School are highly involved in anthroposophy (the philosophy and education of Rudolf Steiner, the "founding father" of the Waldorf school movement). To many parents in the school who are not in the study group, anthroposophy means little, yet the school is guided by these principles, so it was necessary to try to understand them. Thus, many weeks I was in the schools four out of every five school days, and sometimes evenings.

Observations

Time spent in the schools actually in classrooms was considered all important. The principal means of data gathering were observations, in classrooms, meetings, hallways, athletic lessons, lunch rooms, on the playground, and elsewhere. Teachers are able to construct their ideologies intricately, which they may express eloquently in interviews. Administrators can consciously project the public image that they wish the school to have. But in the schools, over a long period of time, such efforts at building a public *face*, to use Goffman's term, break down. The researcher comes to witness and be part of the day-to-day life in schools. There, in the unvarnished, lies the opportunity to see more clearly what schools are about. In an effort to guard against falling into a pattern of easy acceptance of taking what I saw at face value I constantly asked myself, what are the opposing views? It was also important to document thoroughly many details of each event. For instance, instead of writing down "this is a friendly climate," I set out to record specifics such as the exact words spoken by the teacher, as well as facial and bodily expressions.

Intensive classroom observations occurred in the senior elementary grades (Grades 4, 5, 6, and 7), although all the grades were observed and studied. The decision to focus on the senior grades in depth, rather than spending equal time across the classes, was as much an outcome of the schools' needs as any rationale of my own. Both schools considered the older grades least likely to be disrupted by a constant observer. A side benefit was that these students had been at the schools longest and might be expected to be well socialized into the school's cultural milieu. At Waldorf School most of the students in the senior grade were in the original founding class of the school as first graders, so have been with the school throughout its history. Most of the older children at St. Catherine's have also been together since kindergarten.

Observations were recorded in the form of field notes, tape recordings, and, wherever possible, videotape. There were no objections to audiotaping classroom lessons, and it was regular procedure to audiotape all classroom observation periods. At times, however, taping other events was not permitted because of its intrusiveness, for example at faculty meetings, anthroposophical meetings, chapel, open days for parents, and so on. Immediately following these sessions I reconstructed the events from memory. An expressed fear about videotaping was that people would look at the videotape and criticize teaching or the school. For the most part, however, the statement that the tapes would be used only by the researcher, and that all publications would mask the identity of the schools was accepted, and permission to tape was granted in both schools.

The video camera was an indispensable tool in recording detail. Teaching events that are over in the space of a few short minutes are retrievable and available for close study. Bateson (1971, p. 10) makes this point:

We do not notice at which moments in a conversation we cross and uncross our legs or at which moments we puff on our cigarettes or blink our eyes or raise our brows. But the fact that we do not notice these things does not imply that all these details of personal interaction are irrelevant to the ongoing relationship. Just as we are in the main unconscious of the fleeting pacts which we enter into as to how messages are to be understood, so also we are unconscious of the continual dialogue about these pacts.

Tapes were available for repeated study long after memories of actual events had receded. Students mostly became blasé about the videotaping of their classrooms, although they sometimes saw the videocamera as a source of embarrassment —"Oh no, this is all on film," and at other times as a source of pride— "Great. Our play will be on TV." No apparent differences were noted between the schools in this regard. St. Catherine's students would be expected to be more familiar with technology, given the use of educational videotapes and computers in the school, as opposed to Waldorf, which has none. Yet both groups of students responded with interest to the idea of themselves being on videotape.

The use of the videocamera had the consequence of heightening awareness of observation initially, although this decreased as the year progressed. At the same time, however, students and teachers knew me more intimately as the year progressed, and the problem of reacting to my presence remained to a degree. This cannot be entirely overcome. No researcher is an inanimate object. What can be done is to recognize the intersubjective and interactive nature of the research and carefully pay attention to the researcher's role in the creation of data. It is also important to be there often enough to be part of the establishment and to develop a nonthreatening role through verbal assurances of confidentiality, and actions demonstrating trustworthiness. I presented myself to the schools, teachers, parents, and students as an Australian who was at the university learning about different approaches to teaching and learning. A student role is always helpful in fieldwork. People want to help students and delight in teaching them. To some audiences the project was explained in detail. To others, such as a class of fourth graders, "learning about what goes on in schools" was adequate.

During observation sessions it soon became clear that not everything could be recorded. In one sense, analysis is taking place even at the very early stage of data gathering, because the researcher is making conscious decisions about what to include and what to neglect. I decided to follow the teacher at all stages during classroom interaction. At the same time, it was important to insure that the teacher was viewed in the context of his or her whole class and not just in isolation with one or two students, although this was important, too. Some selection in shooting the videotape was of course inevitable. The aim was to include as much of the classroom as possible and to shoot the scene continuously without breaking audio or videotape. While this approach does not yield entertaining viewing, it is more likely to be scientifically useful. Pauses, gaps, time spent on tasks, were all significant aspects of life in the schools.

In field notes the exact times of segments within a lesson were also recorded. This was done to offer clues about what teachers and the schools valued, as indicated by the time spent on a particular activity. I was searching for sequences and processes within a whole event. Beginnings and endings, and points marking a rhythm, were sought for clues to patterns in events. Teachers' schedules provided some of this information, but schedules were frequently altered, and they gave only a paucity of information on what was likely to occur in any particular lesson. Events that appeared likely to offer evidence of values were also sought out and *oversampled*, Glaser and Strauss's (1967) term for theoretical sampling. For instance, chapel at St. Catherine's was studied in depth, because it is an important ritual embodying cultural values. Similarly, at Waldorf School the many festivals that are celebrated throughout the school year were studied.

Interviews, Documents, and Other Data

Formal and informal interviews were conducted with teachers, administrators, parents, board members, and students. The depth and breadth of interviews varied considerably. Sometimes the interview took place on the playground while the teacher was on playground duty. At other times they were conducted after school or in the evenings, lasting as long as 3 hours. All the teachers were interviewed a minimum of three times, and some teachers were interviewed more than a dozen times, depending on the teacher's availability and my perception of his or her usefulness in gaining access to certain types of information. Administrators were interviewed to gain demographic, historical, and other information held in school records, as well as to gauge the official "party line." Interviews with parents and students were also conducted to provide other perspectives.

The reasons for conducting interviews to supplement observation were many. Interviews provided an ideal forum initially for me to provide teachers with feedback on what was observed. It was also an ideal opportunity for me to gain feedback from the interviewees as to whether my emerging ideas were tenable from their point of view. Interview protocols were sometimes used, although it was more often the case that I started with a basic list of questions to ask a particular individual and this was modified as the interview progressed. My task was to be sensitive to issues that required further probing and to recognize when the informant needed to be "off the hook." Then other means of finding out about those sensitive areas had to be found. Interviews also helped build rapport. I was placed in situations of revealing some of my own feelings and ideas, thus building bonds that were invaluable in gaining access to the other's world.

Formal interviews were taped and transcribed. Informal interviews often took the form of a conversation. On these occasions notes were made, either at the time, for everyone knew my role as researcher, or immediately following the interview. An example of this latter type of interview would be at weekly chapel at St. Catherine's, where I sometimes engaged in conversation with chapel mothers or parents attending chapel prior to the event. More often interviews were carefully planned, although I tried to cultivate an informal and nonthreatening climate for every interview.

In addition, school documents were studied for their content, form, and tone. These included: school newsletters, bulletins, the curriculum, parent, faculty and student handbooks, and other documents produced by the schools. "Maps" of social relationships, school structure, use of space, physical setting, layout, and so on, were useful for their explicit and implicit messages. Finally, artifacts, such as wall hangings, art work, posters, murals, and other decorative items on school walls were studied for what they might also reveal about school culture.

Grounded Theory

The purpose of the study was to describe and analyze school cultures, the "little universes of meaning" (Geertz, 1980, p. 171) at Waldorf School and St. Catherine's. To study in cultures necessitated the methods of cultural anthropology, built on the notion of extended fieldwork and the method of "constant comparative analysis" to make sense of the data (see Glaser & Strauss, 1967, pp. 101–117; Goetz & LeCompte, 1984). Fieldnotes, consisting of observations, interview transcripts, video transcripts, school documents, and methodological and self-as-instrument notes, were studied daily and coded tentatively into conceptual units. As these units emerged from the raw data, further questions arose that were used to guide ongoing observations and interviews. The findings from the new fieldwork were compared to the initial units. The unitized data were then organized into categories that provided inferential or descriptive information about the contexts under study. Tentative categories were refined by a constant comparison of data. Of particular usefulness were negative cases and the testing of ideas on participants. Such an inductive process led me toward theory that was "grounded" in the data. In other words, the units and categories were readily, not forcibly, indicated by the data, and they were also recognizable to the people in the situation studied. Thus, the repeated process of coding data and the generation of new ideas from the data continued until the findings could be presented in a way that made sense to the participants in the study and myself.

Problem Solving in the Field

Difficulties encountered in the field were many. The first challenge was the physical and emotional demands of fieldwork. Questions were formulated and gaps in knowledge recognized. Fieldnotes were written up or expanded as soon after events as possible. Videotapes and audiotapes were reviewed, transcribed, and indexed, tapes copied and distributed to the teach-

ers. It was important to do follow up interviews and establish
new leads and connections wherever possible. Then I needed to
find time for reflection and conceptual work. Becoming intimate
with the schools, asking countless questions, and learning their
"codes" required time, patience, and persistence.

Though I had read widely on anthropological research design,
the many accounts of fieldwork and ethnographies, books, and
articles were unable to provide answers to problems that were
locally situated. The general issue I was grappling with at any
one point in time might have been discussed by one or another
researcher, but its enactment was often more complex and
required my own judgment and decision making in quite different circumstances than those described by others. Some of
these problems I had experienced before, having conducted an
ethnographic study of rural schooling in Australia (Henry, 1986,
1989). However, even the "same" problems were quite different
in a different setting.

One issue was that I was by no stretch of the imagination a
native. Neither had I been a native in the rural school study.
There I was an outsider in a community where very few people
were university educated. But I had been an Australian. That
much I shared with my informants, though some were Aboriginal Australians. Here in the U.S. I was distinctly different. I had
spent my whole life, some 34 years at the time of my arrival in
the U.S., in a different culture. Geertz's maxim that the familiar
needs to be seen as strange was helped by my immersion in a
new culture. However, if the researcher is from a different
culture then there is always the possibility of relational difficulties. Fortunately, Australia is not so culturally divorced from the
U.S. that this proved to be a major barrier. There was a Waldorf
school, called Steiner School, in the city in which I lived prior to
my arrival in the States, which I had visited. Episcopal and
college prep schools (though not known by those labels) were
also well known to me in Australia. Nevertheless, there was an
ongoing problem of bringing Australian lenses to bear on American phenomena and misreading people and situations. As far as
possible I tried to assume an initial position of openness, and
have the people in the schools give me their versions through
actions and words of what was going on. These ideas were then

verified with multiple informants and through other techniques of data collection, a practice known as *triangulating data*.

In some ways my Australian identity enhanced my involvement in the schools. At St. Catherine's I gave short talks about Australia—its flora, fauna, environment, geography, history, economy, political system, and so on. For students in both schools I was a source of information about Australia, fielding questions on topics ranging from "Walkabout Creek" (of *Crocodile Dundee* fame) to parakeets. When I set up interviews I sometimes felt that people were agreeing as much out of a sense of hospitality to a non-American as for any other reason. They also felt they had to explain things more completely to me, since it was assumed that I was learning about their school and the American situation.

The problem then became how to be sincere in all these contacts and friendships that developed throughout the course of the study. I tried to be direct and open about my mission in the schools, but there were many occasions when the lines between friendship and professional relations became blurred. Separating what people told me in confidence, or when I was in their home visiting unofficially, from what was part of the study became an issue. Being continually open to new avenues for information, cross checking data with multiple members of the cultures, seeking confirmation of material, all these are maxims for good fieldwork, and they all require a fair degree of aggressive work with informants and a balancing of human concern with research objectives.

What both schools hoped for, I assumed, were favorable reports. Schools, particularly private schools, have a vested interest in maintaining a good public image. Failing to do this almost certainly means closure. While needing to be sensitive to this concern, research can never be a public relations exercise. Educational problems in schools, as well as the admirable, needs to be considered. What I could offer the schools was to try to be involved fully in the school and open to what people were saying and trying to do, so as not to be biased against them. In addition, I needed to be aware of the possibility that the views presented might have been contaminated in some way. Informants can be influenced by the researcher's "leading questions,'' a problem that I tried to guard against by the use of probes that were not suggestive. Other possible problems were that informants would work to present a favorable image of the school, or that they would want to please me (give the researcher what she wants) or distort information because of a fear of retribution from others. Actions such as turning off the tape recorder to clarify a point "off the record" and setting up interviews on personal territory, rather than at school, were possibly significant actions with other stories embedded in them.

I also sought ways in which I could return something of value to the schools. One of the ways I was able to help was as an extra adult in the school. To students I was an adult in whom they could confide without fear of judgment. Students told me when they were planning to lock the teacher out of classrooms or engage in other pranks. When students were having relational problems with friends or were worried about upcoming tests, they frequently shared these concerns with me. I was also an audience for students, who seemed to delight in having an interested observer. At St. Catherine's in particular, I was often greeted with pleas to "Come to our class."

Sometimes teachers took advantage of my presence to leave the room or group, confident that there was an adult available for the children. I was also occasionally used as an extra hand, for instance to drive children places. But it was my role as listener that seemed to be most important. Often when I was in this role I thought back to my own decade of teaching in primary schools and how isolated one can feel. I had particularly enjoyed team teaching ventures because of the comaraderie these situations evoked. In the schools under study there were many teachers who delighted in the telling of their story. Strong emotions surfaced. More than once there were tears quickly blinked away in the course of an interview. Even in good schools with good management, the isolation of teaching and the stresses of working alone with young children for long periods exist.

Another way of giving something back to the schools was to provide the teachers with copies of the videotapes of their teaching. Some teachers used these for personal review, so that they could better understand how they taught and work at improving problem areas. After they had viewed the tapes I

would elicit responses, and the ensuing discussions were helpful. The majority of teachers had never seen themselves teach on
videotape, so the idea of being on tape was of interest, although
they regarded it as a challenge. On receiving the tape some
teachers were embarrassed or nervous about viewing it, saying
things such as "I'll have to psych myself up to this." I was also
thanked by many teachers for asking hard questions and
"keeping them on their toes."

Self-as-Instrument

The ethnographer's hand is evident on every page of the mono-
graph. What is selected, framed, and edited is a reflection of the
author. The researcher's character is in many ways indelibly
etched on the canvas that tells the story. In an effort to lay out the
researcher's biases it is traditional to include a section on self
disclosure in ethnographies. Alan Peshkin's (1986) discussion of
his Jewishness and other aspects of his "self" when studying a
fundamentalist Christian school is an example. While recognizing that attempts to lay out one's biases is inevitably flawed
by the same bias that permeates the research, the tradition is a
useful one.

Ethnographers are not just intellectual voyeurs, as Leslie
Roman (Roman & Christian-Smith, 1988) has suggested. Instead,
they seek to gain an insider's view, at the same time acknowl-
edging their own part in the production and creation of knowledge. Data are produced discursively in association with informants. In every study the "cultural baggage" or "knowledge
position" of the researcher is important. Every researcher needs
to ask himself or herself: Why am I interested in studying this?
Why do we need to know this? What are my assumptions about
the work I am doing? How are those assumptions changing over
time?

One of my assumptions is that studying schools in the field is
critical for the social science of education. Having spent a
decade in schools as a teacher my view of schools and the
importance of bridging the gap between the academician and the
practitioner differs from those who would keep the ivory tower
clean and unsullied. I also believe in private schooling and
parents' right to choose an education, yet this rests uneasily with

my belief in equality of opportunity. The idea of "choice" excludes many people. At the same time I am an idealist and an optimist, someone who holds faith that schools can be better than they are. Private schools provide a welcome relief from a bureaucratic model of schooling. They offer different kinds of education, the choice that we have come to expect in so many other aspects of our lives.

In reflecting on my patterns "for" behavior (the mentalistic component) I am made aware of just how complex this is and how contradictory certain elements are. Although a rebel, a nonconformist in many ways, I have not forsaken entirely my conservative upbringing. I respect my parents' credo (white, Anglo-Saxon, Anglican), but I also admire so many other world-views. To many people, though, I may appear conservative and predictable. In terms of the effects on the research I have to acknowledge this blend in me, the struggle between the conservative who follows the socially acceptable course of action and the rebel. There is a tendency for me to be seen as compliant and "nice" by informants, which has the potential to elicit confidential responses, raising ethical dilemmas. Patterns of behavior (or observable behavior) would have to include my high energy level. I think I am expressive, yet in the American context people often assume I am reserved and disciplined. This could also be my Anglo upbringing. I am attracted to different ways of thinking and being, which have been fed through scholarly reading and time spent in not-so-ordinary places—from Ayers Rock in outback Australia to Istanbul. That I now live in the U.S., studying schools, is witness to my cultural interest.

My identity as a white female is significant. Socialized into the world of womanhood, my perception is shaped in a way that differs from my male counterparts. We need only look at recent advances in anthropology where "cultures previously portrayed only through the eyes of men have been totally recast by ethnographies that address the role and status of women" (Ulin, 1984, p. 157). Also, my life's work as a teacher makes me sympathetic to teachers' situations and concerns in a way that others may not share. It may also make me critical of teaching and aware of its ramifications. Like McLaren's nun who offered prayer in atonement for the suffering teachers inflict on students (1986, p. 189), I share a concern for students and recognize their vulnerability. Another aspect of my "cultural baggage" is that I am an Australian, which led, as previously discussed, to interesting relations with parents, teachers, and students. The eyes of someone not reared to see in American ways invariably filter a different view. Whether this resonates with the experience and knowledge of others reared in a culture depends on my ability to penetrate the social code, and to represent it with its identifying features and with my signature, so that others can see where I have framed the picture.

REFERENCES

Addison, J. T. (1969). *The Episcopal church in the United States: 1789–1931.* Boston: Archon Books.

Anyon, J. (1989). Social class and the hidden curriculum of work, In J. Ballantine (Ed.), *Schools and society* (2nd ed.). Mountain View, CA: Mayfield Publishing Company.

Apple, M. & Weis, L. (Eds.). (1983). *Ideology and practice in schooling.* Philadelphia: Temple University Press.

Armstrong, T. (1988, August). Lessons in wonder: Waldorf schools emphasize what others don't—the fairy tale magic of being a child. *Parenting,* pp. 44–45.

Aronowitz, S. (1973). *False promises: The shaping of American working class consciousness.* New York: McGraw-Hill.

Association of Waldorf Schools of North America (AWSNA). (1988). *Directory of schools 1988–89.* Great Barrington, MA: Author.

Atkin, J. M., Patrick, C., & Kennedy, D. (1989). *Inside schools: A collaborative view.* New York: The Falmer Press.

Baltzell, E. D. (1964). *The protestant establishment.* New York: Random House.

Barnes, H. (1988). *The introduction to Waldorf education.* New York: Hillsdale.

Barr, R., & Dreeben, R. (1983). *How schools work.* Chicago: University of Chicago Press.

Barth, R. (1980). *Run school run.* Cambridge, MA: Cambridge University Press.

Bateson, G. (1955). The message "This is play." In B. Schaffner (Ed.), *Group processes: Transactions of the second conference.* New York: Josiah Macy Jr. Foundation.

Bateson, G. (1971). Introduction. In *The natural history of an interview*. (Series 15, Nos. 95–98). University of Chicago Library Microfilm Collection of Manuscripts in Cultural Anthropology.

Bateson, M. C. (1984). *With a daughter's eye: A memoir of Margaret Mead and Gregory Bateson*. New York: William Morrow and Company, Inc.

Bateson, M. C. (1990, March 23). *Composing a life: Conscious purpose, gender and response*. Lecture at the University of Virginia, Charlottesville, Virginia.

Becker, H. (1986). *Doing things together: Selected papers*. Evanston, IL: Northwestern University Press.

Belenky, M., Clinchy, B., Goldberger, N., & Tarule, J. (1985). Epistemological development and the politics of family talk. *Journal of Education, 167 (3)*, 9–27.

Benamou, M., & Caramello, C. (Eds.). (1977). *Performance in postmodern culture*. Madison, WI: Coda.

Bernstein, B., Elvin, H., & Peters, R. S. (1966). Ritual in education. *Philosophical Transactions of the Royal Society of London*, Series B, 251(772), 429–436.

Bernstein, B. (1971). On the classification and framing of educational knowledge. In M. Young (Ed.), *Knowledge and control: New directions of the sociology of knowledge*. London: Collier-Macmillan.

Bernstein, B. (1977). *Class, codes and control* (Vol. 3). London: Routledge and Kegan Paul.

Boas, D. (Ed.). (1986). *Left, right and babyboom: America's new politics*. Washington, DC: Cato Institute.

Bourdieu, P., & Passeron, J. (1977). *Reproduction: In education, society and culture*. London: Sage.

Bowles, S., & Gintis, H. (1976). *Schooling in capitalist America*. New York: Basic Books.

Bredo, E. (1990). *Games, texts and dramas as metaphors of schooling*. Unpublished manuscript, University of Virginia, Charlottesville, Virginia.

Bredo, E., & Henry, M. (1989, February 24–25). *Alternatives to the one best system*. Paper presented at the Ethnography in Education Research Forum, University of Pennsylvania, Philadelphia.

Buerk, D. (1986, January 30). Shared meanings in mathematics: An approach for teachers. *Radical Teacher*, pp. 26–29.

Carlgren, F. (1972). *Education towards freedom* (Trans. from Erziehumg zur Freiheit). London UK: Lanthorn Press.

Cazden, C. (1988). *Classroom discourse*. Portsmouth, NH: Heinemann.

Chemerinsky, E. (1989). The constitution and private schools. In N. Devins (Ed.), *Public values, private schools*. Philadelphia: The Falmer Press.

Chubb, J., & Moe, T. (1990). *Politics, markets and America's schools*. Washington, DC: The Brookings Institute.

Clifford, J. (1986). On ethnographic allegory. In J. Clifford & G. Marcus (Eds.), *Writing culture: The poetics and politics of ethnography*. Berkeley, CA: University of California Press.

Coleman, J., Hoffer T., & Kilgore, S. (1982). *High school achievement: Public, catholic and private schools compared*. New York: Basic Books.

Connell, R., Ashenden, D., Kessler, S., & Dowsett, G. (1982). *Making the difference: Families and social division.* Sydney: George Allen and Unwin.

Cookson, P., & Persell, C. (1985). *Preparing for power: America's elite boarding schools.* New York: Basic Books.

Cooper, B. (1988a). The changing universe of U.S. private schools. In T. James & H. Levin (Eds.), *Comparing public and private schools* (Vol. 1). New York: The Falmer Press.

Cooper, B. (1988b). The uncertain future of national education policy: private schools and the federal role. In W. Boyd & C. Kerchner (Eds.), *The politics of excellence and choice in education.* New York: The Falmer Press.

Cusick, P. (1973). *Inside high school: The student's world.* New York: Holt, Rinehart and Winston, Inc.

Davies, B. (1982). *Life in the classroom and playground: The accounts of primary school children.* London: Routledge and Kegan Paul.

Deal, T. (1985). The symbolism of effective schools. *The Elementary School Journal, 85* (5), 615.

Deal, T. (1990). Private schools: Bridging Mr. Chips and my captain. *Teachers College Record, 92* (3), 415–424.

Deal, T., & Kennedy, A. (1982). *Corporate cultures.* Reading, MA: Addison-Wesley.

Deal, T., & Peterson, K. (1990). *The principal's role in shaping school culture.* Washington, DC: U.S. Government Printing Office.

Deering, P. (1989, October). *An ethnographic approach for examining participant's construction of a cooperative learning classroom culture.* Paper presented at the Annual Meeting of the American Anthropological Association, Washington, DC.

Dewey, J. (1938). *Experience and education.* New York: Collier.

Dewey, J. (1960). *How we think.* Lexington, MA: D.C. Heath and Company. (Original work published 1933)

Dreeben, R. (1968). *On what is learned in school.* Reading, MA: Addison-Wesley.

Dugan, D. (1990). *Survey of San Francisco Waldorf School parents.* Unpublished manuscript, San Francisco.

Durkheim, E. (1961). *Moral education: A study in the theory and application of the sociology of education.* New York: The Free Press.

Durkheim, E. (1965). *The elementary forms of religious life* (J. W. Swain, Trans.). New York: Free Press.

Eisenhart, M. (1990). Reconsidering cultural differences in American schools. *Educational Foundations, 3* (2), 51–68.

Ely, J. (1976). *The crisis of conservative Virginia.* Knoxville: The University of Tennessee Press.

Erickson, F. (1982a). Classroom discourse as improvisation: Relationships between academic task structure and social participation structure in lessons. In L. C. Wilkinson (Ed.), *Communicating in the classroom.* New York: Academic Press.

Erickson, F. (1982b). Taught cognitive learning in its immediate environment: A neglected topic in the anthropology of education. *Anthropology of Education Quarterly, 13 (2)*, 149–180.

Erickson, F. (1987). Transformation and social success: The politics and culture of educational achievement. *Anthropology and Education Quarterly, 18*, 335–356.

Everhart, R. (1988). *Practical ideology and symbolic community.* New York: The Falmer Press.

Fitzgerald, J., & Brackbill, Y. (1976). Classical conditioning in infancy: Development and constraints. *Psychological Bulletin, 83*, 353–376.

Geertz, C. (1965). The transition to humanity. In S. Tax (Ed.), *Horizons of anthropology.* London: George Allen and Unwin.

Geertz, C. (1966). Religion as a cultural system. In M. Banton (Ed.), *Anthropological approaches to the study of religion.* London: Tavistock.

Geertz, C. (1968). Religion as a cultural system. In D. Cutler (Ed.), *The religious situation.* Boston: Beacon Press.

Geertz, C. (1973). *The interpretation of cultures.* New York: Basic Books.

Geertz, C. (1980). Blurred genres: The refiguration of social thought. *The American Scholar, 49 (2)*, 165–179.

Gehrke, N. (1979). Rituals of the hidden curriculum. In K. Yamomoto (Ed.), *Children in space and time.* New York: Teachers College Press.

Gerholm, T. (1988). On ritual: A postmodernist view. *Ethnos, 53 (3–4)*, 190–203.

Gesell, A. (1977). *The child from five to ten.* New York: Harper and Row.

Giroux, H. (1981). *Ideology, culture, and the process of schooling.* Philadelphia: Temple University Press.

Giroux, H. (1983). *Theory and resistance in education.* South Hadley, MA: Bergin and Garvey.

Giroux, H. (1984). Marxism and schooling: the limits of radical discourse. *Educational theory, 34 (2)*, 113–35.

Giroux, H. (1988). *Teachers as intellectuals.* Granby, MA: Bergin and Garvey.

Glaser, B., & Strauss, A. (1967). *The discovery of grounded theory.* Chicago: Aldine.

Goetz, J., & LeCompte, M. (1984). *Ethnography and qualitative design in educational research.* Orlando, FL: Academic Press.

Goffman, E. (1959). *The presentation of self in everyday life.* Harmondsworth, UK: Penguin.

Goffman, E. (1961). *Asylums: Essays on the social situation of mental patients and other inmates.* Garden City, NJ: Anchor Books.

Goffman, E. (1967). *Interaction ritual: Essays on face-to-face behavior.* Garden City, NY: Doubleday & Company, Anchor Books.

Goldman, S. & McDermott, R. (1987). The culture of competition in American schools. In G. Spindler (Ed.), *Education and cultural process: Anthropological approaches* (2nd ed.). Prospect Heights, IL: Waveland Press.

Grant, G. (1988). *The world we created at Hamilton high.* Cambridge, MA: Harvard University Press.

Greene, M. (1983). Curriculum and consciousness. In Henry Giroux & D. Purpel (Eds.), *The hidden curriculum and moral education*. Berkeley, CA: McCutchan Publishing Corporation.

Grimes, R. (1982). *Beginnings in ritual studies*. Washington, DC: University Press of America.

Haertel, E., James, T., & Levin, H. (1987). Introduction. In E. Haertel, T. James & H. Levin (Eds.), *Comparing public and private schools* (Vol. II). New York: The Falmer Press.

Hall, E. T. (1973). *The silent language*. Garden City, NY: Doubleday. (Original work published 1959)

Hall, E. T. (1984). *The dance of life: The other dimension of time*. New York: Anchor Press.

Hanson, F. (1982). Introduction. In F. Hanson (Ed.), *Studies in symbolism and cultural communication*. Lawrence, KS: University of Kansas.

Harwood, A. (1977). *Portrait of a Waldorf school*. New York: The Myrin Institute.

Harwood, A. (1980). Eurythmy in education. In *Eurythmy: Essays and anecdotes*. Roselle, IL: Schaumburg Publications.

Heath, S. B. (1983). *Ways with words: Language, life and work in communities and classrooms*. New York: Cambridge University Press.

Henry, M. (1986). *Rural schooling: An ethnology*. Unpublished masters dissertation, University of New England, Australia.

Henry, M. (1989, October). *Ideologically diverse schooling and community*. Paper presented at the annual meeting of the American Educational Studies Association, Chicago.

Henry, M. (1990). *Private schools and the hidden curriculum*. Doctoral dissertation, University of Virginia. (*Dissertation Abstracts International*, Vol. 51105–A, p. 1570.)

Henry, M. (1991, April). *The symbolic order of school*. Paper presented at the annual meeting of the American Educational Research Association, Chicago.

Henry, M. (in press). School rituals as educational contexts: Symbolizing the world, others and "self" in Waldorf and College Prep schools. *International Journal of Qualitative Studies in Education*.

Hymes, D. (1980). Educational ethnology. *Anthropology and Education Quarterly, 11*, 1.

Hymes, D. (1982). Narrative form as a "grammar" of experience: Native Americans and a glimpse of English? *Journal of Education, 164*, 121–142.

Jackson, P. (1968). *Life in classrooms*. New York: Holt, Rinehart and Winston.

Jackson, P. (1986). *The practice of teaching*. New York: Teachers College Press.

Jacob, E. (1984, April). *Reading and writing activities at home and school A new perspective*. Paper presented at the American Educational Research Association, New Orleans.

James, T. (1988, November). Totality in private and public schooling. *American Journal of Education*, pp. 1–17.

James, T., & Levin, H. (1988). Introduction. In T. James & H. Levin (Eds.), *Comparing public and private schools* (Vol. I). New York: The Falmer Press.

Kaestle, C. (1983). *Pillars of the republic: Common schools and American society, 1780–1860.* New York: Hill and Wang.

Kane, P. (1991). Independent schools in American education. *Teachers College Record, 92*(3), 396–408.

Kapferer, J. (1981). Socialization and the symbolic order of the school. *Anthropology and Education Quarterly, 11* (3), 258–74.

Kisseleff, T. (1980). Eurythmy: Metamorphosis of temple dance. In *Eurythmy: Essays and anecdotes.* Roselle, IL:Schaumburg Publications.

Kluckhohn, C. (1962). *Culture and behavior* (Richard Kluckhohn, Ed.). New York: The Free Press.

Kraushaar, O. F. (1972). *American non-public schools: Patterns of diversity.* Baltimore, MD: Johns Hopkins University Press.

Leinster-Mackay, D. (1984). *The rise of the English prep school.* London: The Falmer Press.

Lesko, N. (1988). *Symbolizing society: Stories, rites and structure in a Catholic high school.* New York: The Falmer Press.

Levin, B. (1987). The courts as education policy-makers in the USA. In W. Boyd & D. Smart (Eds.), *Educational policy in Australia and America: Comparative perspectives.* New York: The Falmer Press.

Lévi-Strauss, C. (1963). *Structural anthropology* (C. Jacobson & Brooke G. Schoepf, Trans.). New York: Basic Books.

Lévi-Strauss, C. (1979). *Myth and meaning.* New York: Schocken Books.

Lisman, D. (1990, October-November). *The ethical: Socialization, social critique and the community.* Paper presented at the annual meeting of the American Educational Studies Association, Orlando, FL.

Lortie, D. (1975). *Schoolteacher: A sociological study.* Chicago: University of Chicago Press.

Lutheran Church. (1990). *Statistical report summary, 1989-90.* St. Louis, MO:Lutheran Church, International Center.

Marcus, G., & Cushman, D. (1982). Ethnographies as texts. *Annual Review of Anthropology, 11*, 25–69.

Marcus, G. E., & Fischer, M. M. J. (1986). *Anthropology as cultural critique: An experimental moment in the human sciences.* Chicago: University of Chicago Press.

Massad, C. (1979). Time and space in space and time. In K. Yamamoto (Ed.), *Children in time and space.* New York: Teachers College Press.

Mathus, D. (1989). *A comparison of the philosophy of John Dewey and the Episcopal Church.* Unpublished manuscript, University of Virginia, Department of Educational Studies, Charlottesville, VA.

McDermott, R. P. (1974). Achieving school failure. In G. Spindler (Ed.), *Education and cultural process.* New York: Holt, Rinehart and Winston.

McDermott, R.P. (1976). *Kids make sense: An ethnographic account of the interactional management of success and failure in one first grade classroom.* Unpublished doctoral dissertation, Stanford University.

McDermott, R. (1984). *The essential Steiner: Basic writings of Rudolf Steiner.* New York: Anthroposophic Press.

McDermott, R. P., Goldman, S., & Varenne, H. (1984). When school goes home: Some problems in the organization of homework. *Teachers College Record, 85* (3), 391–409.

McDermott, R. P., & Roth, D. (1978). The social organization of behavior: Interactional approaches. *Annual Review of Anthropology, 7,* 321–345.

McLachlan, J. (1970). *American boarding schools: A historical study.* New York: Charles Scribner's Sons.

McLaren, P. (1986). *Schooling as a ritual performance.* London: Routledge and Kegan Paul.

McLaren, P. (1988). Schooling the postmodern body: Critical pedagogy and the politics of enfleshment. *Journal of Education, 170* (3), 530–83.

Mehan, H. (1978). Structuring school structure. *Harvard Educational Review, 48,* 32–46.

Mehan, H. (1979). *Learning lessons.* Cambridge, MA: Harvard University Press.

Mehlman, C. (1991). Walden within. In R. Miller (Ed.), *New directions in education: Selections from Holistic Education Review.* Brandon, VT: Holistic Education Press.

Metz, M. H. (1978). *Classrooms and corridors: The crisis of authority in desegregated secondary schools.* Berkeley, CA: University of California Press.

Meyer, J., & Rowan, B. (1978). The structure of educational organizations. In M. Meyer, J. Freeman, M. Hannan, J. Meyer, W. Ouchi, J. Pfeffer, & W. Scott (Eds.), *Environments and organizations.* San Francisco: Jossey-Bass.

Milton, J. (1967). The tractate on education, 1644. In J. Patrick (Ed.), *The prose of John Milton.* Garden City, NY: Doubleday & Company. (Original work published 1644).

Mitchell, D., Ortiz, F., & Mitchell, T. (1987). *Work orientation and job performance: The cultural basis of teaching rewards and incentives.* Albany: State University of New York Press.

Niederhauser, H., & Frohlich, M. (1984). *Form drawing.* Spring Valley, NY: Mercury Press.

Noblit, G., & Pink, W. (Eds.). (1987). *Schooling in social context: Qualitative studies.* Norwood, NJ: Ablex Publishing Corporation.

Oakes, J. (1985). *Keeping track.* New Haven, CT: Yale University Press.

Olson, L. (1991, February 20). Proposals for private-school choice reviving at all levels of government. *Education Week,* pp. 1, 10, 11.

Ostling, R. (1991, April 29). A revolution hoping for a miracle. *Time,* pp. 52–53.

Oswald, P. (1988). Montessori and Waldorf education. *Communications, 4,* 9–21.

Page, R. (1990). Cultures and curricula: Differences between and within schools. *Educational Foundations, 4* (1), 49–76.

Parsons, T. (1959). The school class as a social system: Some of its functions in American society. *Harvard Educational Review, 29* (4), 297–318.

Persell, C., & Cookson, P. (1989). Power and privilege in education: American boarding schools today. In J. Ballantine (Ed.), *Schools and society.* Mountain View, CA: Mayfield Publishing Company.

Peshkin, A. (1986). *God's choice: The total world of a fundamentalist christian school.* Chicago: The University of Chicago Press.

Pouderoyen, E. (1980). Historical notes on Eurythmy. In *Eurythmy: Essays and anecdotes.* Roselle, IL: Schaumburg Publications.

Rebell, M. (1989). Values inculcation and the schools: The need for a new Pierce compromise. In N. Devins (Ed.), *Public values, private schools.* Philadelphia: The Falmer Press.

Reese, W. (1985). Soldiers for Christ in the army of God: The Christian school movement in America. *Educational Theory, 35* (2), 175–194.

Rice, K. (1980). *Geertz and culture.* Ann Arbor, MI: The University of Michigan Press.

Richards, M. (1980). *Toward wholeness: Rudolf Steiner education in America.* Middletown, CT: Wesleyan University Press.

Ringle, K. (1989, 11 November). The school with a Southern accent. *The Washington Post,* pp. c1, c4.

Rohlen, T. (1983). *Japan's high schools.* Berkeley, CA: University of California Press.

Roman, L., & Christian-Smith, L. (Eds.). (1988). *Becoming feminine: The politics of popular culture.* New York: Falmer Press.

Rorty, R. (1990, March 30). *Dewey, pragmatism and education.* Lecture given at the University of Virginia, Charlottesville, VA.

Sarason, S. (1971). *The culture of the school and the problem of change.* Boston: Allyn & Bacon.

Schechner, R. (1977). *Essays on performance theory 1970–1976.* New York: Drama Book Specialists.

Schein, E. (1985). *Organizational culture & leadership.* San Francisco: Jossey-Bass.

Schofield, J. (1989). *Black and white in school: Trust, tension or tolerance?* New York: Teachers College Press.

Scott, W., & Meyer, J. (1989). Environmental linkages and organizational complexity: Public and private schools. In J. Ballantine (Ed.), *Schools and society.* Mountain View, CA: Mayfield Publishing Company.

Sergiovanni, T. (1990). *Value-added leadership: How to get extraordinary performance in schools.* Orlando, FL: Harcourt, Brace, Jovanovich, Inc.

Shklovsky, V. (1965). Art as technique. In L. Lemon & M. Reis (Trans.), *Formalist criticism: Four essays.* Lincoln: University of Nebraska Press.

Simons, E. (1980). Movement as a language of the soul. In *Eurythmy: Essays and anecdotes.* Roselle, IL: Schaumburg Publications.

Sisson, C. H. (1983). *Anglican essays.* Manchester: Carcanet Press.

Sizer, T. (1964). The academies: An interpretation. In T. Sizer (Ed.), *The age of the academies.* New York: Teachers College Press.

Sommer, R. (1974). *Tight spaces: Hard architecture and how to humanize it.* Englewood Cliffs, NJ: Prentice-Hall.

Southworth, C. (1989, November). *Teacher as poet: A Waldorf image of teacher education*. Paper presented at the American Educational Studies Association, Chicago.

Southworth, C. (1990). Static knowledge, mobile imaginations, and the image of humankind. *Educational Foundations, 4* (3), 59–82.

Spindler, G. (Ed.). (1978). *The making of psychological anthropology*. Berkeley, CA: University of California Press.

Spindler, G. (Ed.). (1982). *Doing the ethnography of schooling: Anthropological approaches* (2nd ed.). New York: Holt, Rinehart and Winston.

Spindler, G., & Spindler, L. (1987a). Ethnography: An anthropological view. In G. Spindler (Ed.). *Education and cultural process: Anthropological approaches* (2nd ed.). Prospect Heights, IL: Waveland Press.

Spindler, G., & Spindler, L. (1987b). Schonhausen revisited and the rediscovery of culture. In G. Spindler & L. Spindler (Eds.), *Interpretive ethnography at home and abroad*. Hillsdale, NJ: Erlbaum.

Spradley, J., & McCurdy, D. (1988). *The cultural experience*. Prospect Heights, IL: Waveland. (Original work published 1972)

Steiner, R. (1907). Autobiographical sketch. In R. A. McDermott (Ed.), *The essential Steiner*. San Franscisco: Harper.

Steiner, R. (1926). *The essentials of education* (H. Collison, Ed.). London: Anthroposophical Publishing Company.

Steiner, R. (1937). *Practical course for teachers*. New York: Anthroposophic Press.

Steiner, R. (1947a). *Knowledge of the higher worlds and its attainment* (H. & L. Monges, Trans.). Spring Valley, NY: Anthroposophic Press.

Steiner, R. (1947b). *Spiritual ground of education*. London: Anthroposophical Publishing Co. (Nine lectures given at Oxford, 16–25 August, 1922)

Steiner, R. (1966). *Study of man*. London: Rudolf Steiner Press.

Steiner, R. (1967). *Discussions with teachers*. London: Rudolf Steiner Press.

Steiner, R. (1968). *The roots of education* (H. Fox, Trans.). London: Rudolf Steiner Press

Steiner, R. (1970). *The philosophy of freedom: The basis for a modern world conception* (M. Wilson, Trans.). New York: Anthroposophic Press.

Steiner, R. (1972). *Occult science: An introduction* (3rd ed.). Spring Valley, NY: Anthroposophic Press.

Steiner, R. (1973). *Theosophy: An introduction to the supersensible knowledge of the world and the destination of man* (4th ed.). London: Rudolf Steiner Press.

Steiner, R. (1977). *Rudolf Steiner: An autobiography* (R. Stebbing, Trans.). New York: Rudolf Steiner Publications.

Steiner, R. (1980). Introductory words for a eurythmy performance. In *Eurythmy*. Roselle, IL: Schaumburg Publications, Inc.

Steiner, R. (1981). *Truth and knowledge: An introduction to philosophy of freedom*. (R. Stebbing, Trans.). Blauvelt, NY: Garber Communications. (Original work published 1892)

Steiner, R. (1982). *The kingdom of childhood*. London: Rudolf Steiner Press.

Stephens, J. (1967). *The process of schooling*. New York: Holt, Rinehart & Winston, Inc.

Stockmeyer, E. (1982). *Rudolf Steiner's curriculum for Waldorf schools.* Forest Row, E. Sussex, UK: Steiner Schools Fellowship Publications.

Tobin, J. J., Wu, D. Y., & Davidson, D. H. (1989). *Preschool in three cultures: Japan, China and the United States.* New Haven, CT: Yale University Press.

Toch. T. (1991, December 9). The exodus. *U.S. News & World Report, 3* (24), 66–77.

Turner, V. (1967). *The forest of symbols.* Ithaca, NY: Cornell University Press.

Turner, V. (1968). *The drums of affliction.* Oxford: Clarendon Press.

Turner, V. (1969). *The ritual process: Structure and anti-structure.* Chicago: Aldine.

Turner, V. (1988). *The anthropology of performance.* New York: PAJ Publications.

Tyack, D., & Hansot, E. (1982). *Managers of virtue: Public school leadership in America, 1820–1980.* New York: Basic Books.

Tyack, D. (1968, October). The perils of pluralism: The background of the Pierce case. *American Historical Review, 74,* 74–98.

Uhrmacher, B. (1989, November). *Knowing-with Social Studies education.* Paper presented at the annual meeting of the National Council for the Social Studies, St. Louis, MO.

Uhrmacher, B. (1991). *Waldorf schools marching quietly unheard.* Unpublished doctoral dissertation, Stanford University.

Ulin, R. (1984). *Understanding cultures: Perspectives in anthropology and social theory.* Austin: University of Texas Press.

U.S. Department of Education. (1989). *Choosing a school for your child.* Washington, DC: U.S. Department of Education.

U.S. Department of Education. (1991). *Digest of education statistics.* Washington, DC: U.S. Department of Education National Center for Education Statistics.

Vallance, E. (1983). Hiding the hidden curriculum: An interpretation of the language of justification in nineteenth century educational reform. In H. Giroux & D. Purpel (Eds.), *The hidden curriculum and moral education.* Berkeley, CA: McCutchan Publishing Company.

VanMaanen, J. (1988). *Tales of the field.* Chicago: University of Chicago Press.

Varenne, H. (1977). *Americans together: Structured diversity in a Midwestern town.* New York: Teachers College Press.

Varenne, H., & McDermott, R. P. (1986). "Why" Sheila can read. In B. Schieffelin & P. Gilmore (Eds.), *The acquisition of literacy: Ethnographic perspectives.* Norwood, NJ: Ablex Publishing Corp.

Waller, W. (1932). *The sociology of teaching.* New York: John Wiley.

Weick, K. (1982, June). Administering education in loosely coupled schools. *Phi Delta Kappan,* pp. 673–676.

Willis, P. (1977). *Learning to labor: How working class kids get working class jobs.* Hampshire, UK: Gower.

Wolcott, H. (1973). *The man in the principal's office: an ethnography.* New York: Holt, Rinehart and Winston.

Wolcott, H. (1976). Criteria for an ethnographic approach to research in schools. In J. I. Roberts & S. K. Akinsanya (Eds.) *Schooling in the cultural context*. New York: McKay.

Wolcott, H. (1977). *Teachers versus technocrats: An educational innovation in anthropological perspective*. Eugene, OR: University of Oregon.

Wolcott, H. (1987). Life's not working: cultural alternatives to career alternatives. In G. Noblit & W. Pink (Eds.) *Schooling in social context: qualitative studies*. Norwood, NJ: Ablex Publishing Corp.

Wolcott, H. (1988). Adequate schools and inadequate education: The life history of a sneaky kid. In R. M. Jaeger (Ed.), *Complementary methods for research in education*. Washington, DC: American Educational Research Association.

Wolcott, H. (1990). *Writing up qualitative research*. Newbury Park, CA: Sage.

Yinger, J. M. (1982). *Countercultures: The promise and peril of a world turned upside down*. New York: The Free Press.

Young, T. W. (1990). *Public alternative education: Options and choices for today's schools*. New York: Teachers College Press.

Yudof, M. (1982). *When government speaks*. Berkeley, CA: University of California Press.

AUTHOR INDEX

SUBJECT INDEX